Low Cholesterol Gourmet

The Healthy Heart Guide

The Fischer/Brown
Low Cholesterol
Gourmet

By Lynn Fischer and W. Virgil Brown, M.D.

ACROPOLIS BOOKS LTD.
WASHINGTON, D.C.

ACROPOLIS BOOKS, LTD.
Alphons J. Hackl, Publisher
Colortone Building, 2400 17th St., N.W.
Washington, D.C. 20009

Attention: Schools and Corporations
ACROPOLIS books are available at quantity discounts with bulk purchase for educational, business, or sales promotional use. For information, please write to: SPECIAL SALES DEPARTMENT, ACROPOLIS BOOKS, LTD., 2400 17th St., N.W., WASHINGTON, D.C. 20009.

Are there Acropolis books you want but cannot find in your local stores?
You can get any Acropolis book title in print. Simply send title and retail price. Be sure to add postage and handling: $2.25 for orders up to $15.00; $3.00 for orders from $15.01 to $30.00; $3.75 for orders from $30.01 to $100.00; $4.50 for orders over $100.00. District of Columbia residents add applicable sales tax. Enclose check or money order only. no cash please, to:
ACROPOLIS BOOKS LTD.
2400 17th St., N.W.
WASHINGTON, D.C. 20009

Library of Congress Cataloging-in-Publication Data
1. Low cholesterol diet—Recipes. I. Brown, W. Virgil. II. Title. III. Title Low cholesterol gourmet.
RM237.75.F55 1988   641.5'631   88-14566
ISBN 0-87491-909-6

Front Cover Photograph
Tom Radcliffe
Point of View Studio, Takoma Park, MD
Interior Photographs
—Tom Radcliffe
—Culinary Hearts Kitchen
  American Heart Association (reproduced with permission)
—United Fruits and Vegetables Association
—Pork Council
—United Fisheries Institute
Rear Cover Photograph
Rob Kinnon

The Recipes in the Fischer/Brown Low Cholesterol Gourmet have been analyzed for cholesterol and saturated fat content by the Nutrition Coordinating Center at the University of Minnesota. These values are listed at the bottom of each recipe and are on a per serving basis.

The Fischer/Brown Low Cholesterol Gourmet is a compendium of information from many sources including doctors, the American Heart Association, the Minnesota Nutrition Coding Center, the Department of Agriculture, the National Institutes of Health and many others.

The book is not intended to be used as the final word in a personal treatment program because individual cases may vary. Your doctor should be contacted for specific problems. It does, however, contain the latest nutrition and diet information concerning a low cholesterol, low saturated fat diet, which is now known to influence cholesterol levels and coronary heart disease, the number one cause of death.

The recipes in the Fischer/Brown Low Cholesterol Gourmet have been tested for cholesterol and saturated fat content by the Minnesota Nutrition Coordinating Center at the University of Minnesota. They are given at the bottom of each recipe.

Preface

This book was written because my then husband, Gif Fischer learned he had very high cholesterol. It was imperative that he lower it immediately. Since I bought and prepared all of the food, I had to educate myself quickly, thoroughly and correctly. To complicate matters, we were feeding teenage and young adult children some of the time, entertaining heavily part of the time, and he was traveling often.

The first step was easy. Eliminate the big offenders! I bought no eggs, organ meats, few dairy products unless they were low or no fat, and no butter at all. Since Gif wanted to enjoy many old favorites like chili, Chinese food, pasta, Caesar salads and the like, I learned through trial and error how to make old favorites with new low cholesterol, low saturated fat guidelines.

It was time to introduce newly invented concotions, some more successful than others. It was a challenge to prepare the most gorgeous meal with no or little cholesterol. Guests weren't told that the delicious food in lush buffet arrangements was also very healthy for their hearts. It was amazing how many would say things to me like, "You know my husband Andy usually can't eat much at parties, and there isn't anything here he can't eat. Did you do that on purpose?" Soon friends began asking me for recipes and even to cater their parties, which I gladly did.

For the most part however, unless asked, I didn't give away my "secret," because some people have been known to react negatively if they think they are being served so-called healthy food. One incident highlighted that rather vividly. My young daughter Lisa brought home (for a sumptious Sunday brunch) a handsome six-foot athlete who was very confident, very friendly, and very hungry. We had French toast, waffles with fresh blueberries and pure maple syrup, mushroom omelets, sausage, biscuits and honey, fresh squeezed orange juice, pineapple, and minted iced tea.

He ate everything, continually complimenting me, asking for seconds, telling funny stories. I beamed; my daughter did too. My husband could hold the secret no longer and proceeded to tell him very proudly, nothing (he exaggerated) was "real." The young man actually turned white, then green, and then headed for the powder room. I don't remember if he ever came back.

Despite this temporary setback, I continued inventing new sauces, dips, vegetable combinations, and soups; I tried new products offered in the grocery store. I read everything I could about the subject. Since I was then and am now a television medical reporter and TV host, I already had a pretty good foundation of medical knowledge, nutrition, and health in general. Plus I had begun cooking when I was twelve or thirteen as my mother traveled a lot, and I was the oldest of five children. My mother was a world-ranking badminton player having won the U.S. Open and my father was a fine athlete in skiing, tennis, ice skating, and golf—as well as a full-time attorney. So my family had talked health and athletics for many years. And as I had to devise ways for little kids to eat all their food when I was very young, cooking and optimum health were a natural to me. I had been doing it all my life. Later, I began writing the recipes down—especially when my husband's cholesterol was indeed lowered by about 15 to 20 percent.

I have always been weight conscious, and my husband although very tall and slender, always (since I've known him) had a weight problem in the stomach area. With this new way of eating he *lost* weight, but still had more energy.

In 1985 I decided to put down on paper all of the low cholesterol recipes I had gathered over the years. Realizing there were many misconceptions and great confusion about cholesterol, I began a search for a doctor who was an expert in the field of cholesterol research but who treated patients at the same time. The American Heart Association directed me to Dr. W. Virgil Brown, their spokesperson and Chairman of the Nutrition Committee of the A.H.A. Virgil was also Chief, Arteriosclerosis and Metabolism at the Mount Sinai School of Medicine in New York City. Most important, it soon became apparent he could explain what cholesterol is and why we should avoid too much. In addition, he was vitally interested in the project right from the start.

Our philosophies on food and health are nearly identical, and neither Virgil nor his wife Alice think you have to give up the good life and fine food to have a low cholesterol, low saturated fat diet. Alice has been buying and preparing low cholesterol foods for many years, and she is particularly pleased that their children, Matt and Peter, prefer these foods. She says as far as buying some prepared foods she would like to see clearer and more specific labeling, and adds, checking labels carefully can bring positive benefits. Some products she had previously not bought because of coconut or palm oils had changed ingredients and only because she read the labels did she realize that some manufacturers were now using unsaturated vegetable fats. An excellent point. Both Alice and Virgil think a cookbook like this increases awareness as well as gives specific information for those who are already knowledgeable.

As you read the science and food chapters, you'll be aware they were written in two different styles. Virgil and I purposely didn't try to blend our writing, but sought instead to express ourselves and our ideas separately. The result is, I think, one of the clearest explanations of cholesterol, saturated fat and heart disease I've ever seen. Conversely, I put in everything I thought a food buyer and preparer would need. We were, however, deeply interested in each other's work. Numerous suggestions were passed back and forth, but the expert in that field always had the final say on what should be included. We felt this approach would give the readers the very best chance to decide to work for good heart health for themselves and for their families. We hope we've achieved that.

This book is really just the beginning. There is no reason why you can't eat wonderfully interesting and delicious food that is healthy at the same time. I hope it won't be long before more restaurants, mothers and fathers who cook, caterers, grocery stores, manufacturers, hosts and hostesses, food suppliers, chefs and cooks, and especially cookbook writers everywhere become knowledgable about how humans need to eat well. Our philosophy isn't to limit your food choices, but to expand the variety; it's to try different ways of preparing previously risky fare with healthier methods; it's to try and incorporate the many new products, both tasty duplications of old favorites like sour cream as well as brand new combinations. It's to make knowledgeable choices about what you eat.

It's a great natural high to eat a meal that's good for you, keeps your weight down, and keeps you feeling good the next day and the next week and hopefully for years. It isn't just how long you live, but how well you live the life you have.

If you have any low cholesterol, low saturated fat recipes you would like to share, please send them to me. I'd love to publish them, and I'll credit you. If you've taken a really good color transparency (35 mm) send that too. We would probably rephotograph it, but we'd like to see it.

Lynn Fischer
Acropolis Books Ltd.
2400 17th St. N.W.
Washington, D.C. 20009

Acknowledgements

First, I wish to thank W. Virgil Brown, a dedicated and very busy doctor who collaborated cheerfully and put aside great blocks of time to devote to a project he enthusiastically believed in right from the start.

I also want to thank gourmet cook Christine Schuyler who contributed to the recipe section many new and original low cholesterol, low saturated fat, culinary masterpieces.

The following friends, relatives, and acquaintances contributed to the book in many ways with listening, encouragement, enthusiasm, time, ideas, endorsements, and recipes.

They are, in no particular order: Terri, Ginnie, John, Gif, Kevin, Sandy, Al, Vicki, Wendy, Diane, Carl, Walter, Susie, Cathy, Kathy, Leonard, Kay, Lillian, Joanne, Laurie, Jeanne, Joan, Henry, Alice, Pamela, Chuck, Marilyn, Judith, Pat, Helen, William, Jack, Malcolm, Joy, Matthew, John, Seppi, Nick, Carol, Nina, Phil, Tom, Susan, Carolyn, Mary, Marty, Larry, Dan, Kathleen, Taddy, Elizabeth, Karl, my children Lisa and Cary, Lisa's husband Bill, and Cary's wife Bryn.

I also thank my long-time typist Val Eichenlaub. Last but hardly least, I thank Sandy Trupp (and her husband Phil whom I first contacted) and publisher Al Hackl. Their ideas and suggestions were greatly appreciated.

TABLE OF CONTENTS

CHAPTER ONE

America, the Land of the Grease

*A*mericans eat too many foods that are bad for their health—foods that contain fat, grease, and oil. We grew up on it, we are used to it; we love it. No wonder we have high cholesterol levels, heart disease, and weight problems.

We come by the use of grease, oil, and fat quite naturally. Years ago, when cattle, lamb, hogs, and poultry were butchered at home in this country, every part of the animal was used. Tallow went for wax, soap, and candles. Fat was left on the meat for people to consume, though these earlier farm and wild animals undoubtedly weren't as fatty as ours have become. Pans were stored with a layer of fat. In fact, some skillets were left unwashed and coated with fat to stay smooth and black.

During the depression, nothing was wasted. Bacon grease was saved to fry chicken or potatoes or scramble eggs. Fat from short ribs put weight on people. Gravy, a staple, was made with leftover grease. Fatback or salt pork (called white pork) was used, particularly in the south, to cook everything from baked beans to green beans, spinach to collards. The fatty skin of pigs, often called "cracklin", was fried to a crisp or peeled from a whole barbecued pig. It was, and still is, relished down south.

In the past, meat could be tough, or if it was from wild animals, it was often tough *and* gamey. Without refrigeration it was frequently slightly spoiled. Sauces were created to help mask the flavor and our great marinades were invented. These served the double purpose of preserving the meat because of the high salt, sugar or vinegar content.

Meat production was greatly improved in the '40s, becoming tender and fatty simultaneously. In our society, there was less and less human physical labor being performed as factories proliferated, so there was no way to burn off the extra calories. Those who grew up poor in a fluctuating and unsteady economy psychologically viewed a meat-laden diet as a luxury; they dreamed of a chicken in every pot. Relatively speaking, we are a very rich country; even our poor have more and better food than the middle classes of many other countries.

Our food habits and traditions die very hard, however. We prefer our hot vegetables laden with regular or sour cream, butter or margarine, bacon fat, and cheese; our cold vegetables with salad oil, bacon grease, sour cream, or with cheese dips. We put oils on or under fruit in the form of cream, pie crusts, or whipped cream; we drizzle it on meat, fish, and chicken in the form of sauces like Béarnaise, Dijonnaise, and mayonnaise. Our gravy, Newburg, chaud-froid, barbecue, garlic butter, Hollandaise, Lyonnaise, Bordelaise, velouté, and the ever-ready white sauce are all made with oil, butter, fat, or grease of one kind or another. Some use chicken fat (*schmaltz*) in chopped liver, put whipped cream on ice cream, triple creme cheese on butter cookies, mayonnaise or margarine on liverwurst sandwiches and clarified butter on lobster. We drink it in the form of whole milk, shakes, eggnogs, cream in coffee or tea, and after-dinner liqueurs with cream.

We stubbornly continue to fry foods. We fry in fat or animal grease, braise in fat, sauté in fat; baste, brown, stew, marinade, and bake in or with fat and oil. You get the point and can probably think of fifty other ways we add oil, grease, or fat to foods like meat or chips that already have their own fat.

Having a diet loaded with fat and grease is implicated in a great many diseases, but particularly in coronary heart disease, obesity, and perhaps diabetes and cancer, all major causes of premature death or disabling infirmity in this country. Obesity and just unwanted weight is a major problem in America. The addition of fats to an already fatty diet contributes to weight gain, particularly when our lives become more sedentary as we age.

In addition, Americans apparently are the world's single largest users of antacids. A diet heavy in fried foods and fats may be connected to upset stomachs, indigestion, gas, heartburn, colon cancers, and perhaps other major intestinal problems.

The key to a better lifestyle, to better health in general, is the way we eat. You can restrict greatly your own buying, preparing, cooking, and serving of foods with cholesterol, saturated oils, fats and gratuitous grease. You can also moderate your intake of cholesterol and fat at restaurants and cocktail parties. You can nearly eliminate it at home. We will show you how to do just that in this book. Most important, this change in diet can reduce your risk of cardiovascular disease, a disease that according to the American Heart Association kills nearly 1,000,000 Americans each year. I read somewhere former first lady Rosalynn Carter said, (and I concur wholeheartedly,) ''For the first time in history, we have the knowledge to be in charge of our own health.''

CHAPTER TWO

Who Should You Believe About Diet, Cholesterol, and Nutrition?

*M*any best-selling diet books say one thing about diet and cholesterol, corporations, advertising and various organizations say something else. Perhaps your family doctor says another thing. Television, medical, and health reporters contribute even more reports on the subject. And one study showed that Americans get 80 percent of their health information from soap operas. So where do you start?

Who Do You Believe?

Start with your doctor, who learns from researchers in the field, nutritionists, *registered* dietitians and writers whose track records deserve your trust. Registered dietitians have spent years in the study of food and how it affects the body. But even those highly trained professionals disagree, however. Be aware the subject of nutrition is like religion—there are many different beliefs and theories among the best of them. However, you can rest assured there is in general, agreement on certain major points, specifically that saturated fats and cholesterol in the diet raise blood cholesterol.

Trained and registered dietitians and nutritionists can also help coronary bypass patients and people with abnormally high blood cholesterol levels by explaining basic health principles, and suggesting new diet selections and new ways to prepare food. They help at-risk children with their special menu needs, and for those who want more information about many special diets for such diseases or problems as high blood pressure, diabetes, allergies, and obesity, their advice is invaluable.

Journals and Studies
What about these Journals and Scientific Studies That Are Always Quoted?

There are about 3,000 journals published each month (if you count foreign issues and the weeklies), which print the findings of scientists, doctors, and researchers. Some of the best known of these journals are *The Journal of the American Medical Association*, *The New England Journal of Medicine*, *The Journal of Clinical Investigation*, and, from the United Kingdom, *The Lancet*. Most journals are fairly specific and report on a particular discipline such as blood, plastic surgery, or psychology. Some journals concentrate on just diet and nutrition such as The American Journal of Clinical Nutrition and The Journal of The American Dietetic Association. Others cover a variety of subjects. These pubcations provide articles on the latest scientific findings, but only after they have been carefully reviewed by other scientists working in the same research area.

How about Cookbook Writers?

Anyone can have an idea about diet so he or she might write a diet book. Some of these books say some food combinations should be avoided and some books advise eating eggs to lower cholesterol. Scientists state these books may be nutritionally imbalanced or just wrong. These are largely fad diets that cannot be used indefinitely for most persons. They are simply boring. More important, they espouse poor overall nutrition or are downright dangerous. Other cookbooks may be written by newspaper or magazine writers. They can be knowledgeable consumers or informed health writers and the books they write have a good scientific base. Medical credentials, then, aren't always the only indicator of sound advice, and the lack of a medical degree doesn't mean the book or recipes should be suspect.

Some people advocate a very stringent, almost tasteless diet that drastically reduces all fat and protein. This is not necessary and could be harmful. And most Americans can't follow it for long. Our book shows blood cholesterol can be lowered dramatically by less severe dietary changes. At the same time the food can be scrumptious and gorgeous as our book will show.

Where Can I Find Answers for Myself Without Reading All these Research Journals?

The Department of Agriculture (USDA) spends millions of dollars to experiment with and test theories—new and old. It prints innumerable booklets on diet and nutrition and food analysis. Anyone can order these books and educate himself or herself. Write for the list of publications to U.S. Department of Agriculture, Room 325A, Federal Building, Hyattsville, MD 20782. More material can be obtained from the Human Nutrition Information Service at the same address. Or write for diet and health information to Consumer Inquiries, TFA-5600, Fisher Lane, Rockville, MD 20857. The Department of Agriculture also has available books that list cholesterol content as well as many fats and nutrients.

Other organizations that can give you information on cholesterol, saturated fat, and diet are the American Heart Association, some hospital outpatient clinics, public health departments, county extension services, state or local medical societies, the local American Red Cross, local diabetes associations, local heart associations, and local health centers and clinics. Organizations like the American Heart Association do a lot of good work in just this area; they take a balanced approach and can be trusted. So do the American Cancer Society and the American Dietetic Association and the American Diabetes Association. Your doctor may also have diet information.

To give you some historical information, the fatty deposits of cholesterol were first pulled out of veins and arteries in the late 1800s. Almost a century later we learned that too much ingested saturated fat found primarily in animals, in coconut and palm products, and some nuts and foods, like chocolate, can be harmful to us.

Food is our fuel. Apparently a few of us can run on almost any fuel, but we may not run as well as we could. The vast majority of us are slowly but fatally harmed by smoking, over-ingestion of saturated fat and cholesterol, and alcoholism. This book can show you how to get the proper kind of fuel by eating delicious food prepared in a healthy way. It takes some relearning and some effort, but what better place to invest effort and relearning than in your own body's health and in the bodies and health of your family?

CHAPTER THREE

We Are What We Eat

by W. Virgil Brown, M.D.

We live in a very special time in history. This latter half of the twentieth century has been called the "Atomic Age," the "Electronic Age," and the "Age of the Computer." But the most important characteristic of this period, by far, is literally right under our noses. This is the "Age of Food."

The average American can eat virtually anything he or she wishes, in amounts limited only by one's pocketbook and appetite. Having fresh meat, fruits, and vegetables on the table in any season of the year has been possible for only the last 40 or 50 years.

How We Got Where We Are

For centuries, most of our calories came from staples—grains and starchy tubers such as the potato—because they could be stored in their natural state. To supplement these, small quantities of meats and fruits were dried, smoked, or preserved in salt or sugar. The birth of the canning industry in the beginning of the twentieth century added new variety to the diet. This improved not only the pleasure of eating, but the nutritional quality of food. Prior to the advent of refrigeration and rapid transportation, however, fresh meat was too expensive for the average family to eat, and fresh produce was available only during the local growing season. It's no wonder that, until recently, warnings about the unbridled consumption of food were more likely to be the subject of jokes than of serious concern.

Today, with refrigerated vehicles that carry fresh vegetables from fields in California to tables in New York and shellfish from African or Alaskan waters to restaurants in Chicago, it is possible to have almost any food year-round.

This tremendous supply of food has made it possible to virtually end protein and calorie malnutrition in economically developed nations. Too much food is now the major problem.

Overconsumption in developed nations has biological origins, encouraged by psychology and tradition. Man evolved with food in short supply most of the time. As a result, our genetic machinery is well-designed to deal with inadequate calories, protein, and other nutrients for days or weeks, then to quickly store them during the brief times of plenty. Such occasions—the kill of a large animal or the harvest of a crop—naturally triggered celebrations. Eventually, huge feasts became the way to celebrate other happy events. It's no wonder that eating with family and friends is closely tied to feelings of protection and love.

Man is not designed, however, to consume food ad infinitum. It is now clear that although an overabundance of food reduces the incidence of certain health problems, it triggers the onset of other equally serious problems. Overeating foods rich in saturated fats and cholesterol, for example, is linked to the number one killer of both men and women in the United States—diseases of the heart and blood vessels, known as cardiovascular disease. Coronary heart disease is a type of vascular disease that affects the coronary arteries, the vessels that supply blood to the heart.

A wide spread misconception holds that if we reduce saturated fats and cholesterol in our diets we will markedly reduce the pleasure of eating. This cookbook will demonstrate that many heart-healthy dishes can indeed be delicious. In fact, changing your diet in this way can be both liberating and adventuresome.

The recipes in this book can be part of a healthy diet for anyone. We believe it's important, however, to determine whether you are one of those persons who has a higher-than-average risk of heart disease. Such people are in need of a more careful diet plan. Your risk level can now be determined by some rather simple blood measurements. It is explained in Chapter 5. The rationale for taking these measurements and using them to monitor your risk of heart disease has a sound scientific basis.

Most of the food we eat is used to provide fuel to run our metabolic machinery. When the major nutrients—proteins, carbohydrates, and fats—combine with oxygen, chemical energy results. It is measured in units known as calories. This energy drives our heart to circulate blood, and fuels other muscles that maintain basic body functions such as breathing and rebuilding tissue proteins.

Calories. Most of us require about 10 calories per pound of body weight each day just to maintain these so-called basal metabolic functions. Additional energy is needed to power skeletal muscles for activity such as walking or running. For example, a man who weighs 150 pounds and works at a desk requires about 1500 calories for basal needs and another 500 calories for the muscle activity in an ordinary day. If he jogs for 45 minutes after work, he might burn another 500 calories.

Most of our calories come from the three basic groups of macronutrients: proteins, carbohydrates, and fats. Alcohol provides some calories as well. According to recent diet surveys, the typical American eats approximately 15 percent of calories as protein, 40 to 45 percent as carbohydrate and 35 to 40 percent as fat. Experts agree we should reduce the fat in our diet and replace it with carbohydrate calories. These dietary changes are discussed in Chapter 6.

Proteins. Each protein is composed of a chain of smaller compounds called amino acids. There are some 22 amino acids; of these, nine cannot be made by the human body and therefore must be supplied by the foods we eat. They are referred to as "essential amino acids." The remainder are called "non-essential amino acids."

Dietary protein must have the proper balance of essential amino acids to be efficiently used by the body. If we consumed only protein that contained large amounts of all the essential amino acids, we could get by eating only enough protein to equal 5 or 6 percent of calories. But since the protein we eat isn't all of this high quality, our current consumption of protein in the amount of 15 percent of calories provides a large safety factor. Eating proteins from different sources helps assure that we obtain all the essential amino acids in adequate amounts.

In order to be absorbed into the body, protein first must be broken down into individual amino acids in the intestines. After they reach body tissues, they are used to build new proteins. Excess amino acids are burned for energy or stored as fat.

Carbohydrates. Carbohydrates occur in nature in two basic forms: 1) simple sugars, such as glucose (blood sugar), sucrose (table sugar), fructose (fruit sugar), and lactose (milk sugar); and 2) complex carbohydrates, such as starches and fibers.

All starches must be broken down into simple sugars before they can be absorbed. But fibers, such as cellulose, pectin, and gums, are not digestible. The human digestive system lacks the enzymes needed to break them down so they can be utilized. As a result, they provide no calories.

After they are absorbed, sugars are removed from the bloodstream by various tissues. They are then converted to glucose and either burned for energy, stored as glycogen (another complex carbohydrate), or converted to fat for long-term storage. The average American eats 25 percent of his calories in the form of simple sugars (mostly sucrose) and about 20 percent as starches and other digestible carbohydrates.

Fats. Lipids—another name for fats—represent a large variety of substances that cannot dissolve in water. Examples include triglycerides and phospholipids. Lipids are essential for the normal functioning of body tissues.

Triglycerides are by far the most common fat in animals and plants, because they are the storage form of fat. Both butter and vegetable oils, for example, are almost pure triglycerides. They are an extremely rich source of energy, or calories. Four to five times as much energy can be stored as fat than can an equivalent weight of carbohydrate or protein because a large amount of water must accompany the stored carbohydrate or protein. Biologically, this offers an advantage. Consider the 150 pound man who has 25 pounds of fat tissue. If he had to store an equivalent amount of energy as glycogen, it would weigh 125 pounds, making him a rather hefty 250 pounds at the same height.

When fats are digested, most of the triglycerides are broken down into fatty acids to be absorbed. They then regroup back into triglycerides and are coated with a layer of protein to make them soluble in blood. It is these lipid-protein particles—called lipoproteins—that transport triglycerides throughout the body. In muscles and other tissues, they are used for energy. In adipose tissue (fat tissue), they are stored for later use.

In total, fats contribute about 40 percent of calories. But more important than total fat is the nature of those fats. The fatty acids that make up each triglyceride are literally chains of carbon atoms linked by chemical bonds. Saturated fats are those in which all the carbon atoms are "saturated" with hydrogen. When a fat is "unsaturated," it has double bonds where there would normally be hydrogen atoms. If it has one double bond it's called a monounsaturated fat. Fats with more than one double bond are polyunsaturated. In practical terms, the more saturated a fat, the more solid it is at room temperature. That's why highly saturated butter is harder to spread than polyunsaturated margarine.

Cholesterol. Cholesterol is a waxy fat-like substance called a sterol. Although it is present in the body in much smaller quantities than triglycerides, it also is essential to life. Cholesterol is needed for the normal functioning of cell membranes, the formation of sex hormones, and the formation of bile acids, which act as the body's "detergent" by helping to digest fats. It is only found in animal tissues; it cannot be made by plants. As a result, fruits, nuts, grains, vegetables and vegetable oils naturally contain no cholesterol.

Despite the fact that we cannot live without cholesterol, we don't need to eat it because our bodies make as much as we need. That's why true vegetarians, who eat virtually no cholesterol, can remain healthy. Nevertheless, the average American consumes about 400 milligrams of cholesterol each day. Men tend to take in more than women, because they eat more calories. Some people who eat large amounts of eggs, meat, and whole dairy products may consume one to two *grams* a day (the same as 1,000 to 2,000 milligrams).

Alcohol. A source of calories often overlooked is alcohol. Surprisingly, each gram of alcohol contributes more calories than a gram of carbohydrate or protein. The average American consumes 5 percent of his total calories as alcohol (the average is 10 percent if you count only those who drink). If taken in moderation, alcohol is burned efficiently and there is no significant accumulation in the blood or ill effects on health. In fact, some research has shown that moderate drinkers have less heart disease and live longer than "teetotalers."

People who drink more than two ounces daily, however, are at increased risk for high blood pressure and stroke. There also is evidence that these levels can cause direct damage to the heart, liver, and brain in some people. As a result, alcohol use cannot be encouraged. On the other hand, there is no medical basis to advise against moderate use of alcoholic beverages in persons with a history of good control. The admonition not to drink and drive is always important advice.

Vitamins and Minerals. Collectively, vitamins and minerals are called micronutrients because the body requires them in much smaller (milligram or microgram) amounts, than macronutrients, which are needed in gram quantities.

Vitamins are specific chemical substances that are ''vital'' to life in animals and generally must be supplied by the diet. Without them, many biochemical reactions in the body could not proceed. Vitamins are made, or synthesized, in other living things (usually bacteria or plants) but, with one or two exceptions, not in humans. The exceptions include vitamin D, which can be manufactured in the skin, provided a person is exposed to enough sunlight. The other is vitamin K, which can be synthesized in the intestines.

Minerals are components of the rock and soil of the earth. They are important to the normal functioning of proteins, as structural components of bone, in the transport of oxygen, and in maintaining fluid balance throughout the body.

The Recommended Dietary Allowances (RDA) are average daily quantities for many of the micronutrients that are specified by the Food and Nutrition Board of the National Academy of Sciences to assure good health and avoid oversupply. The U.S. RDA is simplified for use on food labels. In most cases, the numbers are calculated to include a generous safety allowance, to account for individual differences in requirements. RDA levels are well above the amounts at which a nutritional deficiency might occur in an otherwise healthy person. So consumption of less than the RDA for a single nutrient in an individual is not cause for alarm. With a few exceptions—particularly iron and calcium in women—the great majority of Americans receive adequate quantities of nutrients from their usual diets.

Since vitamins and minerals are needed only in very small amounts, any extra that is consumed is either stored or excreted from the body. Micronutrients

We Are What We Eat

are analogous to the tiny parts in a fine automobile engine. Having the right part in the right place is extremely important, but adding extra parts is a waste of money and may damage the engine. So it is, too, with vitamins and minerals. The purchase of nutrient supplements is generally a waste of money. The use of vitamins in quantities that far exceed the RDAs is discouraged, since it's more likely that toxicity will result than it is that a health benefit will be realized.

The Case Against Cholesterol

People used to die from infectious diseases, usually at a young age, before cardiovascular disease had its chance to kill. In fact, tuberculosis was the number one cause of death among Americans during the 1920s. With the availability of better sewage and water systems, and improved food supplies as well as the discovery of antibiotics, people started living longer. However another major problem, cardiovascular disease began to limit life expectancy. By the 1960s, heart attacks and strokes were causing almost half of all deaths. Today, over 500,000 people die each year of heart attacks, while another 150,000 succumb to strokes.

The underlying problem is the same for both heart attacks and strokes—atherosclerosis—a form of arteriosclerosis that's popularly called "hardening of the arteries." It occurs when blood vessels become thickened and inelastic. In atherosclerosis, deposits made of cholesterol and other material form on the inside of the arteries, blocking blood flow. If a blockage occurs in a major artery to the heart, a heart attack ensues. If the clogged blood vessel leads to the brain, a stroke occurs. Other blocked vessels can result in gangrene of the legs or loss of kidney function. Because the artery deposits—called plaque—develop slowly over many years, victims often have no symptoms until the blood flow is suddenly stopped by a clot that gets caught in a narrowed artery.

It has been known for many years that a build-up of cholesterol is a hallmark of atherosclerosis. Early in this century, it was discovered that rabbits fed large amounts of cholesterol developed fatty deposits. In humans, however, there is a less dramatic rise in blood cholesterol after consumption of cholesterol in food. Post-World War II studies demonstrated the ability of saturated fats to raise blood cholesterol. Finally, it was noted that people with a genetic tendency for high blood cholesterol often became heart attack victims very early in life.

Healthy Artery

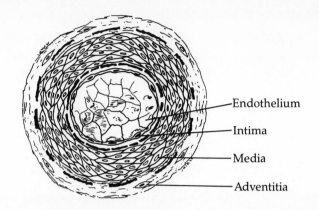

— Endothelium

— Intima

— Media

— Adventitia

Perhaps the Seven Countries Study was the most famous. It compared the lifestyles of different populations to uncover what factors might predict who was likely to develop cardiovascular disease. Among other things, the study examined blood cholesterol levels and the composition of the diet for groups of people in the United States and six other countries. The findings? A very strong relationship was found between the amount of saturated fat in the diet and blood cholesterol levels. An equally strong relationship was found to exist between the incidence of heart disease and blood cholesterol levels.

To compare the extremes, for example, the Japanese group averaged a saturated fat intake of less than 5 percent of calories, with an average blood cholesterol of 165 mg/dl, while in Finland, 20 percent of calories were eaten as saturated fat and blood cholesterol averaged 265 mg/dl. Correspondingly, the heart attack rate was over six times greater in middle-aged Finnish men as compared to Japanese men of the same age.

The possiblity that genetics was mainly responsible for the differences between countries was dispelled by further research. Japanese who migrated to Hawaii and San Francisco were tracked. In both cases, their diets changed to that of the Caucasian population. As predicted, their blood cholesterol levels and rate of heart disease changed as well.

The ongoing Framingham Massachusetts study of nearly 6,000 men and women that was begun in the 1950s continues to provide us with information on coronary "risk factors"—things that increase a person's chances for developing heart disease. Framingham data confirmed that blood cholesterol is a powerful predictor of risk for cardiovascular disease, along with blood pressure,

We Are What We Eat

cigarette smoking, excess body weight, and diabetes.

But it wasn't until the recent U.S. Coronary Primary Prevention Trial that the preventive benefits of lowering blood cholesterol could be demonstrated. The study proved that by lowering elevated blood cholesterol levels in 4,000 men with no evidence of coronary disease, the number of heart attacks could be reduced. Although this study used drugs to lower blood cholesterol, another study done in Oslo Norway has shown a similar reduction by means of diet with similar benefits in the heart attack rates. In the U.S. study men who took the drug reduced their blood cholesterol levels by 25 percent and suffered 50 percent fewer heart attacks and sudden deaths than those who took a placebo, or inactive pill. The study concluded that in people with elevated blood cholesterol levels, every one percent reduction in blood cholesterol reduces the risk of heart attack and sudden death by two percent.

The evidence is now undeniable that atherosclerosis is related to blood cholesterol. The higher the level, the higher the risk of heart disease. And we know blood cholesterol is raised most by eating a diet rich in saturated fats (dietary cholesterol has a similar but less powerful effect.) So it seems logical that if we want to reduce blood cholesterol, we need to focus on avoiding excess saturated fats in the diet.

To confuse matters, several studies have uncovered a particularly provocative finding. As strong as the connection is between *blood* cholesterol and heart disease, *it seems that there's an even stronger relationship between the incidence of heart disease and dietary cholesterol, the cholesterol we eat.* It may turn out that eat-

Abnormal Artery

ing foods high in cholesterol increases one's risk of heart disease beyond just raising blood cholesterol levels. So avoiding dietary cholesterol as well may be wise after all.

Changing for the Better

If consumption of the wrong foods can lead you down the road to heart disease, can changing to the "right" foods protect you, or at least reduce your risk? This, of course, is the key question. The answer appears to be yes.

Studies of men who changed their diets after suffering a heart attack indicate that the chances of a second heart attack can be reduced by lowering blood cholesterol levels. More significant is the now strong evidence that diets lower in saturated fat and cholesterol can markedly reduce the chances of a first heart attack in men who start out with very elevated blood cholesterol levels.

Other dietary factors may be important as well. Recent studies have uncovered the seemingly protective effect of fish. Other research has focused on monounsaturated fats such as olive and canola oils. Water-soluble fibers are capable of lowering dangerously high blood cholesterol levels. Calories and sodium may both have an indirect influence.

It should be kept in mind that blood cholesterol is not the only risk factor for heart disease. Cigarette smoking is the number one preventable cause. High blood pressure, diabetes, and obesity each individually increase one's risk. And all three are strongly affected by diet. Excess body fat predisposes people to developing high blood pressure and diabetes. In fact, even modest obesity is associated with higher blood cholesterol levels and, as a result, to a higher incidence of heart disease. There are excellent reasons, then, to begin by reducing excess body weight.

Osteoporosis

Osteoporosis affects 25 million Americans, mostly women and people of northern European descent, (Scottish, English, Irish, German, Scandinavian, etc.) It also affects those of Chinese and Japanese descent. Thin, white women of small stature, especially those with fair hair and fair complexions and freckles are at greater risk. Your habits can also increase your risk of osteoporosis,

Alcohol intake can lead to calcium deficiency because it interferes with its absorption. The high amount of phosphates contained in most carbonated beverages rob calcium from bones. Smokers are also at greater risk. On the other hand, those who exercise, have had several pregnancies and have a good diet are at decreased risk.

The peak bone density period for women is about 30 years of age. Thereafter, bone thinning begins. Some think that having calcium in our diet may help prevent the development of osteoporisis. Calcium is found in leafy green vegetables such as kale and collards, in oysters and sardines and in salmon. It's in tofu and is abundant in many of the dairy products suggested in this book such as nonfat yogurt, skim milk, low cholesterol cheese like those recommended. It's also in low fat ricotta and cottage cheese. It's even in low fat dry milk products. Getting a little daily sunshine or a small amount of vitamin D helps calcium to be absorbed. Often your physician will give you an osteoporosis risk evaluation and may recommend a calcium supplement as well.

CHAPTER FOUR

Determining Your Personal Cardiovascular Risk

by W. Virgil Brown, M.D.

*W*e are all different, one from the other. Just as the shape of our noses and the color of our hair differs from our neighbors, our functional features also differ. The genetic messages that determine our unique external features also determine our unique internal features, such as blood measures of cholesterol and sugar, and appetite control. As evidence, in communities where dietary patterns and physical activity are very uniform, there still is a wide range of blood values among individuals.

That's not to say that environmental factors, such as diet and lifestyle, don't influence these numbers. Genetics only provide a foundation of favorable or unfavorable tendencies. It's up to the individual to be sure that lifestyle habits tip the scales in the right direction. Although the risk of coronary heart disease clearly runs in families, environmental factors can be very important in reducing an individual's cardiovascular risk factors, even when that person has inherited dangerous tendencies.

Who Is at Risk?

In deciding whether it is important for you to change your diet, it is useful to consider the personal characteristics that have been established as major risk factors for coronary heart disease and stroke. Obviously some of these, such as age and sex, cannot be altered. But fortunately most of the rest can be changed. And diet plays an important role for many of the following risk factors.

Table 1: Desirable Weights for Men and Women – (Ages 25 and Over)					
	Height[2] Feet	Inches	Small Frame	Medium Frame	Large Frame
Men	5	2	112-120	118-129	126-141
	5	3	115-123	121-133	129-144
	5	4	118-126	124-136	132-148
	5	5	121-129	127-139	135-152
	5	6	124-133	130-143	138-156
	5	7	128-137	134-147	142-161
	5	8	132-141	138-152	147-166
	5	9	136-145	142-156	151-170
	5	10	140-150	146-160	155-174
	5	11	144-154	150-165	159-179
	6	0	148-158	154-170	164-184
	6	1	152-162	158-175	168-189
	6	2	156-167	162-180	173-194
	6	3	160-171	167-185	178-199
	6	4	164-175	172-190	182-204
Women	4	10	92- 98	96-107	104-119
	4	11	94-101	98-110	106-122
	5	0	96-104	101-113	109-125
	5	1	99-107	104-116	112-128
	5	2	102-110	107-119	115-131
	5	3	105-113	110-122	118-134
	5	4	108-116	113-126	121-138
	5	5	111-119	116-130	125-142
	5	6	114-123	120-135	129-146
	5	7	118-127	124-139	133-150
	5	8	122-131	128-142	137-154
	5	9	126-135	132-147	141-158
	5	10	130-140	136-151	145-163
	5	11	134-144	140-155	149-168
	6	0	138-148	144-159	153-173

[1]Weight in pounds according to frame (indoor clothing).
[2]With 1-inch heel shoes on for men and 2-inch heel shoes on for women.

SOURCE: Metropolitan Life Insurance Company Actuarial Tables, 1959.

Determining Your Personal Cardiovascular Risk

Age. Heart attacks are very rare before 40 years of age. After 40, the number of coronary events in men rises sharply, peaking in their late 50s. It's similar in women, but there's a 10- to 12-year delay. Clearly, atherosclerosis is a very slow process in most people. So although changes in blood vessels have been documented as early as the teenage years, the effects of this naturally appear later in life. Yet it's just as clear that heart attacks and strokes are not the inevitable outcome of aging. In populations where blood cholesterol levels are low, cardiovascular disease is quite uncommon even in people as old as 80 and 90 years of age.

Sex. By the time they reach their 40s and 50s, five to 10 times more men suffer heart disease than women. The reason for this is not clear. Some of it may be due to differences in blood cholesterol levels or to the fact that, before 1980, more men than women smoked cigarettes. But it is also possible that there is a negative effect of male sex hormones or a positive effect of female hormones.

Blood Cholesterol. As discussed in Chapter 1, blood cholesterol is a powerful predictor of heart disease risk. We'll examine this further in Chapter 5.

Blood Pressure. The higher a person's blood pressure, the greater the risk of a heart attack and even greater the risk of stroke. The lower the blood pressure the better, as long as there are no symptoms. The higher number in a blood pressure reading, or the systolic value, is the better predictor of heart attacks. It measures the peak pressure in the coronary arteries as the heart contracts. The diastolic value, the lower reading, measure the lowest pressure, as the heart relaxes. High blood pressure—or hypertension— is defined as a blood pressure that is consistently 140/90 or higher.

Cigarette Smoking. Most people aren't aware that cigarettes cause more deaths from cardiovascular disease than from cancer. Smoking is a strong predictor of heart attack, stroke, and diseased leg arteries. Fortunately, the risk appears to diminish rapidly when smoking stops. Perhaps 90 percent of the risk is gone five years after quitting. After 15 years, there is no detectable risk.

Obesity. People who are more than 20 percent over their ideal weight—defined as obese—are at increased risk for hypertension, elevated blood cholesterol, and diabetes and other diseases. As a result, they are risking cardiovascular disease as well. Obese individuals tend to be more sedentary—whether it's a cause or a result of being overweight—which further increases their risk. It now appears that being overweight, even without these other risk factors, still is associated with more heart disease. It is not clear yet how much a person's risk is reduced when one loses weight.

Exercise. People who exercise regularly tend to suffer fewer heart attacks. Fit persons who do suffer heart attacks are more likely to survive. In animals with similar blood cholesterol levels, the ones who exercise show less damage to their heart. Perhaps an important benefit of exercise is enlargement of coronary arteries, enabling blood to flow more easily, even when atherosclerosis exists.

''Type A'' Personality. Certain characteristics of personality, as measured by particular questionnaires, were shown in the past to be predictive of who develops heart disease. The so-called ''Type A'' personality is characterized by intense time-consciousness and a sense of intense competitiveness. In contrast, a person with a ''Type B'' personality is more relaxed. Few scientists believe that external stress actually causes heart disease. What may be important is how an individual responds to perceived stress. The rise in blood pressure and and heart rate that some people experience when ''under the gun'' may be detrimental. Stressful situations, in fact, can cause higher blood cholesterol readings.

Subsequent studies have contradicted the earlier ''Type A'' findings, suggesting an association with heart disease only for people who hold in hostile feelings. Obviously, more research is needed to delineate exactly what personality characteristics may be predictive of heart disease risk.

Diabetes. Atherosclerosis is a common and very serious disease for diabetics, especially women. While diabetic men have twice as many blood vessel problems as non diabetics, women with diabetes suffer vascular disease five to six times more often. It appears that the advantage women enjoy over men regarding the incidence of heart disease is completely lost if diabetes develops.

Getting Started: Self Assessment

The first step in determining if you are personally at risk for cardiovascular disease is to take stock of your obvious characteristics. You may be surprised to learn that some of the most important risk factors can be tackled without professional help. Since virtually all the changes that need to be made will ultimately be your responsibility, you might as well get started right now.

Quit Smoking. If you smoke cigarettes, this is the most obvious and important risk factor to change. Besides reducing your risk of cardiovascular disease, it will benefit your family, friends, and associates. The enjoyment of food is markedly affected by smoking, which can hinder smell and taste perception. If you smoke at the table, you may ruin the experience for your dining companions as well.

The great majority of smokers want to quit, but have a sense that they've lost control. Some may be truly addicted. Nevertheless, persons with long histories of heavy smoking are stopping every day. Consider that in the mid-1940s over half of all physicians smoked cigarettes, while today less than 10 percent of physicians and less than 2 percent of medical students do. Repeated attempts to quit, even if only short-lived, often lead to success in the long run.

Are You Obese? Although determining actual body fat content is complicated, deciding if you weigh too much is usually not difficult. Most people already know the answer to that. For those who don't, an objective guide that's often used is the Table of Desirable Weights published by the Metropolitan Life Insurance Company in 1959 (see Table 1). Although it was revised in 1983, the newer table allows much heavier weights, particularly for women. We discourage its use. Even weighing only 10 percent over the 1959 Table's weight for your sex, height, and body build is associated with a measureable increase in the risk of a heart attack. Being 20 percent overweight—defined as obese—is even riskier. In either case, it's wise to reduce your weight.

Start Exercising. An effective way to begin a weight loss program is to exercise more frequently. The major goal is to burn extra calories, but you also want to become more fit. Choosing an activity that's aerobic will accomplish both. Tying your exercise program to some regular essential function, such as commuting to work, helps establish it as a habit. Try parking your car a greater distance from where you work or shop so you are forced to walk farther. Shun escalators and elevators; take the stairs. Have walking meetings rather than sitting meetings whenever possible. Enjoy a sport with a partner who encourages your self-improvement.

A cardinal rule for the middle-aged and older individual is to check with a physician before attempting any major change in one's activity level. We suggest you start slowly with an activity that you know will not exhaust you. Walking is a wonderful exercise—easy on the knees and back and easy to control. Fast walking can be as vigorous as jogging. A common error is to begin an overly ambitious program of running, aerobic exercises, or weight lifting. You may find that you are not motivated enough to continue such activities for very long. Moreover, you may injure yourself. If, after the first week, you can pleasantly visualize regularly participating in the activity you've chosen for at least five years, then it has a good chance of being a successful program for you. Aim for an hour three times a week.

Getting the Most from Your Doctor

Your family physician can be a great help in assessing your remaining risk factors, giving you a sense of their importance and in helping you make the necessary changes to reduce your risk of developing vascular disease. If you already have evidence of atherosclerosis—a previous heart attack or surgery for a diseased coronary or leg artery—reducing your risk factors can be effective in preventing further trouble.

The following information is intended to give you a better understanding of your doctor's evaluation and advice. Think of your physician as a counselor who can provide you with the information you need to control your risk factors. Just remember, there are no magic cures. It will be your job to make the daily decisions necessary to avoid life's booby traps: food rich in cholesterol and saturated fats, cigarettes at every check-out stand, entertainment that takes time away from physical activity, and transportation that reduces walking to a minimum.

The Medical Work-Up. The most valuable tool your physician can use to evaluate your cardiovascular risk is a thorough and systematic interview. The questions likely to be asked of you include: important illnesses and causes of death in relatives, significant medical events in your past, current and past medications, unusual signs and symptoms that may be bothering you, and relevant social information, such as the nature of your employment, hobbies, and the important support persons in your life (spouse, children, friends).

Laboratory tests likely to be performed include a urinalysis and a complete blood count. Certain chemistry values reveal your blood sugar level, cholesterol count, and information about your liver and kidney function.

If you're a healthy person, the most valuable measurements are your blood pressure and your blood cholesterol count. That's because either one can be abnormal without your having a single clue. And that could be serious trouble. So it's important to find out if you're one of the 15 percent of middle-aged Americans whose blood pressure is too high and/or one of the 50 percent of Americans whose blood cholesterol is high enough to warrant treatment.

High Blood Pressure. Despite its medical name—hypertension—people with high blood pressure are not necessarily "hyper" or nervous. The disease is known as the "silent killer" because it can exist without causing any symptoms. Almost one in every 12 middle-aged persons has a blood pressure that's high enough to require drug treatment for control.

When blood pressure is measured, the physician or nurse routinely uses the right arm. On the first visit, however, both of your arms may be checked since vascular disease can reduce the pressure in either extremity. The higher reading is assumed to be the correct one. In some people, blood pressure varies considerably from one reading to the next. Anxiety can contribute to this phenomenon. That's why hypertension is never diagnosed from one blood pressure reading alone. Several measurements are usually recorded, noting the sequence and position of the patient. Medication should not be considered until high readings are measured on at least three consecutive visits at weekly intervals.

Although hypertension is defined as systolic blood pressure over 140 and diastolic pressure over 90, drug therapy is not usually begun unless your measurements are more than 160 for systolic or more than 95 for diastolic. If they are between 140/90 and 160/95, several months of dietary treatment is appropriate, allowing time for weight loss to occur and new eating habits to be adopted. These measures include using less salt or sodium, and eating more foods rich in potassium and calcium, two minerals that recent research suggests may be important to maintaining a normal blood pressure. If you drink, alcohol consumption should be reduced to less than two ounces a day. About 20 percent of patients are able to lower their blood pressure by limiting their sodium intake. Even more people respond if they are able to lose excess weight.

If diet does not do the job, there are many excellent drugs available to treat high blood pressure. Your physician will probably first prescribe the drug with the fewest side effects. The exact dose may need to be adjusted several times or a different medication may need to be tried. Sometimes, low doses of several different drugs may work best. The key is to cooperate with the physician, making certain that all your questions are answered and that you understand the dose and purpose of each drug. Then take the medication exactly as prescribed. If you don't, your doctor won't be able to judge how effective it is. Remember, hypertension can only be "controlled," not cured. If you are on blood pressure medication, it must be taken every day. Don't discontinue it just because you feel good.

Very High Blood Cholesterol. Most people have a total blood cholesterol between 150 and 300 mg/dl, although it can be lower than 100 or higher than 400. If your physician discovers that your blood cholesterol is extremely elevated, certain reasons for it should be considered. It can be caused by underlying disease, such as low thyroid function (hypothyroidism), kidney disease (nephrosis), or a liver disorder. Blood tests can usually rule these out.

But in cases of extremely high cholesterol values—anything over 300 mg/dl —it's likely that a metabolic disorder has been inherited. It's important to find out as early as possible whether you are one of these people, so treatment can begin right away. Dietary change is always the first treatment but drugs are usually necessary as well. Often, just reviewing your family history may reveal clues that something is awry. Your physician might suspect a possible genetic problem if any of your close relatives suffered heart attacks before the age of 60 or were known to have high blood cholesterol.

Extremely high blood cholesterol values should trigger consideration of Familial Hypercholesterolemia, literally meaning high blood cholesterol inherited from a parent. This disorder, which affects one in every 500 men and women, is the result of inheriting a defective gene from one parent. The major concern is early heart disease. It's not uncommon for such people to suffer heart attacks at the age of 40 in men and 50 in women. Even rarer is the child who inherits defective genes from both parents. In such cases, blood cholesterol soars in the 600 to 1,000 mg/dl range and may trigger a heart attack by age six. Obviously, such children require drugs and medical care. Even so, they may not live beyond age 20. Newer treatments are making longer lives possible, even with these extreme cases.

People with very high blood cholesterol levels often exhibit some rather distinctive findings which the physician may notice on physical examination. The most obvious are small yellow nodules filled with cholesterol. These xanthomas can be found anywhere, but are often located around the elbows, knees, ankles and buttocks. When they appear in clusters on the eyelids they are referred to as xanthelasmas. The physician also looks for small lines around the clear front window of the eye called corneal arcus. Finally, a thickening and lumpy feel of certain tendons may be apparent. Usually involved are the Achilles tendon at the back of the heel and the long tendons that connect the back of the hand to the fingers. These are an almost sure sign of Familial Hyper-cholesterolemia.

While diet certainly doesn't cause a genetically abnormal cholesterol level, eating the wrong foods can still adversely affect it, often with extreme results. As we will discuss later, selecting a healthy diet is important to everyone with undesirable cholesterol levels, no matter how high or what the underlying cause.

Moderately High Blood Cholesterol. Cholesterol counts between 200 and 300 mg/dl may be less dramatic, but are far more common and still worrisome. Heart attacks and strokes that occur in middle to late life are the result of life-long exposure of our arteries to these seemingly benign moderately high cholesterol levels. Indeed, research has documented an increase in the number of heart attacks as blood cholesterol rises above 200 mg/dl.

The recently established National Cholesterol Education Program has released guildelines to help guide us in the management of these potentially risky levels of cholesterol. These will be discussed in some detail in the next chapter. Experts have determined that persons with blood cholesterol values over 240 mg/dl may be at high risk for a heart attack. People with values between 200 and 240 are in a borderline risk category. A desirable count is below 200. It is important for you, especially if you are a high-risk individual, to have your blood "fractionated" for a total lipoprotein profile. This enables the doctor to more accurately predict your level of risk because the ratio of LDL-cholesterol to HDL-cholesterol is considered to be a better predictor of cardiovascular risk than just total cholesterol alone. The various lipoproteins and their significance will be discussed in Chapter 5.

Table 2

Initial Classification Based on Total Cholesterol

< 200 mg/dl	Desirable Blood Cholesterol
200-239 mg/dl	Borderline-High Blood Cholesterol
≥ 240 mg/dl	High Blood Cholesterol

It's important that diet be the first line of defense against elevated blood cholesterol because it is the least invasive treatment, with no adverse side effects. Drugs should not be used until dietary modification has been given a chance to succeed. Since results cannot be expected overnight, this may take some patience. But diet change may be expected in most Americans to lower elevated blood cholesterol by 10 to 15 percent in four to eight weeks.

If your physician prescribes a cholesterol-lowering diet, it is likely that you will first be instructed by a designated member of the medical team with prepared information. Supplemental materials from the American Heart Association can help to insure that a change in diet habits is successful. If your blood levels do not show an adequate response when retested, a nutritionist should then be consulted. It is useful to decide on a goal cholesterol (or a goal for the more specific LDL cholesterol) so that you and your physicians agree on the target—then work toward that as a team. You are the most important member of that team.

Ask your physician to refer you to a nutritionist who is a registered dietitian (R.D.), preferably someone with experience in counseling cardiovascular patients. If after four to six months on a cholesterol-lowering diet the goal has not been reached, then it is appropriate for your doctor to prescribe a lipid-lowering drug.

CHAPTER FIVE

Why Cholesterol Is Confusing

by W. Virgil Brown, M.D.

*W*hy do so many people equate cholesterol with poison when, in fact, it is essential to life? The confusion may be due, in part, to a lack of understanding about the difference between *blood* cholesterol — that which circulates in the bloodstream — and *dietary* cholesterol — that which we eat in food.

It's *blood* cholesterol that we need for a variety of functions. It is a structural component of cell membranes and the protective sheath around nerves. It's also required for the manufacture of sex hormones and vitamin D. Yet there's no need for *dietary* cholesterol because the body can make as much cholesterol as it needs. In fact, the amount of cholesterol eaten isn't strongly related to the amount in the blood. To understand why, let's first discuss blood cholesterol.

It's not so much the total of cholesterol in the body that worries physicians, but problems that occur during it's transport through the body's blood vessels. Cholesterol is carried around by fat-protein packages called lipoproteins. The various types of lipoproteins, like vehicles on the highway, differ in size, shape, and function. In just the past few years, researchers have improved their understanding of how each one affects the development of atherosclerosis.

Understanding Lipoproteins

Lipoproteins are tiny spheres, with protein and fat forming an outer coat much like the jacket on a baseball. Most of the cholesterol is inside, combining with triglycerides to form a core. Different types of lipoproteins contain different amounts of cholesterol, triglycerides, and protein.

There are four major groups of lipoproteins: 1) chylomicrons, 2) very-low-density lipoproteins (VLDL), 3) low-density lipoproteins (LDL), and 4) high-density lipoproteins (HDL). Chylomicrons are the largest. In fact, one chylomicron may contain one million times more triglyceride than an HDL particle. As their names imply, the other lipoproteins differ in density, or weight per unit of volume. Researchers can isolate the lipoproteins from blood and separate them from each other using a machine called an ultracentrifuge. This is called "fractionating" the blood, or obtaining a "lipoprotein levels."

The analysis of an individual blood sample by using the ultracentrifuge is a very slow and costly process. Fortunately, more rapid methods for measuring the levels of lipoproteins have been developed. Today, doctors have this type of laboratory analysis at their disposal. They know how different levels of each of these lipoproteins affect the risk of cardiovascular disease and how other diseases such as diabetes may change their levels. Your physician can determine your lipoprotein levels and use them to predict your risk of a heart attack and to devise a plan to reduce that risk. The following information may help you understand why these tests are performed and why diet changes are necessary.

Chylomicrons. These large fat-filled lipoproteins are formed in the intestines from the triglycerides and cholesterol in digested food. In graphic terms, the amount of triglycerides the average person absorbs each day is equivalent to about a stick of margarine, and the cholesterol absorbed is enough to fit into one-and-a-half aspirin tablets.

Once each chylomicron is formed, various proteins known as apo-proteins are placed on its surface. In effect, the chylomicron acts like a little oil tanker with tiny hooks that can link up only to certain storage depots or filling stations. The surface proteins are needed to direct the chylomicron to certain tissues where it can unload its fat. In adipose, or fat, tissue, the triglycerides are unloaded for storage. In muscle, they are rapidly burned as a major source of energy.

An enzyme (called a lipase) and its corresponding apo-protein are both needed to unload the triglycerides. In rare genetic disorders either the enzyme or the protein is absent or inactive. As a result, chylomicrons float around in the bloodstream for hours with no place to dock for unloading.

After the lipase does its job and triglycerides are removed, the chylomicron remnant is now just a hull of the original tanker. But since it still contains all its cholesterol, it is potentially damaging to blood vessels as it circulates through the bloodstream on its way to deposit cholesterol in the liver.

Very-Low-Density Lipoproteins. Structurally, VLDLs are similar to chylomicrons. They, too, contain mostly triglycerides. They originate in the liver, which is the main switching station for fuel distribution for the entire body. The liver constantly receives fatty acids from adipose tissue and burns them for energy. But the liver is not prepared to be a warehouse for storage of large amounts of fuel, so leftover fats are repackaged into lipoproteins, (VLDLs) in the process. These lipoproteins are the main vehicles for shipping energy rich fat to the rest of the body. If the other organs (i.e., muscles, kidneys, lungs) don't use the triglycerides, the fatty tissue will take it up and store it.

As with chylomicrons, the delivery of triglycerides to body tissues depends upon the presence of the same enzyme (lipase) and the lipoprotein that allows the VLDL carrier to dock. A genetic defect can block this step as well. But normally, after the triglycerides have been removed, the VLDL is converted into LDL (Low Density Lipoprotein) by getting rid of excess protein. What's left is mostly cholesterol with one major protein called ''Apo-B.''

Low-Density Lipoproteins. LDLs are the major cholesterol carriers in the bloodstream. LDL-cholesterol is sometimes referred to as ''bad'' cholesterol. That's because, after being formed from VLDLs, LDLs circulate in the blood for several days and during this time, they can accumulate in susceptible blood vessels. Most LDLs eventually find their way to specific protein receptors on cells, most of which are in the liver, for uptake and destruction. This process normally regulates the blood level of LDL keeping it safely low—unless the system is altered by a bad diet or bad genes.

Most of the tissues in the body can regulate the cholesterol content of their cells, in much the same way a thermostat controls the temperature in a room. When the cells run low in cholesterol, they signal for production of more receptors on their surface. This, in turn, increases the uptake of LDL-cholesterol from blood. If the cells have too much cholesterol, receptor production shuts down.

There are several genetic disorders that can cause abnormally high LDL blood levels. In Familial Hypercholesterolemia, described in Chapter 4, two or three times the normal number of LDLs are present, accounting for the extremely high cholesterol levels that are characteristic of this disease. Because they have inherited a defective gene, such people are unable to make enough receptors. As a result, LDLs, and the cholesterol they carry, accumulate in the bloodstream. Such people often suffer cardiovascular disease in their 40's or 50's.

Those who inherit two defective genes cannot make *any* receptors, causing a life-threatening situation in childhood. If not treated, they rapidly develop clogged arteries and suffer heart attacks. This genetic disorder has provided some of the strongest evidence that high blood levels of LDL-cholesterol can directly cause atherosclerosis without other risk factors being present.

High LDL levels can also be the result of too many VLDLs being made by the liver. If this is the case, a person's triglyceride blood count is usually high as well, since VLDLs are rich in this fat.

High-Density Lipoproteins. Each protein-rich HDL particle contains at least eight different apo-proteins on its surface. One of HDL's functions is to provide some of these proteins to chylomicrons and VLDLs, which need them to clear fat from the bloodstream. If HDL levels are low, triglycerides in chylomicrons and VLDL build up in the blood.

The second known function of HDLs is to transport cholesterol from other tissues to the liver so it can be excreted from the body. This role is crucial in regulating the overall balance of cholesterol into and out of tissues—including the artery walls where atherosclerosis takes place. In fact, HDL-cholesterol is often referred to as "good" cholesterol, because its presence means cholesterol is being removed from arteries that would otherwise be damaged by a build up.

Without an adequate quantity of HDLs, the normal flow of fats through the bloodstream is disrupted. Since removal of cholesterol from artery walls is part of this process, it's not surprising that people with very low HDL-cholesterol blood values are at increased risk for heart disease. This can be the result of inheriting a genetic disorder. In some cases the problem is an inability to make enough HDLs, while others may have unusually fast removal of HDLs from the bloodstream.

Recently, attention has been focused on the fact that HDLs exist in two sizes, the larger HDL-2, and the smaller HDL-3. People who are blessed with high blood levels of HDL, including women, seem to have more HDL-2. People with low blood HDL levels—in general, men—possess mostly HDL-3. It's possible that HDL-2 may offer some unique protective value against atherosclerosis, making its measurement more important than total HDL levels. This is still being debated among scientists.

What Are Normal Lipoprotein Levels?

It's important to realize that *normal* or *average* values are not necessarily *desirable* values. In fact, half of all American adults have cholesterol levels that are not in the desirable range, which is below 200. And 25 percent of us have levels over 240 mg/dl, signaling the need for medical evaluation and monitoring.

Laboratory Test Results. Measurement of the LDL and HDL levels in the blood present an accurate picture of cardiovascular risk. Your physician should order this comprehensive blood test if your total cholesterol measures more than 240 mg/dl, or if it is over 200 and you have any two of the other risk factors for heart disease (family history, smoking, high blood pressure, diabetes, or obesity). Remember, being male is a risk factor, so a man needs only one more risk factor to be placed in this category.

Unfortunately, many of the laboratories that test for cholesterol are not yet standardized, and test results can vary. In addition, the body's cholesterol levels normally vary according to the time of year, the time of month (in women), the time of day, and the position of the body during blood sampling. Finger-prick screening tests — the type offered in malls or health fairs — are reasonably accurate for total cholesterol, but they can't yet test for the various lipoprotein fractions. When having blood drawn for a lipoprotein levels (HDL and LDL), it's best to have fasted for 12 hours beforehand.

One solution to all this variation is to be tested for total cholesterol at least twice. If the values are now within 30 mg/dl of each other, another test should be performed. Much the same as with high blood pressure, a high blood cholesterol should not be treated on one reading alone. Persons with values in the desirable range below 200 mg/dl should be re-tested with each physical examination, or at least every five years.

Everyone should know his or her own cholesterol count, the actual number, not just whether it's in the normal range. That's because laboratories use average values as their standards, not desirable levels. Some even list up to 300 mg/dl as "normal." Yet such values are clearly associated with a very high risk of heart disease. Knowing your number allows you to keep track of whether it declines as you improve your diet. It also provides a base number with which to compare values in the years ahead.

Currently, there is a national campaign underway to have all adults tested for their cholesterol levels. Those over the age of 18 should have their blood tested for total cholesterol at least once every five years. The National Cholesterol Education Program has issued new guidelines for classification of total blood cholesterol values (*see* Table 2). If the number is over 200 mg/dl, further testing and treatment should be followed.

Total Cholesterol Values. As we grow older, total blood cholesterol rises. By age 70, our cholesterol count may be 60 mg/dl higher than when we were 20 years old. Men's values tend to increase sooner, during their 30s and 40s. Women eventually catch up when they reach their 50s and 60s. Most of the rise in total cholesterol levels as we age is due to an increase in LDL-cholesterol, the undesirable fraction.

A "desirable" total blood cholesterol is below 200 mg/dl Values between 200 and 239 are classified as "borderline-high," while counts of 240 and over are "high."

Table 3

Classification Based on LDL-Cholesterol

130 mg/dl	Desirable LDL-Cholesterol
130-159 mg/dl	Borderline-High-Risk LDL-Cholesterol
160 mg/dl	High-Risk LDL-Cholesterol

LDL-Cholesterol Values. This is the most significant number of all the lipoprotein fractions, because it is the most directly related to cardiovascular risk. If your initial screening for total blood cholesterol reveals a count higher than 200 mg/dl, then your physician may check your LDL-cholesterol level.

Why Cholesterol Is Confusing

The lower your LDL-cholesterol the better. A value below 130 mg/dl is "desirable." For individuals with no other risk factors, experts believe up to 160 is the upper limit of safety. This range, between 130-159, is classified as "borderline-high-risk." Individuals with values of 160 and above, are at "high-risk." At least 25 percent of American adults need to lower their LDL-cholesterol levels according to these criteria. Specific goals for LDL reduction are provided in Table 3.

HDL-Cholesterol Values. Boys and girls start out with similar HDL values, until puberty, when it drops 10 mg/dl in boys. Men's HDL-cholesterol levels average about 45 mg/dl, while women's values average 55, rising to about 60 in the sixth decade of life. The fact that women in their 70s actually have higher total cholesterol counts than men is due, in part, to their higher HDL levels. In this case, having higher cholesterol levels actually results in lower risk.

The higher your HDL-cholesterol the better. People with values below 35 mg/dl are classified as "at risk" because such blood levels are associated with increased risk of heart disease. In fact, the risk of developing heart disease or stroke is significantly reduced as HDL rises. Exercise has been shown to help increase the amount of HDL cholesterol circulating in the blood, as has quitting smoking and losing excess weight. Although alcohol also can raise HDL levels, its use is not a recommended method of reducing cardiovascular risk.

Triglyceride Values. High blood triglyceride levels—above 250 mg/dl—are associated with a greater risk of vascular disease, but it's not as strong as the blood cholesterol connection. In fact, it might be explained by the fact that people with high triglyceride values often have high LDL-cholesterol values, and many also have low HDL-cholesterol values. So there's usually no need to consider triglycerides separately; assessing risk based on LDL and HDL values alone is adequate.

That does not mean triglycerides shouldn't be measured at all, however, since a high level may be a clue to some other underlying disease, such as diabetes or a thyroid, kidney, or liver disorder. If the triglyceride level measures above 500 mg/dl, it needs to be carefully monitored to be sure it does not rapidly rise higher. People with levels over 1,000 are at risk for a severe inflammation of the pancreas, a serious condition with the threat of shock and even death. Diet and medications may be needed to keep triglycerides below 1,000.

How Do Liproproteins Damage Blood Vessels?

We know now that when a person's LDL-cholesterol level is high there's a good chance that he or she will develop the disease called atherosclerosis. As a result, arteries will be dangerously clogged with cholesterol and the growth of cells that result from the ongoing damage. We know that the process is accentuated if the HDL-cholesterol level is low, if blood pressure is high, if there is too much body fat or the habit of cigarette smoking exists. But just how all these factors actually damage the wall of the artery is much harder to explain.

Most of what we know about arterial lesions—the fatty deposits that build up on the inside of artery walls—comes from studying animals. It is easy to induce atheriosclerosis in primates, both monkeys and apes, by feeding large amounts of cholesterol and saturated fat. This raises their LDL-cholesterol blood levels and they develop clogged arteries similar to those seen in humans during surgery or at autopsy.

The Healthy Artery. The artery wall consists of four layers, each with its own characteristic cells. The innermost layer, called the **endothelium,** is only one cell thick. These specialized cells are flat and tightly stuck together, like tiles on a floor.

The next layer, the **intima,** is very thin, containing mostly protein fibers and very few cells. Next to that is the **media,** the thickest layer in coronary arteries. It provides the flexibility that such muscular blood vessels require. The final outermost layer is the **adventia,** tougher than the other layers. It provides strength and helps to separate the artery from the tissues through which it passes. **(page 16)**

The Diseased Artery. It is in the intima that the atherosclerotic disease process is first noticeable. With a microscope, it's possible to see cholesterol-filled cells in this thin layer that usually has few, if any, cells. As the disease progresses, the cells accumulate and eventually die. As they do, they release their cholesterol into the artery wall.

The presence of the cholesterol stimulates a process to clean up the debris. This leads to a clump of cells, debris, and scar tissue that builds up in the intima, producing the characteristic atherosclerotic lesion, or plaque. This is not harmful until the mass of cells grows large enough to slow the flow of blood through the artery.

Although the disease process is first noticed in the intima, it doesn't begin there. Animal research has provided strong evidence to suggest that damage to the endothelium is the first step in development of the atherosclerotic lesion. It appears that a rise in blood cholesterol triggers the endothelial damage. But damage to the endothelium occurs so quickly after cholesterol is eaten in animal experiments, that some researchers have suggested that dietary cholesterol might have a deleterious effect even before it causes a rise in LDL-cholesterol, perhaps as it circulates in the remnants of chylomicrons. If this is the case, people might want to consider limiting dietary cholesterol even if their LDL-cholesterol is in an apparently safe range.

Indeed, studies of populations show that the amount of cholesterol in the diet is a powerful predictor of future heart attacks. Obviously, more research is needed to clarify the effects of dietary cholesterol on blood cholesterol.

Once damage to the endothelial lining occurs, many blood constituents have access to the inner artery wall. Many more LDL particles get into the intima carrying their heavy load of cholesterol. The debris-clearing cells take up excess cholesterol, accounting for the cholesterol-filled cells that appear in the intima. There's some evidence that oxygen-damaged LDL particles clog arteries more quickly and smoking may promote this process by generating more such damaged LDL particles. If there are high levels of circulating HDLs, however, they may be able to come to the rescue to pick up the accumulating cholesterol and carry it back to the liver.

A damaged endothelium is ripe for trouble because the artery lining now has rough spots where sticky blood particles called platelets quickly accumulate, causing blood vessels to spasm. This also stimulates the blood to form a clot. As this blood clot gets bigger, there's a danger of it completely obstructing the vessel and suddenly cutting off blood flow to the heart or brain, causing a heart attack or stroke.

Understanding the complex particles called lipoproteins gives insight into the relationship between blood cholesterol and the development of atherosclerosis. We understand more about how diet and other risk factors can change these lipoprotein levels. Most important, we now have evidence that we can change our diets in very specific ways to improve our lipoprotein profile and reduce the risk of vascular disease.

CHAPTER SIX

Dietary Changes to Lower Your Cardiovascular Risk

by W. Virgil Brown, M.D.

By changing your diet, you can reduce several of the risk factors for cardiovascular diesease. Chief among these is lowering your LDL-cholesterol level. If you are currently eating the usual American diet and you alter your diet to meet the American Heart Association guidelines (see Tables 5 and 6) you can expect a 10 to 15 percent reduction in your LDL-cholesterol value. This is thought to translate to a 20 to 30 percent reduction in your risk of a heart attack.

Some of the dietary changes recommended here may raise your blood level of HDL-cholestrol, while others may lower it. Although higher HDL levels are desirable, it's probably better not to choose dietary treatments based on what happens to the HDL level. Too little is known about HDLs to make major dietary changes based on their fluctuation.

Other risk factors that can be tackled by diet include reducing excess body fat, lowering elevated blood pressure, improving diabetic control of blood sugar, and reducing the tendency of blood to clot. Although research has not shown that heart disease can be prevented by such measures, we do know that people who have these problems, but do nothing about them, suffer more heart attacks. We also know that lowering blood pressure reduces the chances of having a stroke—remarkably so.

When changing your diet to achieve these goals, you should focus on reducing total calories, total fat, saturated fat, dietary cholesterol, and sodium. Many individuals may also need to limit their intake of sugar and alcohol. In addition, most Americans would benefit from a concomitant increase in complex carbohydrates, soluble fiber, and fish. To do all this, just follow the relatively simple rules that we've outlined here.

Reducing Total Calories

If you weigh 10 percent or more over the Metropolitan weight guidelines (see Table 1 in Chapter 4) you are at greater risk for a heart attack, but don't panic into trying an irrational fad diet. If you need to reduce your weight, do so slowly. One to two pounds per month is reasonable. This can be done by cutting down on foods rich in fat and alcohol as we suggest in this book, without compromising the palatability of your diet. If you can keep up this slow weight loss pace, you've probably succeeded in establishing new dietary habits.

Weight loss can be hastened if you exercise regularly in addition to cutting calories. It's best to look for an activity that will burn about 300 extra calories every day, rather than choose an intermittent heavy activity. As with changing food habits, the small and easily accomplished daily exercise routine is more likely to be sustained than an all-out effort that quickly loses its appeal. People who maintain an exercise habit are more likely to stick to good eating habits as well.

Reducing Total Fat

Currently, Americans eat almost 40 percent of their calories as fat. That's too much. By cutting down on the total fat in your diet, you automatically reduce your intake of saturated fats, cholesterol, and total calories, all of which will likely benefit your heart.

You can reduce your fat intake to 30 percent with relatively simple changes in your diet such as switching to skim milk and low fat dairy products; halving your intake of margarine, mayonnaise and other high fat spreads, choosing lean cuts and trimming the fat from meat; removing the skin and fat from poultry (before cooking); and steaming, baking, microwaving or broiling instead of frying.

Americans eat more protein than we need, and meat contributes an untoward share of both protein and fat. Try cutting down on portion sizes, by thinking of meat as a side dish and making complex carbohydrates the focus of the meal. A perfect example of this is a bowl of pasta with a marinara sauce containing a small amount of lean meat.

Reducing Saturated Fats

Of everything that we eat, saturated fats have the most powerful effect on raising LDL-cholesterol levels. Currently, Americans eat about 15 percent of calories as saturated fat. That should be reduced by about 30 to 50 percent to less than 10 percent. By following the simple rules in Table 4, you should be able to significantly reduce the amount of saturated fat you eat to within acceptable limits.

By switching to low-fat dairy products and cutting out butter you can trim 20 percent off your saturated fat intake. Drinking skim milk can become second nature if the switch is made gradually, first getting used to 2 percent milk, then 1 percent, then skim. Cheese is a bit more of a problem. There aren't that many low fat choices available. Several are mentioned on page 57. Hard cheeses such as Cheddar should be limited, since they contain a large amount of saturated fat.

Cutting down on your intake of hot dogs, cold cuts, and beef fat by at least two-thirds may also reduce saturated fat intake in a meaningful way. Look for lean cuts of meat with the new 'Select' grade and trim the fat. Cutting in half the amount of egg yolks, doughnuts, and cookies you eat eliminates 5 percent more.

Particular caution is due for coconut and palm kernel oils. Despite being vegetable oils, they are more saturated than even beef fat or lard (pig fat). They are commonly found in commercial baked goods, often with labels that proclaim, ''Made with vegetable shortening. No cholesterol!'' This implies that these products are healthy for your heart, when the evidence suggests just the opposite. We believe the wise move is to read labels and avoid those foods that list coconut, palm kernel, or palm oils. Of the three, coconut oil is by far the worst.

Substituting Unsaturated Fats

Many people have the mistaken notion that polyunsaturates can do no harm and are actually good for you. This myth is perpetuated by the advertising of margarines and vegetable oils such as corn and soybean oils. Polyunsaturated fats do, in fact, help to lower blood cholesterol levels when they are substituted for saturated fats. In other words, don't add extra fat to your diet, just switch from a saturated fat source to an unsaturated one. A good example is to substitute margarine for butter.

But while polyunsaturated fats lower LDL-cholesterol, if substituted for saturated fats they also lower HDL-cholesterol. This may blunt some of the beneficial effect, but the actual meaning of this fall in HDL has not been established. Furthermore, the long-term effects of a high polyunsaturated fat diet is unknown. Current recommendations are to keep polyunsaturated fats to no more than 10 percent of calories. This would allow a small increase from our current average intake of about 7 percent.

Monounsaturates, such as that found in olive, canola, and peanut oils, have recently gained in favor. It was thought that they had a neutral effect on blood cholesterol. But new research indicates that, when substituted for saturated fat in the diet, monounsaturates can also lower LDL-cholesterol with less lowering of HDL-cholesterol when compared to polyunsaturates. Current recommendations are that monounsaturates should make up the balance of calories, after saturated and polyunsaturated fats are considered. This ends up being about 10 to 15 percent of calories, similar to current consumption.

Reducing Dietary Cholesterol

The average American man eats between 400 and 500 milligrams of cholesterol a day; women consume somewhat less. Because the body can regulate how much cholesterol it manufactures, blood cholesterol won't necessarily decrease on a low-cholesterol diet. Some people will see a response; some won't. But since we can't easily identify who will respond, it's best if everyone tries to limit dietary cholesterol.

The major portion of our saturated fat comes from beef and dairy products. These also are major contributors of our dietary cholesterol. With a few exceptions, foods that are high in saturated fats are high in cholesterol as well. So by concentrating on reducing saturated and total fat, you will automatically be reducing your intake of dietary cholesterol; the oils from coconuts and palm trees are the chief exception.

As most people know, the egg yolk is a rich source of cholesterol, containing 275 milligrams; the entire day's recommended limit is between 250 and 300 milligrams. Organ meats, such as liver, brains, and sweetbreads, are also extremely high in cholesterol. Neither eggs or organ meats need be totally forsaken, however, because they are rich in nutrients. Rather, they should be viewed as occasional foods.

As with saturated fats, switching from whole to low-fat dairy products can reduce cholesterol substantially. Ounce for ounce, the muscle in meat contains nearly as much cholesterol as the fat portion. So the most effective way to reduce fat *and* cholesterol when eating meat is to reduce your portion size. Three ounces of cooked lean meat, poultry or fish is a reasonable portion.

Table 4: 11 Tips to Reduce Saturated Fat and Dietary Cholesterol Intake

1. Choose new "Select" grade of lean cuts of meat; trim all visible fat; broil, grill, steam, microwave, bake or pan cook without added fat.
2. Limit meat portions to 4 ounces raw (3 to 3½ ounces cooked), about the size of deck of cards.
3. Eat less processed meats (hot dogs, luncheon meats, sausage).
4. Remove the skin from poultry *before* cooking.
5. Use skim milk and skim or nonfat milk dairy products.
6. Substitute margarine for butter.
7. Reduce your intake of fatty cheeses (most hard cheeses such as Cheddar); substitute low-fat varieties (read labels for brands with no more than 2 to 6 grams of total fat per ounce of cheese).
8. Eat few egg yolks: Substitute imitation eggs when whole eggs are called for in recipes.
9. Read labels of potato chips, microwave popcorn, poultry stuffing, cookies, donuts, pastries, etc. to avoid coconut, palm kernal, and palm oils in processed foods. If it's purchased in cellophane, read the labels.
10. Limit your intake of liver, kidney, and other organ meats to once a month at the most.
11. Increase legumes (dried peas and beans), leafy green vegetables, fruits and grains.

The recipes that follow will illustrate how these rules can be followed assiduously while maintaining a very attractive diet.

Reducing Sodium

The value of reducing sodium in our diet—primarily by cutting down on the amount of salt we eat—has been the source of debate for years. The evidence now suggests that reducing dietary sodium from the current average of five grams a day to three grams will help lower blood pressure in only 20 percent of hypertensives.

On the other hand, there is strong evidence from studies in countries around the world that a life-long diet high in sodium correlates with a higher probability of developing high blood pressure. This suggests that people who eat a diet that's low in sodium from early childhood will be less likely to develop hypertension. For this reason, the current recommendation is to limit sodium to about three grams per day.

By not adding any salt at the table, you can probably reduce your sodium intake to four grams or less. To reduce it further requires avoiding many processed foods, which typically are high in sodium. Especially watch out for condiments, commercial breads, hot dogs, cold cuts, and cured meats. Reading ingredient labels is essential, since not all high-sodium foods taste salty. Look for any words that have salt or sodium in them. The closer to the end of the list they are, the better, since ingredients must be listed in descending order of their weight.

Reducing Sugar

About 20 percent of calories in the typical American diet come from sucrose, or common table sugar. While the only evidence of direct harm is its contribution to dental decay, there is an additional subtle effect. "Empty" sugar calories—which otherwise provide no nutrients—take up space in the diet, reducing the intake of more nutritious foods that would provide vitamins, minerals, and protein.

A reasonable goal is to reduce sucrose so it contributes no more than 10 percent of calories. This can be accomplished by 1) not adding sugar at the table, 2) choosing fruit instead of sweets for snacks and desserts, 3) avoiding condiments, such as ketchup, that contain sugar, and 4) reading labels for "hidden" sugar, such as that in commercial breadings and breakfast cereals, even adult types.

Drinking Alcohol in Moderation

In moderation, alcohol is associated with higher HDL levels and seems to correlate with fewer deaths from vascular disease, although the relationship is questionable. What *is* certain, are the damaging effects of excessive alcohol. People who drink more than two ounces a day suffer more high blood pressure and stroke. Moreover, direct damage to the liver, brain, and the entire nervous system are well documented.

Since drinking "just a little" can often lead to drinking a lot, it is inadvisable to recommend alcohol as part of a healthy diet. The additional social disruption and accidental deaths that accompany alcohol abuse make it even more unwise to recommend alcoholic beverages for health purposes. In essence, alcohol is a drug whose side effects preclude its prescription. Yet there's no medical basis to advise against moderate and responsible consumption of alcohol. It is a component of many fine wines and other beverages that may add to the enjoyment of food. For those who can control their intake of alcohol, here's to your health!

Increasing Complex Carbohydrates

Starches are often mistakenly blamed for our obesity and ill health. Quite the contrary, over the past half-century, as our intake of cereals and other whole grains has fallen, we have gotten fatter. In actuality, starches, such as bread, potatoes, and pasta, are relatively low in calories. The accompanying butter, margarine, and fat containing sauces are the real calorie culprits.

Experts agree that Americans should increase their intake of carbohydrates from the current 45 percent of calories to 55 or 60 percent, primarily by increasing vegetable consumption. This will assure adequate vitamins, minerals, and fiber intake.

Increasing Fiber

Complex carbohydrates that are not digestible contribute fiber to our diets. Examples of fiber sources include cellulose, hemicellulose, pectin, gums, and lignins. Over the years, as we have eaten more fat and sugar, we've consumed less fiber. There's some evidence that this has contributed to a number of disease processes.

There are two types of fiber—soluble and insoluble—and it's best to ob-

Table 5		
	Average American Diet	Cholesterol-Lowering Diet
Saturated	15-20%	Less than 10%
Monounsaturated	14-16%	10-15%
Polyunsaturated	7%	Up to 10%
Carbohydrate	47%	50-60%
Protein	16%	Up to 20%
Cholesterol	300-600 mg	Less than 300 mg

The differences between these two diets are subtle and appear to be small, but they are very important for lowering your blood cholesterol level. All of these small changes add up to big improvements in your blood cholesterol level. Take a look at the sample menus.

tain a mixture of the two. Insoluble fiber, such as that found in wheat bran, can improve bowel function. It's soluble fiber, however, that's particularly beneficial in this case because it apparently reduces LDL-cholesterol levels, without reducing HDL levels. To obtain this benefit, eat more oat and corn bran, dried peas and beans, fruits and vegetables. Some nutritionists recommend increasing total fiber from a current low of 12 grams a day to over 40 grams daily. If you do this, you can expect an elevated blood cholesterol to fall as much as 10 percent.

Increasing Fish

Recently, there's been a flurry of interest in the health benefits of fish. It all started when researchers noticed that Greenland Eskimos and Japanese fisherman—who eat large amounts of fish—have extremely low rates of heart disease.

Subsequent animal studies identified the type of fat in fish—known as omega-3 fatty acids—as the apparent beneficial substance. Animals fed large amounts of fish oils show fewer atherosclerotic lesions, even when on high cholesterol diets. It's thought that fish oil actually reduces the stickiness of the blood platelets that otherwise would cling to damaged blood vessel walls and form dangerous clots.

A common misconception is that fish oil lowers LDL-cholesterol. In fact, it has little effect on either LDL-or HDL-cholesterol, compared to that of vegetable oils. It has been shown to markedly lower high triglyceride levels in people. In animal studies that used fish oil in amounts up to 30 percent of calories—the equivalent of 40 to 60 fish oil capsules a day—VLDL levels fell, which can indirectly reduce the number of LDL particles. In more usual doses of two to six grams daily, it's reasonable to expect a measurable effect on blood platelets, but not on blood cholesterol levels.

Additional studies have helped confirm that eating fish is clearly associated with fewer heart attacks. But the exact mechanism for reduced damage to blood vessels is not yet known. In a Dutch study, people who ate as little as six to ten ounces of fish each *week* suffered *half* the coronary heart disease of those who ate no fish. The fascinating finding in this study was that most of the fish eaten was not fatty fish, and total fish oil consumption averaged less than one gram per day. So perhaps there is something else that's beneficial in fish besides omega-3 fatty acids.

This argues against popping fish oil capsules, since they may not contain all the benefits of fish. Ironically, some fish oil brands contain large amounts of cholesterol, which may defeat the supposed purpose of the pills. Moreover, long-term use of such supplements has not been adequately studied. Eating fish two or three times a week, however, seems sensible and offers the additional benefit of providing a low-fat but tasty substitute for meat.

In Summary

There is overwhelming evidence that the typical fat laden diet most Americans eat contributes to heart disease. It does this primarily by increasing LDL-cholesterol levels in the blood. Our current dietary habits also promote obesity, hypertension, and adult-onset diabetes, all of which further contribute to the risk of developing atherosclerosis.

Changing our diet toward a healthier eating pattern is not only feasible, but is, in fact, occuring in the United States at an impressive pace. So far, the evidence suggests that such dietary changes will continue to reduce the incidence of cardiovascular disease.

Table 6: American Heart Association Dietary Guildelines
1. Reduce saturated fat intake to less than 10 percent of calories.
2. Reduce total fat intake to less than 30 percent of calories.
3. Limit dietary cholesterol to less than 300 milligrams/day.
4. Maintain protein intake at 15 percent of calories.
5. Increase carbohydrate intake to more than 50 percent of calories, emphasizing complex varieties.
6. Limit sodium intake to less than 3 grams/day.
7. Limit alcohol intake to a maximum of two ounces/day.
8. Eat enough calories to maintain best body weight (as specified by the 1959 Metropolitan Life Company tables).
9. Consume a wide variety of foods.

CHAPTER SEVEN

Cooking Methods and Food Substitutions

*E*ven those of us who are knowledgeable about food and have always had healthy diets or have adopted healthier eating habits over time still have a few high cholesterol holdovers we love. It may be a BLT sandwich or a hot fudge sundae.

What we've done in this book, besides offering many low cholesterol and low fat recipes, is to use excellent low cholesterol substitutes such as Bright Day™ dressing for mayonnaise with a small amount of very lean or defatted bacon or Morningstar Farms Breakfast Strips™, to make a terrific BLT with no flavor loss. Or vanilla or wildberry Tofutti™ as a substitute for high cholesterol dairy ice cream.

We've compiled a list of foods that can be used in the transition phase or even permanently to enhance a low cholesterol diet. As an example, using Dorman's Lo-Chol™ cheese. A toasted cheese sandwich with this lowered cholesterol, less saturated fat cheese is delicious and tastes no different from the usual high cholesterol fried cheese sandwich.

Once you begin to switch over to these healthier foods, a couple of very important things begin to happen. You no longer like fat as much. In fact, what normally would be considered only a moderate amount of fat in a meal can make you very tired, lethargic, and sometimes even nauseous the next day. Fatty foods and rich desserts just don't look very good to you anymore because you equate them with how you are going to feel. Also, your cravings begin to change, and salads and vegetables take on a new appeal.

Many so-called food substitutes work very well and in many cases supplant the original. Using the substitutes also helps to keep us from feeling deprived. For instance, flavor and texture differences between part or all skim-milk mozzarella or ricotta cheese and whole milk mozzarella or ricotta cheese are indiscernible, especially when used on spicy foods like pizza.

Diet changes start with knowledge, then build on acceptance and a change in thinking, then a reorientation to the foods you buy in grocery stores and order in restaurants. Finally, you change the way you prepare food. It's very difficult to change eating habits. Some people read, and-presto!—they make all the internal mental adjustments and remember all the tips necessary to eat healthier. But for many, changing food habits is traumatic. One study showed immigrants change dress and language long before they change their food. Food habits often continue for generations.

Again, most doctors, scientists, and researchers now agree, according to a consensus conference at the National Institutes of Health, that high cholesterol levels are a major indicator of coronary heart disease and most blood cholesterol levels can be affected by diet alone.

A Complete Heart-Health Guide

This book offers information about cholesterol and gourmet recipes. We hope the Fischer/Brown Low Cholesterol Gourmet will answer many of your questions about cholesterol and saturated fat. We want to make it as easy as possible for you to change to a healthier diet. And even with cholesterol-lowering drugs, diet will still have a great impact on lowering your cholesterol level and is always the first level of defense. Other factors that may involve cholesterol are exercise (one hour a day three days a week is recommended, with some hours being devoted to cardiovascular exercises, such as walking, jogging or aerobics, other hours to toning). Smoking lowers the HDL-cholesterol levels and adversely affects the heart, and lungs, (among other parts of the body). Alcoholism and obesity are severe health problems that, like smoking, may need intervention to overcome. Each one will affect your heart health.

Calories

Calories are often important to people on a reduced cholesterol diet. Most of these recipes are extremely low in calories because there is so little fat. To give you an idea, stuffed flank steak (on page 167) has 184 calories per serving, beef stew, 352; beef and tangerines, 207; pasta primavera, 212; two oat bran cookies, 163; a glass of eggnog has a higher 471; tuna salad 213. But, most are exceptionally low in calories. Most servings of meat are three and one-half ounces or a portion about the size of the palm of your hand or a deck of cards.

Salt

There are many differences of opinion on the use of salt; check with your doctor. Particularly, if you have hypertension, you should lower your salt intake. All the recipes can be made without salt and salt is an option in most. Additional notations are made throughout the book to alert you to hidden salt, such as in commercial bread, and recipes with such high salt foods as anchovies are noted so you can omit them if you wish. Because it is so important, there is more about salt in Dr. Brown's chapters (page 45).

Sugar

Sugar substitutes are numerous. I don't usually recommend brands because in this book our use of sugar is generally limited. Look under sugar substitutes for more information. We've suggested kinds and brands such as maple or the English Demerera for specific flavors. In some cases you can omit sugar, but most people use both sugar and sugar substitutes on a daily basis with no ill effects.

Substitutes in General

To make substitutions easily, a list of products is included so that you can exchange safely and deliciously for such high cholesterol items as butter, egg yolks, sour cream, ice cream, cream cheese, whole cream and other cheeses, whole milk, mayonnaise, and more. We've taken traditional recipes and adapted them to invent fabulous new low cholesterol, low saturated fat meals; we've offered ways to make holiday food with less cholesterol and saturated fat and shown how to eat out with these new guidelines. Again, this is a complete guide for those who want to lower their cholesterol and saturated fat and still enjoy the pleasure of eating.

Cooking Changes, Use of Microwave Ovens

The single biggest change you'll make (besides buying different foods) is in the use of fat and oil when you cook. Almost all standard recipes have superfluous or simply gratuitous fat. A tablespoon here, a quarter of a cup there. And they often say, "sauté the onions in a tablespoon of butter" (or margarine, olive oil, etc.). I've found that nearly any vegetable recipe that says sauté or fry can be changed successfully to "simmer in water," or microwave with a few drop of water in a plastic bag with beneficial health results. When it says "simmer green beans in water," use about four teaspoons of water. The food is actually steamed because it's cooked or microwaved covered. You have to be careful that the water doesn't evaporate, but once you get used to substituting water for oil or fat, really a very simple step, you will find it tastier, cleaner, cheaper, and, most important, healthier. To cook this way successfully you need a certain kind of cookware and, if possible, a microwave oven too. Many cooks use both, often simultaneously. Microwave cooking can be used often as it offers a no fat and no grease alternative to frying, braising and baking. Many of our recipes give microwave instructions as an alternative or to be used in conjunction with other forms of cooking.

Cookware

Because you will be using little or no grease or fat to cook, you'll need cookware that has a good non-stick surface. Of the variety of non-stick cookware currently available, my favorite is Silverstone™, made by DuPont. I use a heavy version and all of my pots, pans, cookie sheets, and skillets have a Silverstone™ coating. This type of cookware is available at department and kitchen stores. It also has the advantages of being incredibly easy to clean.

Product Use and Brand Designation

The cooking section of this book (which took three years to write), entailed the use of many products and many different brands. This is not a *routine* gourmet cookbook in that our first responsibility and interest is in improving health and nutrition. This requires substitutions, new methods of cooking foods, and a greater use of foods that don't contain saturated fat or cholesterol.

In several instances specific brands are recommended because they will enable the reader to complete the recipe with the best taste or lowest fat. For instance, the flavor of I Can't Believe It's Not Butter™ is excellent and closer to butter for those who like butter, so we have sometimes recommended that brand. Two brands, Weight Watchers™ and Soft Diet Parkey™ margarine, had the lowest amount of saturated fat at the time the book was written so we've recommended those products, as well.

Several substitutions, such as King Cholesterol Free™ imitation sour cream, or Tofutti's ''Better Than Cream Cheese,''™ are suggested because we don't wish to swear off stuffed celery permanently, yet we can't handle the cholesterol in real sour cream or cream cheese. We use these special foods only occasionally, yet some cookbook writers and food editors criticize them.

I made it a point at my own expense to visit several companies offering low cholesterol, low fat products. Those companies included Worthington Food in Worthington, Ohio, which makes a variety of excellent foods, especially meatless sausage patties and links. Another is United Foods Brand in Baltimore, Maryland which makes the best mayonnaise available without egg yolks. Tofutti Brands in Rahway, New Jersey, is another. They make many fine products, devoted to delicious low cholesterol, low saturated fat eating; several are recommended in this book.

Why Food Substitutes Work

We like the taste of, and are used to eating, many foods that are high in saturated animal and vegetable fats and cholesterol, therefore, eliminating them from the diet completely, especially eliminating them quickly, is very difficult for most people.

There is a also a highly emotional side to even the most minor food changes that is better recognized and worked with instead of against. People feel deprived or that something is wrong when they change foods. Eating so-called real butter or having marbled beef is a goal that many people have strived for for years, especially those who grew up poor. Children from the depression years of the 30s want real butter. Now, just when they can afford it, or they have gotten used to the taste of butter and fatty meat, someone comes along and says it isn't good for them. Because of our traditions, butter is erroneously considered real; margarine is not. There is nothing more real or natural about butter, a fat from cows, than there is about butter from a whale or a mouse. We simply have a more convenient dairy and cattle industry and not a whale or mouse one. What we call real is just a taste we're used to.

We must change, but changing is hard. In fact, the body rebels physically when we change food habits too quickly. In another example, both smoking and drinking aren't good for the body. They can cause permanent damage and premature death. Yet the body protests violently when you stop either of these dangerous practices abruptly. It's the same with food. The body reaches a comfort level even on a poor diet consisting of lots of fatty animal products, fried foods, simple carbohydrates, and calories devoid of nutrients such as those in potato chips, candy, and alcohol. Switch that person abruptly to a high-fiber, low-fat, high complex carbohydrate diet such as the one recommended in this book for a healthy heart and healthy arteries, and he or she may have some stomach irritation while the body readjusts. But it does adjust if you're patient, and it's well worth the effort.

These food substitutes will help make that adjustment smoother. In some cases, you may want to use the substitutes permanently. Just don't get hung up on the words real or natural. It's all real and surely isn't natural to drink another animal's milk into adulthood. Make dietary changes comfortably and find out what you especially enjoy.

Specifically Speaking

Egg Yolks	Egg yolks are considered one of the primary culprits in raising cholesterol in the American diet. Good substitutes are Egg Watchers™ by Tofutti, Scramblers™ by Morningstar Farms, and Egg Beaters™ by Nabisco, found in the frozen dairy section of most stores. Beware of dried eggs and dried egg yolks. They have *more* cholesterol per serving.
Butter	Butter Buds™, a powdered butter flavoring, it is found in the package goods department of most grocery stores. It is produced by Cumberland Packing Corporation of Brooklyn, NY. Molly McButter™, another butter substitute, comes in granular form.

I Can't Believe It's Not Butter™ is a margarine that has excellent flavor. Like all partially hydrogenated margarines, I Can't Believe It's Not Butter™ has no cholesterol but it does have some saturated fat.

The margarines with the least saturated fat per serving are Weight Watchers™ and Soft Diet Parkay™ brands, which come in tubs.

Parkay Squeeze Margarine™ helps you to control the amount where scoops and patties of margarine often don't. Liquid margarines usually have less hydrogenation so less saturated fat. Country Crock™ makes one, too.

Shedd's Spread™ and Promise™ are also fine butter substitutes, as is Fleishman's Corn Oil Margarine™ , and there are others. Read labels for saturated fat content as they change often.

Cheese

Lo-Chol™ is made by Dorman's from the N. Dorman Company, Syosset, NY. It tastes good and melts well and is very low in cholesterol and somewhat low in fat. The amount of cholesterol in a one-ounce serving is 3 milligrams compared to 25 in regular Muenster. There are many other lowered cholesterol cheeses, such as Borden's Lite Line Cheddar™, which has 10 milligrams. But it is important to check the cholesterol count per ounce, not per serving, to make valid comparisons. Dorman's also makes low salt Swiss and lowered fat Muenster cheeses. Weight Watchers™ makes a fine Cheddar-like product, but it gives no cholesterol value on the packages, which could be misleading. Ricotta and mozzarella, when both are made with skim milk, are two good choices in a low cholesterol, low saturated fat diet. A good mozzarella made with no dairy products is distributed by Schreeber Foods, Inc., Green Bay, WI. Dry curd cottage cheese is healthy, but slightly dry and bitter. Hoop and pot cheese are other selections. Grated Parmesan and Romano cheese are also on the list. Like some hard cheeses, they are lower in cholesterol but they do have a lot of salt. Because they are usually grated, we don't use as much. Parmesan is lower than Romano. No-fat cottage cheese is excellent and hard to discern from the usual high fat variety.

Cream Cheese   Tofutti brand has a new cream cheese substitute, Better Than Cream Cheese™, which doesn't break down when cooked. It is available in major markets. If your grocer doesn't have it, it can be ordered by your grocer. It's from Tofutti in Rahway, N.J. There are other substitute cream cheeses, but they are hard to find.

Milk, Cream   Skim milk (regular milk has 4 percent fat) is the lowest cholesterol milk you can get, and 2 percent milk still has more than half the fat of regular whole milk. Some milk says *skim milk* but a closer examination of the label will reveal it has 1 percent fat. Buy the brand that has zero fat. Evaporated skim milk is a possible choice and dry powdered dairy creamers can be used if low in coconut oil and palm oil (both have no cholesterol but are high saturated fat). These mixed with skim milk make excellent substitutes in recipes that call for cream (just as they do in coffee), although you should take into account, that they tend to be slightly sweeter than cream for whipping cream. Any milk, even skim milk will whip eventually if it's cold enough.

For whipping cream, use Cool Whip™-type products if they don't contain palm, palm kernel, or coconut oil, though unfortunately most do. Powdered cream such as Dream Whip™ has to be reconstituted, but it is a good alternative. Dream Whip™ has a miniscule amount of saturated fat. Low fat or no-fat yogurt can be substitued for milk and sour cream in some dishes. If the yogurt is to be cooked, whisk a bit of flour into it. Regular yogurt has a lot of cholesterol and saturated fat.

Low-fat buttermilk is very low in cholesterol and saturated fat and can be used in soup and dips. It has a different taste though, and it might be too bitter for some. Note that buttermilk isn't always lowfat or skim.

Nonfat dry milk is an excellent milk substitute which when cold, depending on the brand, is quite acceptable, say, over cereal. Carnation™ is a good brand.

Ice Cream

There are several. Tofutti™, distributed to Torj Time, is outstanding, especially the Wild Berry flavor. You can add fresh blueberries or raspberries. Their other flavors are also excellent. Although it has no cholesterol, Tofutti does contain some fat and sugar.

Ice milk can also be used but examine the labels for specific fat and cholesterol content. Most contain both in varying degrees.

Sour Cream

King Sour Imitation Sour Cream™, is also made by American Whipped Products, Newburgh, NY. (This company makes two sour cream type dressings.) King Cholesterol Free™, a sour cream alternative, has only 3 grams of saturated fat per ounce and is delicious and an appropriate sour cream substitute for a low cholesterol, low saturated fat diet. It contains no cholesterol. Their King Sour™ label however contains coconut oil as the primary fat in their flex-labeling and *should be* avoided in a low *saturated fat diet.* (It also contains no cholesterol.)

Salt

Lite Salt™, which is part salt and part potassium chloride, by Morton, No Salt™ (which is all potassium), or other salt substitutes are offered by several manufacturers or distributors. Renal patients may wish to contact their doctors before using potassium; however extra potassium can be considered beneficial to those without renal disease.

Lite Salt™, which has an excellent flavor (probably because it is half salt), only comes with iodine mixed in. Iodine helps keep people from developing goiters; however many people are allergic to it. (It is also in shellfish). In fact, a recent medical journal article stated that 8 percent of all Americans, and especially those of English, Irish, Scottish, and German descent, have Rosacea, a skin disease that flairs up when too much iodine (among other chemicals) is ingested. You could make your own salt-potassium mixture with part potassium/chloride (No Salt™) and part iodine-free salt, adding other flavors you and your family like, such as garlic powder, pepper, or paprika.

Mrs. Dash's™ is a flavored salt substitute. It is quite good and is by Alberto Culver. There are several other spice, salt-free mixtures as well. Another option is to use fresh lemon juice.

Sugar   There are numerous sugar substitutes. But sugar is sugar. Substituting such items as honey, sucrose, glucose, fructose, molasses, dark brown sugar, or Demerera sugar (from England) doesn't lessen the sugar content. If the label has an ingredient that ends in "ose", it's probably still sugar and does the same thing in your system (which isn't necessarily bad unless you eat too much or have a disorder such as hypoglycemia or diabetes). One study indicated that excessive sugar tends to have a synergistic effect on cholesterol, raising it higher than it otherwise would be. Sugar substitutes such as saccharin in Sweet & Low ™ or as aspartame in Nutrasweet™,—two chemically different, sweet-tasting sugar substitutes are readily available. (There are others: in fact there's even a brown sugar substitute by Sweet and Low™. Both products eaten in great excess have shown to cause problems in laboratory animals; however, currently they are both deemed safe when used occasionally or in small amounts, and in fact are an important and safe substitute for those with sugar-related health problems. Many people use both regular sugar in some food preparation and either Equal™ (Nutrasweet) or Sweet & Low™ (saccharin) in lemonade, coffee, tea, and other foods.

Salad Dressing   Many excellent brands in the diet department use no oil, or you can just use plain or spiced vinegars. Most of our recipes can be made without any oil, or just limited amounts. The old rule of two-thirds oil to one third vinegar is not only reversed but one-fourth to one eighth oil (if any), is more the rule.

Mayonnaise

Bright Day Dressing™ is an excellent mayonnaise substitute, and it is one of only two commercially prepared dressings of its type that is egg-yolk free. It is made by United Food Industries, Baltimore, MD. The other is made by Hain ™. If you like a sweet mayonnaise, you may prefer Hain. Hain incidently makes literally hundreds of low salt, low saturated fat, low cholesterol foods. They are in Los Angeles, CA 90061. Most other commercial imitation mayonnaises (such as Weight Watchers™) are made with egg yolks, although their fat content is minimal. This is one of the hardest products to duplicate using cholesterol-free products.

Meat

Substitutes for meat vary. There are quite a few, but often they appear on a shelf one day and disappear the next, so I haven't listed any. Most aren't very good yet. The frozen sausage link, and pork sausage patty substitutes made by Morningstar Farms™ are excellent, with the patty being the best. They also make a hamburger-like product called Grillers™, which is also excellent. Most canned meat substitute products, like franks, haven't been perfected yet. Ground meat can be extended by several fillers. For instance, lean hamburger can be extended with soy products available in grocery stores made especially for that purpose. Bread crumbs, rice, oat bran, wheat germ, and other products can also be used to extend the meat content in such dishes as meatloaf, tamale pies, and quick hamburger skillet dishes. Bacon type pieces for salads etc., are often made without animal products. Check the label. The taste is acceptable but the pink color can be disagreeable. They can also be high in salt.

Vegetarian Paté™, made by Swiss Bonavita, is quite delicious, however it contains palm kernal oil and should be avoided on a low satured fat diet. It contains no cholesterol.

Hot dogs, like most prepared meats, are higher in saturated fat and cholesterol than whole meat; usually they are about 60 percent fat. Turkey or chicken franks may or may not be lower in cholesterol. But because turkey and chicken are lower in saturated fat, they may be an alternative although not a substitute. Most turkey and chicken franks are higher in fat. Check the label when it says ''Lower Fat,'' and ask yourself, lower than what? If the hot dog is lean beef or pork, it may be better than a chicken or turkey frank.

Shellfish

Since most shellfish is somewhat high in cholesterol (although the new figures show that it is lower than previously thought), there are acceptable shrimp and crab products that look like and have the consistency of the real thing. The imitation shrimp is fair, and with the addition of white fishes (pollock) and color, they're certainly usable. Ask at your local fish market or grocery store. One brand is Tasty Tails™ supplied by JAC Creative Foods, Inc., Los Angeles, CA. Pollock is one of the higher cholesterol fishes, however, although lower than beef. Shellfish has little saturated fat. Crab mixtures, shaped and colored like crab legs, have been around awhile. They are a mixture of various white fishes such as pollock and snow crab, and are presently used by many sushi chefs, and are aesthetically pleasing. The taste and texture is more than acceptable, and the cholesterol count is considerably lower than that of solid crab. Sea Majesty™ is one brand of Alaskan fish and crab. A product of Japan, it is packed for the SN International Corp. in Seattle WA. Ask your grocer.

Bulk crab and white fish mixtures are intended to look like back-fin or other parts of the blue crab. The bulk crab available today looks and tastes *least* like the delicious Virginia or Maryland Chesapeake Bay crab. It can still be used, particularly if there are many other ingredients in the dish to mask its flavor. Lobster is lower in cholesterol than previously thought. It is still higher than red meat however, so eat it judiciously. "Fake" lobster tails are available but really fall short of the real thing.

CHAPTER EIGHT

Recipes: More Than 200 for a Healthy Heart

*T*he recipes in the Fischer/Brown Low Cholesterol Gourmet have been analyzed for cholesterol and saturated fat content by the Nutrition Center at the University of Minnesota. They are given at the bottom of each recipe. The values are for one serving and are based on cooked foods. Cholesterol values are rounded off to the nearest multiples of five, such as 80 mg, or 85 mg. (Mg stands for *milligrams*.) Saturated fat is rounded off to the nearest whole number. If the recipe was 8.76 g, we will have it as 9 g, (g is for *grams*).

If there are variations in the recipe, the cholesterol and saturated numbers are always given for the variation that would give the highest value.

Calories

Calories in these recipes are nearly always lower than those from traditional recipes because we have significantly reduced the fat. Most of our meat dishes average 280 calories. Meat has comparatively high calories. Fat has the highest calories ounce per ounce of any food. We suggest smaller portions of meat, about 3½ ounces, (the size of a deck of cards), and fewer meals with animal protein. We eliminate all gratuitous oil and suggest less oil in salad dressing, less use of margarines and almost no fats and oils when cooking.

Salt

Salt is always listed as ''Lite Salt™ (optional),'' to alert you but to allow you some salt if you so desire. Lite Salt™ is half salt and half potassium chloride. See Page 45 for a more complete explanation. Salt containing foods used for flavor such as green olives, catsup, or anchovies, etc. are not always listed as optional. Salt can be eliminated or reduced further in most recipes if necessary.

Sugar

Sugar is clearly marked and is reduced in almost all recipes including many desserts. It can be successfully substituted with an imitation sweetener in most recipes if you choose. Moderate amounts of sugar are not harmful on a low cholesterol diet according to most experts. Excessive amounts (30 teaspoons a day or more, or what is in three to four bottles of soda with sugar) could be detrimental and are a source of calories which provide no vitamins or minerals.

Calcium

Because osteoporosis is a problem for one out of four women (and some men) affecting as many as 25 million Americans including 200,000 hip fractures yearly, special attention has to be paid to calcium. This book has only reduced the use of *whole* milk and cream and fatty cheeses. We substitute low fat and non fat dairy products, including cheese. The calcium is not lost when using non fat dairy foods. See page 18 for more information on osteoporosis. To add extra calcium to soups, see page 99.

Hors d'Oeuvre, Appetizers, and Dips

One of the most challenging areas in which to serve low cholesterol food is in appetizers, hors d'oeuvre, and party fare. After the usual fresh vegetables and dips, many hostesses are lost. We offer some suggestions and recipes that we believe you will find fun and exciting.

One style of hors d'oeuvre, Spanish tapas, works beautifully at a party. Just take several of our recipes and serve small amounts of them throughout the afternoon or evening. Simple or fancy, appetizers can be a pleasant substitute for a formal meal. Before buying and using crackers, pretzels, cheese sticks, potato chips or corn chips, check the package for the inclusion of palm oil, coconut oil or palm kernel oil. Many contain these oils which are very high in saturated fat. Look out for some potato chips, fried in animal fat.

Dips are no problem for the low cholesterol cook. Most dips in the average household have sour cream or cream cheese as a base (sour cream has less cholesterol and saturated fat than cream cheese). Low fat yogurt and buttermilk are very low in saturated fat and also make great bases for dips. You can now eliminate all cholesterol from your favorite cream-based stand-bys by using tofu or the imitation sour cream made by American Whipped Products, or alternatives to cream cheeses, made by Tofutti. But remember, some are high in fat and should be used judiciously. Also you may have to ask your grocer to order these products. Most will. The same may also be true of many egg-free dressings or mayonnaises, so check the labels for fat content.

My ideal cocktail party is an indoor or outdoor seated version with only six or eight people around a low cocktail table. On the table is a huge tray covered with a layer of lettuce. Piled on the lettuce are bundles of blanched and chilled asparagus, green beans, zucchini strips, raw snow peas or sugar snaps, carrots, cauliflower, broccoli, jicama slices, cherry tomatoes, several kinds of olives, small roast chicken pieces, cooked beef strips, a group of canned sardines or tuna chunks, every kind of pickle, a variety of dips in small wooden bowls placed among the vegetables, with bunches of grapes and fresh fruit at either end. Top it all with flower blossoms or a whole roasted chicken (instead of the roast chicken pieces), or avocado or cooked artichoke halves, something wonderful! It makes a stunning centerpiece, where the host or hostess never moves except to refill glasses. My kind of party!

Curry and Chutney Dip

This is a marvelous dip for vegetables and can be made very quickly. It can also be served with vegetables or crackers.

1 medium Spanish onion, chopped fine

1 clove garlic, minced

1 tablespoon curry powder

1 scallion cut into 1/4-inch pieces, including tips

1/2 cup Major Grey's™ chutney, cut fine, or, for more spice, 1/2 cup Sharwood's™ Bengal Hot Chutney

1 cup King Cholesterol Free™ imitation sour cream

Mix all ingredients together and serve cold. Makes 2 cups.

Per Serving: 0 mg cholesterol; 3 gm saturated fat for each 2 1/2 ounces

Eggplant Caviar

This is a Middle Eastern and Sicilian dish, and the ingredients can be varied to suit your taste. Serve cold with crackers or vegetables. It can be served at room temperature but it isn't as good. It can also be stuffed in hard-boiled egg halves without the yolks. It is absolutely scrumptious.

1 large eggplant, trimmed and unpeeled, (chopped or sliced and cooked in oven, microwave oven, or on top of stove in a Silverstone™ non-stick pan until soft.)

1 large Spanish onion, chopped fine and simmered for 5 minutes in small amount of water or microwaved in a plastic bag 2-3 minutes

2 large cloves garlic, minced and simmered with the large onion

1 medium onion, quartered

2 large stalks celery, cut in 4 or 5 pieces

8 large pitted ripe olives

8 large stuffed green olives

1/2 green pepper

1/2 red pepper

2 tablespoons cider vinegar

1/4 cup freshly squeezed lemon juice

1 teaspoon ground cumin

1/2 teaspoon sugar

2 tablespoons chopped fresh parsley

2 teaspoons capers, drained

For Garnish:

1/2 cup finely chopped scallions

paprika

Freshly ground pepper

Lemon, thinly sliced

Add cooked eggplant, onion, and garlic to food processor and puree. Add other vegetables, except capers, to processor chopping only until vegetables are small but not pureed. Add all other ingredients except capers and mix well. Stir in capers last. Scallions and paprika may be sprinkled on top before serving.

Several other vegetables and spices such as chili or oregano may be added if you wish to make it more piquant.

Serves 6 to 8 as hors d'oeuvre or 3 to 4 as a first course.

Per Serving: 0 mg cholesterol; less than 1 gm saturated fat

Stuffed Deviled Eggs
a la Virginia von Fremd

This is the traditional stuffed deviled eggs, now made without the egg yolks (and without the cholesterol). The hard-cooked egg halves can also be filled with eggplant caviar, page 69, or duxelles, page 225. But for deviled egg fanciers, this is a tour de force. Ginnie made these at Easter and got raves. She didn't tell anyone she'd substituted the egg yolks.

16 Egg Watcher™ eggs
1/2 cup tofu (optional)
3/4 teaspoon dry mustard
2 tablespoons vinegar
1/2 cup Bright Day Dressing™
  imitation mayonnaise
Lite Salt™ (optional)
Freshly ground black pepper
1/4 cup Better Than Cream
  Cheese™ imitation cream
  cheese

1/4 cup sweet pickle relish
1 dozen hard-cooked eggs, cut in
  half, yolks discarded
For Garnish:
  Paprika
  Parsley sprigs
  Red or yellow pepper strips
  Capers, drained
  Greek olives or other black
  olives

Cook imitation eggs (in package) in microwave on high until solid or remove from box and pour into a non-stick Silverstone™ pan sprayed with PAM™. Heat without stirring, until cooked and solid (about 3 minutes, covered, on low heat). Lift bottom to be sure it doesn't burn. Add tofu (optional), mustard, vinegar, mayonnaise, salt and pepper and imitation cream cheese. Add relish. Whip in blender or food processor until perfectly smooth and push through strainer to remove all lumps. Adjust seasonings. (Mixture will be slightly more liquid than usual deviled eggs.) Pipe or spoon into egg white halves, garnish each with paprika, tiny sprig parsley, tiny piece red pepper or 1 to 3 capers. Arrange on a platter. Serve cold
  Makes 2 dozen egg halves.

Per Serving: 0 mg cholesterol; 1 gm saturated fat for 2 halves

Cold Salad Couscous

Exotic or country style, couscous can be elaborate or simple. It's better without the usual fat. This can be served hot or cold. We've selected a cold version. There's no cholesterol or saturated fat in the meatless version.

1 large sweet onion, chopped fine
1 large clove garlic, minced
2 scallions including green, cut in 1/4-inch slices
3 carrots, finely diced
2 stalks celery, finely chopped
10 apricots, chopped coarse
1/2 cup raisins

2 cups cooked couscous (as per package directions)
For Garnish:
  Dark green lettuce leaves
  Red pepper slices
  Capers or chopped green olives

Simmer chopped onions, garlic, scallions, carrots, and celery in 3 to 4 teaspoons water for 3 to 4 minutes, adding scallions during the last 10 to 20 seconds. Add spices to the mixture, drain and cool. Add raisins and apricots to cooled couscous. Mix well.

On lettuce-lined plate, spoon a couscous mound. Garnish with red pepper slices arranged lengthwise on the lettuce, around the edges. Crisscross two or three on top, or garnish with capers, or olives or all three. Serve cold or hot with poultry or lamb.

Variation:

Hot with chicken and tomatoes

1 pound chicken (cooked breast cuts) or 1 pound cubes of very lean cooked lamb

Add chicken or lamb to garlic and onion when vegetables are simmering. Mix in couscous, spices, apricots, and raisins until hot. Remove immediately and serve hot, garnishing with chopped tomatoes.

Serves 4

Per Serving: 55 mg cholesterol for lamb (45 mg for chicken); 2 gm saturated fat for lamb (1 gm for chicken)

Belgian Endive, Smithfield Ham and Walnut Appetizer

Take this fair-haired Scottish chef, Norman Preedy (complete with brogue), put him in Dallas, give him some food to work with and you'll get a delicious treat. No question about it. Norman gave us this recipe and we thank him.

12 leaves Belgian endive
1/4 pound Smithfield ham, all fat removed, sliced very thin and cut in slivers (julienned)

32 toasted walnut halves
Honey and lemon dressing

Place 3 endive leaves on each individual plate. Fill leaves with ham strips and walnuts. Dot with mixture of honey and lemon.
Serves 4

Per Serving: 20 mg cholesterol; 2 gm saturated fat

Stuffed Endive

Cooked wild rice, seasoned with finely chopped raw onion and moistened with Bright Day™ imitation mayonnaise, tofu, or pureed cottage cheese, makes a lively hors d'oeuvre.

20 endive leaves, washed and patted dry
1 cup cooked wild rice
4 teaspoons finely chopped onions
1 teaspoon Bright Day™ imitation mayonnaise

20 very tiny mushrooms or 20 mushroom slices
For Garnish:
   Sliced red pepper
   Peppercorns, drained

Stuff endive with one or two teaspoons cooked wild rice, mixed with onions, imitation mayonnaise, and raw mushrooms. Garnish with a strip of thinly sliced red pepper and peppercorns.
Serves 10 to 20

Per Serving: 0 mg cholesterol; less than 1 gm saturated fat (for 2 each)

Stuffed Tomato

This is a very simple but luscious appetizer. The trick is not to use any oil or butter. It isn't needed and it just adds calories and cholesterol (if you use butter). Tiny flecks of sun dried tomatoes, sweet basil, oregano, scallions, even tuna or other fish can vary this versatile dish. The cholesterol and saturated fat content are for the highest cholesterol and saturated fat fish version.

4 large ripe, tomatoes, trimmed and halved, or 12 canned tomato wedges
1/2 onion, finely chopped
1 small clove garlic, minced

1/2 cup cooked green spinach, egg-free noodles
2 teaspoons freshly grated Parmesan cheese

Never peel or seed tomatoes, but if you can't get fresh, homegrown varieties, good quality canned whole or wedged tomatoes can be used. Just pour the stuffing on top and garnish.

Remove some pulp from halved tomatoes; heat halves slightly. Chop the pulp. Lightly simmer onions, garlic, and the cooked green spinach noodles and pulp. Drain and heap into the tomato half, microwave for a few minutes more, and sprinkle on a small amount of grated Parmesan cheese. You may wish to brown the cheese by passing halves under a broiler.

Serves 4

Per Serving: 5 mg cholesterol; 1 gm saturated fat

Carrots and Other Vegetables with Grains

The "holders" for these bite-sized hors d'oeuvre can be almost any firm vegetable like zucchini, partially cooked carrot slices of large, diagonally sliced raw carrots; sliced, raw summer squash; opened blanched snow peas; sliced water chestnuts; sliced baked acorn squash; raw celery, or sun dried tomatoes. The grain filling can be cooked wild rice, brown rice, tiny rice pasta, cooked kasha or couscous, topped with diced onion or sliced scallions, chopped green or black, Nicoise or cracked olives (pits removed), or grated garlic.

1 cup cooked wild rice (or brown rice, kasha, rice, angel hair pasta or couscous)
1/4 cup finely chopped onion
1/8 cup finely chopped scallions
1 teaspoon freshly squeezed lemon
2 teaspoons chopped seedless cracked olives
1 clove garlic, finely chopped
1 teaspoon Bright Day™ dressing

2 large and fat carrots, partially cooked and cooled
1 parsnip, partially cooked and cooled
6 cucumber slices
6 blanched and opened snow peas
4 sun dried tomatoes, patted dry
For Garnish:
　Blanched asparagus tips
　Drained capers

Mix everything but the carrots, parsnips, cucumbers, snow peas and sun dried tomatoes. Chill.

Diagonally slice cooked (but firm) carrots, parsnips, uncooked cucumbers, etc. Open and fill snow peas with mixture. Mound mixture on sun dried tomatoes (or even a slice of firm cooked squash or sweet potato). In order to be sure these softer vegetables stay firm when cooked, slice them before cooking and bake them on a rack. Top these vegetables with little mounds of the other vegetables, kasha with onion, cooked rice, or angel hair pasta mixed with a little Parmesan cheese. Garnish with asparagus tips and a few capers.

Serves 6 to 8.

Per Serving: 0 mg cholesterol; 0 gm saturated fat
(5 mg cholesterol if Parmesan cheese is used, and just under 1 gm saturated fat per serving)

Cream Cheese and Chutney

The tangy flavor of a spicy chutney, crisp onions, and cool cream cheese needn't be given up because you're on a low cholesterol diet. I also like this hors d'oeuvre because it is quick to prepare for unexpected guests.

1 6-oz package Better Than Cream Cheese™ imitation cream cheese
1 teaspoon sherry (optional)
1 cup Sharwood's Bengal™ Hot Chutney

2 scallions, including an inch of the green, chopped in 1/2-inch slices
1 avocado, peeled, seeded, diced, and coated with lemon juice
Crackers and celery cut for dipping

Cream the cheese with sherry. Line a mold with plastic wrap and press soft cream cheese into it. Chill. Now invert it onto a plate so the plastic film can be removed. If sherry is not used, just place the block or imitation cheese on a plate and mold by hand into a mound or loaf.

Spread the cheese with the chutney to make a layer of 1/2 inch, letting it drip down the side. Sprinkle with scallions. Insert avocado in on top.

Serves 4 to 6

Per Serving: less than 5 mg cholesterol; 1 gm saturated fat

Dried Fruit Mixture

Most of us love to snack on munchies of dried fruits and nuts. Walnuts are both delicious and low in saturated fat. Commercially prepared dried fruit mixtures often have coconut and other high saturated fat ingredients, so it's best to make your own. Dried cherries, tart and sweet, are especially good in snack mixtures. By using equal amounts of the following, with half as many almonds (because almonds have more saturated fat), you can make any amount of the fruit mixture you want. I give away this treat to friends, varying the fruit. Dried figs and dates are also good.

1/2 cup walnuts	1/2 cup chopped, dried apples
1/2 cup dried sour cherries	1/2 cup dried, chopped mango
1/2 cup dried currants	1/4 cup almonds (optional)

Add other fruits of your choice. Dried strawberries are delicious. Dried apricots, figs or prunes should be cut up. Keep the mixture mainly fruit, but a small amount of seeds may be added (though seeds are high in oil).

Makes 3 cups.

Per 1 cup Serving: 0 mg cholesterol; 2 gm saturated fat per 1/2 cup

Humus

Canned chick peas work well with this Middle Eastern cocktail dip. This is moderately high in fat. Use as a dip for vegetables or with pita bread.

1 small onion, cut in quarters	1/4 cup Tahini (available in
2 cloves garlic	Middle Eastern markets), drain
1 1/2 cups canned chick peas,	off excess liquid
drained	Juice of one large lemon
1/4 cup toasted sesame seeds	

Puree all of the ingredients in a food processor. Serve cold or at room temperature.

Serves 4 to 6

Per Serving: 0 mg cholesterol; 1 gm saturated fat

Dim Sum

I've seen this served both at the most formal and elegant cocktail parties and around a cozy fireplace. Large wrappers are used. A couple of 6-inch scallions are placed in the wrapper on which the plum sauce has been spread. Slivers of skinless lean cooked poultry are placed on the scallions and sauce. It's then rolled and sliced into bite size pieces, each skewered with a toothpick. Sometimes a chef does it right before you.

Small dim sum wrappers (available in Oriental groceries) may also be used. Very slender steamed and cooled asparagus, or green beans, may be added and rolled with the plum sauce, scallion, and poultry.

4 large dim sum wrappers, steamed, using steamer and 1/2-inch of water with a tea towel wrapped lid after water has reached boiling point and heat turned off. (Towel keeps water from dripping on wrappers.)

1/2 cup plum sauce (can be found in Oriental markets)
4 to 6 scallions, trimmed, slivered lengthwise and cut into 3-inch pieces
Any optional vegetables such as a green beans or asparagus
1 cup julienned cooked lean duck or chicken

Take a dim sum or egg roll wrapper that has been lightly steamed, brush plum sauce on one side, place a piece of scallion and some thin slivers of lean chicken or duck inside (and optional vegetables). Wrap and serve.

Serves 4

Per Serving: less than 5 mg cholesterol; 3 gm saturated fat

Stuffed Cherry Tomatoes

One of the easiest, freshest, and most colorful hors d'oeuvre is stuffed cherry tomatoes. With such new artificial cream cheeses and those made with skim milk cottage cheese, pot cheese, skim milk ricotta and others, there are wide choices for low cholesterol but "cream" type stuffings.

Cherry tomatoes stay fresh quite a while so you can keep them on hand. I suggest selecting very tiny ones if they are to be eaten whole (with a dollop of sauce on top or with a dip), and not stuffed. I've seen many a surprised guest squirted from a too-big mouthful of exploding tomato.

30 large cherry tomatoes
1 cup Better Than Cream Cheese™ imitation cream cheese or 1 cup King Cholesterol Free™ imitation sour cream
1 12-ounce package Hidden Valley™ party dip mix (This has salt so you may wish to substitute 1/8 cup minced onions and 1/8 cup minced celery.)

For Garnish:
Parsley

For stuffing, select larger cherry tomatoes. Remove stems and scoop out small amount of tomato in order to stuff. Mix imitation cream cheese or sour cream and either the Hidden Valley™ mix or the fresh vegetables (or both). Heap on each tomato. Arrange on a platter or tray mingled and ringed with small bunches of parsley.

Variation: Try minced tuna or salmon moistened with pureed skim milk cottage cheese, or puree both together in a food processor. Add some minced onion or celery. Stuff tomatoes with eggplant caviar (page 69) and garnish with tiny sprig of dill, mint, or parsley.

Variation: Add chili powder and cumin mixed with whole kernels of cooked corn mixed in imitation cream cheese for a Tex-Mex variation.

Variation: Stuff cherry tomatoes with chopped raw onions, chopped ripe olives moistened with imitation cream cheese, and garnish with tiny parsley sprig.

Serves 8 to 10

Per Serving: 5 mg cholesterol; less than 1 gm saturated fat

Dill Sauce for Dip

If used for dip, place small dill sprig on top for garnish.

1/2 cup King Cholesterol Free™ imitation sour cream

1/2 cup skim milk or low fat buttermilk

3 large sprigs dill, chopped

1 clove garlic, mashed

1/2 teaspoon vinegar

Mix everything and refrigerate. Garnish with dill.
Makes 1 cup

Per Serving: less than 5 mg cholesterol; 2 gm saturated fat for each 2 ounces

Mustard Dip

Mustard dips are wonderful for vegetables. For a variation, add 1/2-cup skim milk yogurt and whip. An equal amount of tofu may be substituted for the sour cream and skim milk. It is lower in fat, but the taste is a bit more bland. You may also wish to experiment with the amounts of mustard and sugar.

1 cup King Cholesterol Free™ imitation sour cream

4 tablespoons skim milk or buttermilk

3 teaspoons Dijon mustard or 1 teaspoon dry mustard

1 teaspoon vinegar

3 tablespoons beer (optional)

1 teaspoon sugar or honey

Whip everything well and serve cold.
Makes 1 1/4 cups

Per Serving: less than 1 mg cholesterol; 3 gm saturated fat for each 2 ounces

Salads and Salad Dressings

Let your imagination go wild with salads. Salads are an ideal way to add complex carbohydrates, a great variety of high fiber, and low cholesterol foods; the kind of diet we recommend. Lettuce, cabbage and other greens, exotic vegetables, slivers of meat, beans, rice, some nuts or grains, and hard-cooked egg white chunks can make salads into a complete meal.

Salad dressings don't have to contain oil. Many diet varieties don't. Omitting the oil reduces the calories in your diet. In the oil section we've included the saturated fat content of many oils to help guide you in your selections. Some of the lowest are rapeseed oil (Puritan Brand™), walnut oil, and olive oil. Eating excessive amounts of unsaturated oil does not help lower cholesterol. Unsaturated fat and oil are also to be used as a substitute for animal fat, palm, and coconut oil. These safer oils make for a more palatable diet without raising cholesterol, but fat and oil are always the greatest sources of calories. Again, my motto is "Fat in, fat on!"

Have fun with salads. Try new ones and if a Caesar is your favorite, we have a wonderful version without egg yolks.

Chilled Potato Salad

This potato salad is full of vegetables that crunch and blend with the potatoes. To dress it up or make it a complete meal, tuck freshly cooked cold artichoke hearts partially in around the edge, and fill each artichoke heart cup with a pickled baby corn or a cherry tomato. Or cut the artichoke in wedges and poke in around edge alternating with a ripe olive or parsley sprig.

8 to 12 small red potatoes, sliced in halves or fourths and boiled or microwaved in a plastic bag with skins on, until cooked

5 hard-cooked eggs, discard yolks after cooking, slice egg whites in fourths, eighths, or just large chunks or slices

1 large Spanish or Vidalia onion, coarsely chopped

3 to 4 scallions, including green stems, diagonally sliced, 1/2-inch wide

1 stalk celery, cut in 1/2-inch pieces

1/4 cup chopped parsley

2 to 4 sprigs watercress, finely chopped

1/4 cup chopped dill pickles (optional because of salt)

2 teaspoons vinegar

3/4 cup Bright Day™ imitation mayonnaise or King Cholesterol Free™ imitation sour cream

1/2 teaspoon sugar

1/4 teaspoon dry mustard

2 tablespoons capers, drained (optional because of salt)

Freshly ground black pepper

1/4 cup sweet red pepper, sliced thin

Lettuce leaves

For Garnish:
   Black olives
   Red pepper slices and red pepper seeds
   Chopped scallions
   Artichoke hearts (optional)
   Paprika

Combine all ingredients and gently toss. Serve on a bed of lettuce surrounded with garnishes. Sprinkle with paprika.

Serves 6 to 8

Per Serving: 0 mg cholesterol; 1 gm saturated fat

Coleslaw, Plain and Fancy

There are many ways to make your favorite coleslaw and all of them are delicious. In the fancy version, add only one of the seeds: celery or poppy. If you use sugar, omit the raisins or currants. If you use onions, omit the scallions and chives. Make a blend that appeals to you. I like the version with poppy seed, currant, vinegar, onions or scallions, mustard and celery.

Plain:

1 cabbage, finely chopped
1 cup King Cholesterol Free™ imitation sour cream or 1 cup Bright Day™ imitation mayonnaise (more may be necessary as cabbage sizes differ) thin with skim milk, if necessary

For Garnish:
Paprika

Mix cabbage and sour cream. Garnish with paprika.
Serves 8 to 12

Per serving: 0 mg cholesterol; 1 gm saturated fat

Fancy:

1 cabbage, finely chopped
1 cup Bright Day™ imitation mayonnaise or 1 cup King Cholesterol Free™ imitation sour cream and any of the following variations (more may be necessary as cabbage sizes differ). Thin with skim milk, if necessary
2 teaspoons celery seed or 2 teaspoons poppy seed
1/2 cup raisins or currants
1 teaspoon freshly squeezed lemon juice or 2 teaspoons vinegar
1/2 cup chopped onions

4 teaspoons chopped chives
2 teaspoons finely chopped parsley
2 apples, cut into small pieces
4 jalapeno peppers, chopped
1/2 cup chopped green pepper with seeds
1/2 cup chopped red pepper with seeds
1/2 cup chopped scallions
1/2 cup quartered ripe or green olives (optional)
1/2 cup finely sliced carrots
1 teaspoon dry mustard
1/2 cup corn, freshly steamed and cooled

1/2 cup chopped celery
12 to 15 green grapes, halved
Grape leaves

For Garnish:
Red pepper, chopped

Mix all ingredients well into the chopped cabbage. Serve on grape leaves.

Serves 8 to 12
Per Serving: 0 mg cholesterol; 2 gm saturated fat

Mixed Greens and Walnut Salad

Walnuts are one of the lowest nuts in saturated fat. This recipe can be used as the salad course, or by greatly increasing the nuts and grapefruit, it can be used as an hors d'oeuvre. To do so, place a bed of lettuce on a large platter . Toothpicks will be needed. Try a different variety of toothpick for the bite sized grapefruit segments. If served as an hors d'oeuvre, garnish with some finely chopped mint or fresh parsley.

For the dressing:
3 tablespoons walnut oil
1/4 teaspoon dry mustard, mixed
    well in 3 tablespoons red wine
    vinegar
Lite Salt™ (optional)
Freshly ground black pepper
1/2 to 2/3 cup walnut halves

3 bunches of watercress, tough
    stems pinched off
2 Belgian endives, cored and
    sliced crosswise
1 grapefruit, peeled and
    segmented (or try a delicious
    fruit called 'UGLY' or 'UGLI')
1 head red leaf lettuce, leaves
    cleaned and patted dry

Slowly whisk walnut oil into the mustard and vinegar. Add the Lite Salt™ (optional) and freshly ground black pepper to taste. Marinate the walnut halves in the dressing for an hour or so; then remove. Lightly toss the remaining ingredients with the dressing and arrange on the lettuce leaves. Scatter the marinated nuts over the salad and serve.

Serves 4 to 6

Per Serving: 0 mg cholesterol; 1 gm saturated fat

Big Bean/Small Avocado Salad

This is a lovely blend of flavors and textures with avocado, kidney beans, and raisins. I add whatever I have on hand, always keeping the beans, avocados, and raisins. Cider vinegar is the only dressing. Tart but great. You may however, want to add some Puritan™ oil or walnut oil.

1 cup dark red canned kidney beans, drained and rinsed (or homemade according to directions on package of dried beans)

2 sliced pepperoncini peppers (pickled peppers)

1 carrot, sliced diagonally into pieces 1/8-inch by 1 1/2-inch

4 scallions, cut in 1/4-inch pieces, including green

1 avocado, diced, tossed with fresh lemon juice to prevent darkening

10 to 12 slivers of fresh horseradish (optional)

2 tablespoons yellow raisins or currants

8 to 12 large pitted ripe olives, sliced into fourths

12 to 15 raw green beans, sliced into 1/2-inch pieces

1 roasted red pepper, sliced into 1/2-inch by 1-inch slices (homemade or canned)

Freshly ground black pepper

2 cups chopped green such as savoy cabbage, lettuce, or *watercress (*if you want more bite)

Mix all ingredients, blending carefully so as not to bruise the avocado. Or, place all ingredients carefully and artistically on each plate and sprinkle vinegar on top. Serve cold.

Variation (Add one or more of the following):

1 hard cooked egg white, sliced lengthwise into slivers

1 very ripe tomato

Capers, drained (optional because of salt)

Canned tuna in chunks

Cold, previously blanched or steamed asparagus, cut into 1/2-inch pieces

Cooked Canadian bacon, cut in slivers

Mix all ingredients, blending carefully so as not to bruise avocado. Or, place all ingredients carefully and artistically on each plate and sprinkle vinegar on top. Serve cold.

Serves 4 to 6

Per Serving: 0 mg cholesterol; 0 gm saturated fat (without tuna or Canadian bacon); 15 mg cholesterol with tuna; less than 1 gm saturated fat or 10 mg cholesterol with Canadian bacon; 2 gm saturated fat

Salade Nicoise

We've combined some of the ingredients in a traditional Southern French Nicoise salad and added a few that the French were not known to do. For those on a low-salt diet, sliver the anchovies, using just one tiny sliver for each serving, or omit entirely.

Romaine lettuce
Boston lettuce
2 ripe red tomatoes, cut into
    wedges
8 cooked cold red potatoes with
    skins left on, sliced
20 cold green beans that have
    been lightly steamed
1 cucumber, finely cut
2 6 1/2-ounce cans tuna, packed
    in water, drained

3 hard-boiled eggs, (yolks
    discarded), sliced
12 pitted black olives, drained
2 teaspoons capers, drained
Herbed vinaigrette, recipe page
    95
For Garnish:
    Freshly ground black pepper
    4 anchovies (optional)

Place the romaine around plate and break up the Boston lettuce, mounding it on top. Place tomatoes on one side, slices of potatoes next to them, then the green beans and then the cucumbers. Place the tuna in the center, the egg whites next to something dark, like the beans, and the olives around the edge or near the egg whites. Sprinkle with capers and freshly ground black pepper. Garnish with anchovies (optional). The herbed vinaigrette dressing combines well with this hearty salad. Pass it separately.

Serves 4

Per Serving: 35 mg cholesterol; 1 gm saturated fat

The Low Cholesterol Gourmet

Chicken and Fruit Salad

I've served this for a casual lunch, at an afternoon wedding reception, and for a baby shower for my friend Sandy Canada. It is always a hit. The reason for its great success is that the chicken is home roasted with sage, bread, celery and onion stuffing, page 000, which makes it very succulent and flavorful. It's then cut into generous, but still mouth-sized chunks. The pineapple should be at the peak of sweet freshness. I garnish the edge of the platter with a lavish presentation of kumquats, Concord grapes, whole walnuts, and other seasonal fruits such as pomegranates or apples, papaya, and some bright leaves, perhaps even from the pineapple. It can also be served in a scooped out pineapple or orange halves.

1/2 cup Better Than Cream Cheese™ imitation cream cheese
1/2 cup fresh orange juice
1 cup sliced celery
2 cups cooked chicken, diced, deboned, defatted, and skinned (see page 178 to roast chicken)

1/2 cup chopped walnuts
1 1/2 cups diced pineapple
1 cup green grapes or small bunch of grapes
Lettuce leaves
For Garnish:
Several walnut halves

Beat together cream cheese and orange juice until smooth. Blend in celery, chicken, nuts and, lastly, pineapple, so as not to break the pieces. Refrigerate 1 to 2 hours to blend flavors. Arrange on lettuce leaves. Top with individual grapes or serve small bunches on the side. Place one or several walnut halves on top. Serve cold.
Serves 6

Per Serving: 40 mg cholesterol; 2 gm saturated fat

Mixed Green Salad with Jicama

Jicama, for those who aren't familiar with it, looks a bit like a big, round white potato. It is crispy, a little sweet, and mild in flavor.

Place spinach on bottom of each individual large bowl or platter with smaller green lettuces on top. Let spinach leaves show from the bottom. Strew jicama on top. Place dark olives (3 or 5—an uneven number) around edge. Horseradish bits can be sprinkled on top. Serve cold with extra vinaigrette dressing from the marinated jicama.

8 to 12 large whole spinach
   leaves, stems removed
1 head baby romaine lettuce, torn
   or cut into pieces
1 head red leafed lettuce, torn or
   cut into pieces
1 head butter lettuce (or Boston
   lettuce)

1 jicama, peeled and julienned
   and marinated in herb
   vinaigrette dressing, page 89,
   for 1 hour
12 to 18 ripe olives
1/4 cup fresh horseradish,
   julienned

Serves 4 to 6

Per Serving: 0 mg cholesterol; less than 1 gm saturated fat

Carrot and Raisin Salad

A recipe we all remember from childhood, and it's still just as good.

4 to 6 carrots, trimmed
1/2 cup raisins
2 teaspoons fresh lemon juice
1 teaspoon sugar (or sugar
   substitute)

1/2 cup Bright Day™ imitation
   mayonnaise or King
   Cholesterol Free™ imitation
   sour cream

Scrape carrots; shred or grate. Add raisins, lemon juice, sugar (or sugar substitute) and imitation dressing. Mix everything well, chill and serve.

Serves 4 to 6 (depending on carrot size)

Per Serving: 0 mg cholesterol; 2 gm saturated fat

Cold Macaroni Salad

Macaroni salads are old stand-bys, and lots of other favorite ingredients can be added, such as cooked corn or even canned, drained, kidney beans. If you want a more tart flavor, add a half teaspoon of cider vinegar.

2 cups cooked macaroni, cold
1/2 cup Bright Day Dressing™
    imitation mayonnaise
1/2 cup chopped onions
1/2 teaspoon vinegar
1/4 cup chopped celery

1/4 cup chopped green salad
    olives (optional, because of
    salt content)
1/2 teaspoon sugar (optional)
For Garnish:
    Red pepper slivers
    Freshly ground black pepper

Blend all ingredients together. Serve cold, garnished with red pepper slices and ground black pepper.
Serves 4

Per Serving: 0 mg cholesterol; 2 gm saturated fat

Oranges, Avocado, and Onions

Avocados are high in monounsaturated fat, and although high in fat, they have little saturated fat and are fine on a low cholesterol diet. Substitute grapefruit segments for the orange, if you like.

2 ripe avocados
1 Bermuda onion, sliced paper
    thin

1 cup orange segments, cut each
    segment in half
Lettuce
Celery seed dressing (page 97)

Peel and halve avocados, discarding pit. Pile oranges and onions in (and on) avocado halves. Serve on lettuce with celery seed dressing. For a different version, toss diced avocados, orange segments, and onion with dressing. Chill and serve on lettuce or curly escarole.
Serves 4

Per Serving: 0 mg cholesterol; 2 gm saturated fat

Recipes: More Than 200 for a Healthy Heart

Balsamic and Peppercorn Vinaigrette

This is a tangy dressing. For an option, add 1 clove of minced garlic.

1 cup balsamic vinegar
2 tablespoons Dijon mustard
1/2 teaspoon dry mustard
1 to 15 teaspoons olive oil

2 tablespoons rinsed and drained
  pickled peppercorns
1 cup champagne vinegar
1 tablespoon lemon juice

Whisk everything together except the peppercorns so as not to break them. Add them last. Shake or stir before using.

Makes 1 to 1 1/2 cups, depending on amount of oil.

Per Serving: 0 mg cholesterol; less than 1 gm saturated fat

Stuffed Mushrooms

These stuffed mushrooms are versatile and wonderful as a main dish, cold salad, an appetizer or as an hors d'oeuvre. They're easy to prepare and require no attention once the cooking begins. If there's too much stuffing, just let it spill over into the pan. The chopped raw onion and mushroom mixture used for the stuffing does need three to four minutes of pre-cooking before stuffing.

12 very large mushrooms
1 small onion, chopped fine

For Garnish:
  Chopped parsley
  Lettuce

Take large mushrooms, remove stems and chop stems with equal amount of chopped onions. Cook onion and stem mushroom mixture in tiny amount of water for 3 to 4 minutes. Add to mushroom cavity. Cover and let mushrooms simmer in 1 teaspoon of water (mushrooms leach water, too) over low heat for 15 minutes or cook covered in microwave for 8 minutes. Top with chopped parsley before serving. Serve hot or cold. If cold, serve on lettuce with vinaigrette dressing (page 94).

Serves 4

Per Serving: 0 mg cholesterol; 0 gm saturated fat

Persian Beet and Yogurt Salad

Beets and yogurt are a favorite when preparing Middle Eastern food. A minced garlic clove can be mixed in the yogurt to spice it. This same salad can be made substituting cold, uncooked cucumber slices for the beets.

1 bunch fresh beets (4 to 5 medium sized beets)
1 pint of nonfat yogurt or King Cholesterol Free™ imitation sour cream
1/2 teaspoon Lite Salt™ (optional)

1 clove garlic, minced
1/4 teaspoon white pepper
2 tablespoons chopped fresh mint (or 1 teaspoon dried mint)
For Garnish:
Whole mint leaves

Peel beets and cook in small amount of water until tender. Drain beets and chill. Slice into rounds. Add garlic, mint, and seasonings to the yogurt. Put beet slices on plate; add a few tablespoons of dressing on top. Garnish with mint leaf. If making it with cucumbers, fold cucumbers into dressing and let chill for an hour.

Serves 3 to 4
Per Serving: 5 mg cholesterol; 1 gm saturated fat

Champagne-Lemon Vinaigrette

The amount of oil may be greatly varied from none to 16 tablespoons. This dressing can make an excellent Caesar salad dressing by increasing the lemon and decreasing the vinegar. The Caesar would also require a teaspoon Worcestershire sauce and 1 to 2 anchovies. Recipe page 93.

1 cup champagne vinegar
1 tablespoon lemon juice
1 tablespoon Dijon mustard
1 tablespoon freshly grated Parmesan cheese

1/2 clove garlic, minced
2 to 16 tablespoons olive oil (or none)

Mix well and chill.
Makes about 1 1/2 to 2 cups

Per Serving: 0 mg cholesterol; less than 1 gm saturated fat

Tangy Tuna Salad

Tuna is a lower cholesterol and saturated fat fish, perfect for a low cholesterol diet. Serve this salad on toast, stuff it in a tomato or pile on half of an avocado. You can also use it to stuff other vegetables, such as a small cooked eggplant, halved and chilled, with a few scoops removed to make room for the tuna. Or serve tuna salad on a plate with other vegetables. Try carrots, zucchini, and jicama strips, with some olives or pickled okra around the edge.

1 cup flaked, water-packed tuna, drained, or freshly cooked flaked tuna

2 tablespoons chopped sweet pickles

3 tablespoons Bright Day Dressing™ imitation mayonnaise

1 teaspoon fresh lemon juice

1/4 cup chopped celery

1/4 cup chopped scallions

For Garnish:
   Poppy seeds sprinkled on top

Mix everything well and serve, or refrigerate, covered, until needed.
Serves 2 to 3

Per Serving: 50 mg cholesterol; 2 gm saturated fat

Chicken and Avocado Salad

As a variation, this recipe can be served on bread, or toast with lettuce. Or stuff it in a scooped-out pineapple or melon half. It can also be stuffed in a tomato; or omit the diced avocado and pile on avocado halves. To make a sweeter version, add 3/4 cup diced fresh pineapple and garnish with some seedless red or green grapes. You can use canned Lychee nuts, well drained. If you sweeten it with fruit, omit the capers and onions.

**2 cups diced cooked boneless
  skinless chicken (fat trimmed),
  page 178**
2/3 cup chopped celery
1/2 cup chopped onion
1/2 cup chopped olives
1/4 cup capers, drained
**1/2 cup Bright Day Dressing™
  imitation mayonnaise**

1 avocado, peeled and diced
Lettuce or escarole leaves
For Garnish:
  Scallion, julienned and placed
  on top
  For fruit version, a mandarin
  orange segment

Mix well, being careful not to bruise the avocado. Serve on lettuce or escarole.

Serves 4

Per Serving: 60 mg cholesterol; 7 gm saturated fat

Caesar Salad

Caesar salads are incredibly satisfying with their crisp, big hunks of dark green romaine, the crunchy lighter center ribs—all blended with the tang of garlic, pepper, and lemon. It must be freshly made and served very cold. Croutons may be added.

1 large head romaine lettuce, washed, dried and chilled
1/3 cup lemon juice, freshly squeezed
1/2 teaspoon Worcestershire™ sauce
1/4 teaspoon dry mustard (optional)
2 large cloves garlic, minced

1/2 teaspoon vinegar
1 to 2 tablespoons olive oil (optional)
1/4 cup freshly grated Parmesan cheese
Freshly ground black pepper
4 anchovies, well drained and patted dry (one per person) (optional)

Break romaine into 3-inch hunks (or keep leaves whole). Place in large salad bowl and chill. In another bowl, mix all remaining ingredients except cheese, pepper, and anchovies. Toss salad well with dressing, adding cheese, and top with pepper and one anchovy per serving.

Serves 4

Per Serving: 10 mg cholesterol; 2 gm saturated fat

Black-Eyed Pea Salad

This is simple and delicious Texas fare that can be kept for up to two weeks in the refrigerator.

2 cups cooked black eyed peas or 1 18-ounce can, black-eyed peas, rinsed and drained
1 large onion, finely chopped
1/4 cup wine vinegar and 1/4 cup water
Cayenne pepper

Freshly ground black pepper
Lite Salt™ (optional)
1 garlic clove, peeled
For Garnish:
  Red peppers, chopped
  Scallions, chopped

Mix everything and refrigerate, remove the garlic clove after a day. Garnish with peppers and scallions and serve cold.
Serves 4 to 6

Per Serving: 0 mg cholesterol; 0 gm saturated fat

Vinaigrette Dressing

You can use almost any kind of vinegar you like for this salad dressing.

1/2 cup sherry vinegar or other vinegar
1/4 teaspoon dry mustard

Lite Salt™ (optional)
Freshly ground black pepper
1 to 6 teaspoons walnut oil

Mix well.
Makes 2/3 cup

Per Serving: 0 mg cholesterol; 1 gm saturated fat

Raspberry Vinegar Dressing

One of my favorite restaurants is Scotland Yard, an authentic Scottish restaurant in Alexandria, Virginia. Owner James Graham knows that I like low cholesterol, low saturated fat foods, and one evening he read my mind and whipped up one of the best dressings I've ever had. He served it over lettuce and ripe garden tomatoes, sliced in very thin slivers and twisted attractively.

1/4 cup walnut oil
1 cup cider vinegar
1/4 teaspoon savory
1/4 teaspoon dried thyme
1/4 teaspoon dried tarragon
1/2 teaspoon chopped chives
1 teaspoon fresh chopped parsley

3 to 4 frozen sweetened raspberries (add 1/4 teaspoon sugar if fresh raspberries are used)
1-inch of leek, cleaned and sliced very thin

Blend all ingredients except leeks in a food processor. Add the sliced leeks. Makes 1 1/3 cups

Per Serving: 0 mg cholesterol; less than 1 gm saturated fat for each 3 ounces

Basil Vinaigrette

Some of these ingredients—garlic and shallots—can be doubled or tripled. An equal amount of oregano is wonderful too. The type of vinegar may be changed. Avoid too spicy a vinegar because you want to taste the basil. The oregano/basil version is especially good over the first crop of home grown tomatoes in about July, picked while warm from the sun, cut in chunks, doused with the dressing and devoured immediately.

1 cup cider vinegar
1/2 teaspoon dry mustard
1 teaspoon fresh basil or 1/2
    teaspoon dried basil
1 teaspoon fresh oregano or 1/2
    teaspoon dried oregano
    (optional)

1/2 teaspoon sugar
1 teaspoon minced garlic
1 teaspoon chopped shallots
Freshly ground black pepper
1 to 10 teaspoons olive oil, or
    none

Mix well.
Makes about 1 cup

Per Serving: 0 mg cholesterol; 0 gm saturated fat

Yogurt, Dill, and Cucumber Dressing

This dressing may be used for dips or, if thinned with skim milk or low fat buttermilk, as a salad dressing.

2 cups nonfat yogurt
1 small to medium cucumber,
    peeled and chopped very fine
1/4 cup chopped fresh dill

1/2 teaspoon chervil
For Garnish:
    Fresh dill sprigs

Mix all ingredients well and garnish with dill sprigs.
Makes about 3 cups

Per Serving: 5 mg cholesterol; 1 gm saturated fat for each 2 ounces

Celery Seed Dressing

Celery seed dressing is usually sweet, and therefore somewhat higher in calories than those that are mainly vinegar. Lessen the amount of honey or sugar, or use a sugar substitute to cut down. For variety, half a teaspoon of lemon juice can be added. Serve on fruit salads and cooked chilled poultry salads.

1/2 cup least flavored commercial light or diet dressing or

1 teaspoon gelatin, softened in 1 teaspoon water, then dissolved in 1/2 cup boiling water and cooked for 3 minutes over low heat.

1/2 cup sugar or honey

1 teaspoon dry mustard

2 teaspoons celery seed

1 teaspoon pureed or grated raw celery

1 tablespoon pureed or grated raw onion

1/2 cup vinegar

Mix well and chill.
Makes 1 3/4 cups

Per Serving: 0 mg cholesterol; 0 gm saturated fat

Faux   Mayonnaise

The trick to achieving a mayonnaise-like consistency lies in gradually whisking the ingredients together. This mayonnaise has a wonderful, pungent, onion flavor. Omit onion if you're using the dressing for fruit. If you want store-bought mayonnaise, try United Foods Bright Day™ which has no egg yolks. Hain also makes a no-egg yolk variety, but it is a little sweeter.

2 teaspoons Dijon mustard
1 teaspoon fresh lemon juice
1/2 cup virgin olive oil
2 tablespoons finely minced
  scallions

1 cup King Cholesterol Free™
  imitation sour cream
Dash cayenne pepper to taste
Lite Salt™ (optional) to taste
Freshly ground black pepper to
  taste

Place mustard and lemon juice in a bowl and combine. Add oil in 3 stages, whisking well after each addition. Whisk in the scallions and then gradually whisk in the imitation sour cream. Add the seasonings.

Variation: Fold in 2 tablespoons sieved fresh tomato.

Variation: Clean and blanch watercress or spinach, drain under cold water, squeeze dry and chop very fine. Fold in mayonnaise.

Variation: Finely chop fresh herbs and whisk into mixture. Use a fruit vinegar to replace the lemon juice.

Makes 1 1/2 cups

Per Serving: 0 mg cholesterol; 3 gm saturated fat for each 2 ounces

Soups and Sauces

Soups are a great way to eat healthy, low cholesterol foods, and they're easy to prepare. Just combine good food, some stock or water and simmer on a back burner.

You can prepare most traditional cream soups using thickened fresh skim milk, evaporated skim milk, nonfat dry skim milk, imitation cream cheese and even coffee creamers for cream substitutes (if there isn't palm oil in the creamer). You can also thicken soups with pureed potatoes, rice, pasta, even French bread, as well as other thickeners.

For the low cholesterol cook, making great sauces without all the traditional butter or cream is easy and you'll see how here. Incidently, to add more calcium to your diet, whenever you're making stock or soup, if it doesn't already have a soup bone in the ingredients, add one along with a couple of teaspoons of vinegar. The vinegar cooks off and leaves no taste but is necessary to help pull the calcium from the bones during cooking (according to some scientists and as advised in the book, *Stand Tall* by Marsha Ware and Dr. Morris Notelovitz, Triad).

South American Kale Soup

What may strike you when traveling in South America is the wide variety of soups. Many contain bits of fatty pork or pork rind. This version of kale soup is healthier and has just as much taste. I love the fresh surprise of a chunk of raw tomato or, more often, a huge piece of avocado plopped in the middle of these wonderful soups, which you always find in Ecuador. Aji, a spicy hot sauce (page 134), can be added for zest and authenticity.

1 tomato, cut in large pieces (do not peel or seed, but remove stem area)

1 avocado, peeled and cut in fourths, lengthwise, sprinkle with lemon juice to preserve its color

4 potatoes, diced

1 small onion, finely chopped

Pinch of nutmeg

5 cups defatted chicken stock

4 cups shredded kale, collard greens, or cabbage

Freshly ground black pepper

Juice from 1/2 fresh lemon

For Garnish:

2 tablespoons chopped parsley

Place cut tomato and avocado in warm oven or microwave to heat slightly. Cook potatoes, onion, and nutmeg in stock until nearly soft. Add greens the last 10 minutes. Season with lemon juice and pepper.

To serve, place a piece of slightly heated tomato chunk and slightly heated avocado chunk in center of each bowl of soup and sprinkle with parsley. Serve hot with Aji sauce on the side.

Serves 8

Per Serving: 0 mg cholesterol; less than 1 gm saturated fat

Black Bean, Onion, and Rice Soup

This hearty soup is a Puerto Rican basic. It is spicy and good even in hot weather. When in a hurry, I've been know to open a can of black beans, add cream sherry and orange liqueur, microwave it and garnish with diced raw onions and cayenne and eat it all myself. If you don't have Spanish rice (a small grained white rice), any white rice will do. Serve with oranges, tangerines, and pineapple and a cold green vegetable like green beans vinaigrette.

2 1/2 cups uncooked black beans (or canned and drained)
4 cups water or defatted chicken stock
1 large Spanish onion, finely chopped
2 cloves garlic, minced
1 large carrot, trimmed, peeled and finely chopped
1 small stalk celery with leaves, finely chopped

Freshly ground black pepper
Lite Salt™ (optional)
1/4 teaspoon grated orange zest
1/8 teaspoon cinnamon
1/8 teaspoon cayenne or several shakes Tabasco™
1/4 cup vinegar
For Garnish:
  2 cups cooked rice
  2 large Spanish onions, finely chopped

Cook beans in the stock with onion, garlic, carrot, celery, pepper, optional salt, orange zest, cinnamon, cayenne, and vinegar for 1 1/2 hours. (If beans have already been cooked and drained, first simmer all the above vegetables in a few tablespoons of stock for 5 minutes. Or if canned, drain and add 1 1/2 cups stock and cook down liquid over high heat for 10 to 20 minutes). Heat the rice.

Serve soup hot in a cup or bowl in the center of a large individual plate. On one side of the platter pile a mound of rice, on the other side a mound of raw onion. Each person than adds rice and raw onion to the black bean soup in the amounts they prefer. Vidalia onions, a less pungent, sweet onion available in May and June, may be preferred.

Serves 4 to 6

Per Serving: 5 mg cholesterol; less than 1 gm saturated fat

Squash, Wild Rice, and Apple Soup

This thick soup is wonderful on a cool autumn day. It can be topped with a mandarin orange slice and slivers of ginger and small steamed asparagus, or just sprinkled with parsley.

If you don't use more liquid when adding the wild rice, the mixture is thick and is a fine side dish or accompaniment for thin slices of lean duck. Serve the poultry version with steamed Chinese beans, tied at the top with another bean (they are long and thin), or just use regular green beans. If the duck is too fatty, ask the butcher to find lean wild duck, or use skinless chicken or turkey breast.

If you choose to omit meat, serve this hearty soup with slices of brown bread and a green vegetable. If you can get squash flowers (they are edible), they can be blanched (or left uncooked) and placed atop the thick soup with parboiled snow peas for the leaves. It's quite a spectacular touch. Another way of serving this soup is to offer extra wild rice, chopped scallions, chopped raisins, and the seeds of the squash that have been steamed, baked or microwaved. Place these along with 1/4-inch slices of green beans around the soup dish, on a plate in separate mounds. People may then serve themselves.

1 small hubbard or butternut squash (about 1 1/2 pounds)	1 cup defatted chicken stock
1 tart apple	1/4 cup water
1/2 small, sweet onion	1/8 teaspoon cinnamon
2 small inner stalks of celery, with leaves	1/2 teaspoon brown sugar
1/2 teaspoon minced garlic	2 tablespoons cream sherry
1/8 teaspoon grated lemon rind	2 tablespoons uncooked wild rice
	For Garnish:
	Toasted squash seeds

Peel squash with apple peeler, remove seeds and membrane, reserving 3 tablespoons of seeds. Cut squash into 1-inch cubes. Cut apple into eighths, removing core and seeds, but do not peel. Slice onion into coarse pieces; cut celery into 1/2-inch slices, including leaves. Cut the carrot into smaller, 1/4-inch round slices.

Combine all ingredients, except reserved seeds, and sherry and simmer; covered, for 20 minutes; or microwave in a covered bowl for 10 minutes.

Add wild rice, slightly more water, breaking up vegetables into smaller pieces with the back of a spoon. Cook covered an additional 20 minutes (or microwave covered for 15 minutes). Toast reserved squash seeds.

Just before serving, add sherry and sprinkle the toasted seeds over soup. Serves 4

Per Serving: 0 mg cholesterol; 0 gm saturated fat

Parsnip, Carrot, and Green Bean Soup

This soup is very hearty yet not too heavy, like a farm soup used to start a meal. It can be a rich side dish if the stock is both reduced and thickened with cornstarch.

10 parsnips, scraped and trimmed, cut in 1/2-inch slices
7 carrots, scraped and trimmed, cut in 1/2-inch rounds
1 large onion, chopped fine
2 large cloves garlic, peeled and bruised (smash lightly with the side of a knife blade)
3/4 cup white wine
4 cups water or defatted chicken stock
2 teaspoons Dijon mustard
2 teaspoons pickled green peppercorns, drained

4 tablespoons Harvey's Bristol Cream™ sherry
1 tablespoon Lea & Perrins™ white wine Worcestershire sauce
1/4 cup white rice
1 1/2 cups sliced green beans
3 to 4 small nests of green spinach pasta (about 1 cup cooked)
Freshly ground black pepper to taste
For Garnish:
1/4 cup chopped parsley

Put all ingredients except green beans, pasta, and parsley garnish in a large pot and simmer for 30 minutes or microwave for 15 to 20 minutes. Add spinach pasta and simmer for 10 to 12 minutes more, adding green beans for the last 5 minutes. If microwaving, cut the times by one third. If the pasta is cooked, add pasta and beans together and cook for 5 minutes. Remove bruised garlic, sprinkle with parsley, and serve hot.

Serves 8

Per Serving: 0 mg cholesterol; less than 1 gm saturated fat

Tomato Soup

Tomato soup made from fresh, homegrown tomatoes picked at the peak of ripeness is not to be beat.

1/2 cup finely chopped onion
1/2 cup finely chopped celery
1/4 cup water
2 cups finely chopped fresh tomatoes
2 teaspoons lemon juice
1/4 teaspoon Tabasco™
1/4 teaspoon Lea & Perrins™ Worcestershire sauce
1 teaspoon brown sugar
4 cups water or defatted chicken stock

Lite Salt™ (optional)
Freshly ground black pepper
1/4 cup chopped fresh basil (1/2 tsp reserved for garnish)
1/2 cup coarsely chopped tomatoes
1/4 cup scallions cut into 1/4-inch pieces
For Garnish:
   1/2 teaspoon chopped basil
   1/4 cup chopped parsley

Simmer onions and celery in 1/4 cup water or microwave in a covered glass bowl until soft, 1 to 3 minutes. When onions are clear, add tomatoes and all other ingredients (including stock) except for the tomatoes, parsley, and scallions. Add optional salt, pepper, and basil (reserving 1/2 teaspoon of basil). Simmer for 20 minutes, or microwave for 10 minutes.

Just before serving, stir in scallions and coarsely chopped tomatoes. Heat until soup is hot but not boiling. Ladle into individual bowls. Garnish with basil and parsley. Serve immediately.

Variation: If making tomato noodle or tomato rice soup, add hot noodles cooked al dente or cooked wild, white, or brown rice. Stir in just before serving.

Variation: Cream of tomato soup can be made by whipping in 1/2 cup Better Than Cream Cheese™ imitation cream cheese just before adding tomatoes and scallions. The cholesterol will still be zero and saturated fat 1 gm.

Serves 6

Per Serving: 0 mg cholesterol; 0 gm saturated fat

New England Clam Chowder

This is, of course, the "cream" version of clam chowder. Serve hot with toasty-warm bread and a big salad for a fall or winter meal.

1 large Spanish onion, chopped fine
3 cups diced white potatoes
1/2 cup water
1 quart raw clams, chopped fine (if there is clam juice, use it at the time clams are used)
3 tablespoons flour
2 tablespoons "I Can't Believe It's Not Butter"™ margarine
1 1/2 cups skim milk
1/2 cup nonfat dry milk

Pinch of nutmeg
2 1/2 ounce packages Butter Buds™ (optional)
1/8 teaspoon ground mace
Freshly ground black pepper
Lite Salt™ (optional)
For Garnish:
   Chopped chives or parsley
   Lightly cooked very small whole okra

Simmer onion and potatoes in 1/2 cup water for 10 minutes. Add clams (and clam juice) and simmer 3 to 4 minutes more. In a separate non-stick pan, make a roux of flour and margarine. Add 1 cup skim milk, slowly stirring constantly until mixture thickens. Add the rest of the milk, whisked together with the dry milk, optional imitation butter and all of the spices, clams, onions and potatoes. (The imitation butter definitely gives a more buttery flavor, if you like that.) Cook over low heat, not boiling, for 10 minutes. Serve hot. Garnish with chopped chives or parsley or a steamed whole okra floated on top.

Variation: While simmering the onion and potatoes, add 1/2 cup sliced carrots and 1/2 cup sliced green beans.

Serves 6

Per Serving: 60 mg cholesterol; less than 1 gm saturated fat

Gingered Carrot and Snow Pea Soup

This soup, really two soups, is stunning in a shallow, wide soup bowl. The orange carrot soup is on one side and the fresh green snow pea soup is on the other side; half orange and half green. Obviously, they both have to be thick to do this, but it works and your guests will be duly impressed. This one fulfills that ''cream soup'' hunger without the cholesterol. Of course, each soup can be prepared separately.

Carrot Soup:

1/2 teaspoon Weight Watchers™ margarine

4 carrots, trimmed, peeled, and diced

1 onion, diced

1 stalk celery, chopped

1 small leek, peeled and diced

4 cups water or defatted chicken stock

1 cup orange juice

1 teaspoon Better Than Cream Cheese™ imitation cream cheese

Lite Salt™ (optional)

Freshly ground white pepper

For Garnish:

Slivered ginger

Strips of blanched snow peas

Strips of raw carrots

Melt margarine in a pan; add 1/4 cup water; add vegetables and cook gently for approximately 20 minutes. Add stock and orange juice and simmer gently for one hour. Place in a food processor or blender; puree and strain. Adjust consistency and finish by whisking in 1 teaspoon imitation whipped cream cheese.

Snow Pea Soup

1/2 teaspoon Weight Watchers™ margarine

1 pound snow peas, trimmed, chopped fine

1 onion, chopped fine

2 stalks celery, chopped

1 small leek, peeled and chopped

1 large potato, peeled and diced

4 cups water or defatted chicken stock

1/2 bay leaf

Pinch of thyme

Lite Salt™ (optional)

Freshly ground white pepper

1 teaspoon Better Than Cream Cheese™ imitation cream cheese

Melt margarine in a pan, add 1/4 cup water and the vegetables, and cook gently for approximately 20 minutes. Add water and celery stalks and simmer gently for 1 hour. Place in food processor or blender; puree and strain through a strainer. Adjust consistency and finish by whisking in imitation cream cheese.

To serve, place carrot soup and snow pea soup in two jugs and pour the two—at the same time—into each half of shallow soup plate. Serve hot or cold.

Garnish with fine strips of blanched snow peas, blanched carrots or strips of ginger and sprinkle with white pepper.

Serves 4 to 6

Per Serving: 0 mg cholesterol; less than 1 gm saturated fat

Brown Lentil and Smoked Beef Soup

Simple and secure. A no-fuss delicious soup that's perfect for a cool day. A crisp green salad with raspberry vinegar dressing, page 95, and hunks of dark bread make a complete meal.

1 large sweet onion, chopped very fine
1 carrot, chopped very fine
2 cloves garlic, minced very fine
1 cup lentils
3 cups defatted beef broth

3/4 pound cubed smoked defatted beef
1 teaspoon thyme
Pepper to taste
For Garnish:
Raw onion ring slivers
Lemon slivers

Simmer all ingredients covered until lentils are tender (about 1 hour). Serve hot with wafer thin onion rings and lemon slices floating on top of each portion.

Serves 4 to 6

Per Serving: 80 mg cholesterol; 4 gm saturated fat

Manhattan Clam Chowder

This classic is ideal for a low cholesterol meal or soup course. A spicier version can be made by adding a few drops of Tabasco™ sauce.

1 onion, chopped fine
2 cups diced white potatoes
1/2 cup water
1 quart clams, finely chopped, with their liquid
3 cups diced tomatoes
1/2 cup finely chopped green pepper with seeds
2 cups defatted fish stock or water

1/2 cup white wine
For Garnish:
   Chopped scallions
   Freshly chopped parsley
   Serve each portion in a shallow dish with one whole steamed clam or steamed large mussels in shell in center of soup.

Simmer onions and potatoes covered in small amount of water for 10 minutes. (Add more water if necessary.) Add clams and clam liquid and simmer for 5 to 8 minutes. Add everything else and simmer for 10 minutes more

Clam chowder is one of the few dishes that is better refrigerated overnight, then reheated and eaten the next day. Reheat it, garnish with scallions, parsley, or a hot whole clam or mussel in the shell.

Serves 6 to 8

Per Serving: 50 mg cholesterol; less than 1 gm saturated fat

Fresh Garden Pea Soup

Most pea soups are made from dried peas, but this creamed fresh pea soup has a refreshing flavor. Imitation cream cheese is excellent though it does contain vegetable fat. Just a dollop can be added in the center if the soup bowl is shallow, so it can be seen.

2 pounds sweet peas or sugar
    snaps, unshelled
1 head iceberg lettuce, shredded
3 scallions, chopped
2 cups water or defatted chicken
    stock
1 cup Better Than Cream
    Cheese™ imitation cream
    cheese

Pinch of sugar
2 1/2-ounce packages Butter
    Buds™ or several shakes Molly
    McButter™ whisked with 1/2
    cup skim milk
For Garnish:
    1 teaspoon finely chopped mint

Unless the peas are very old and stringy, use the pods. If using sugar snaps, then definitely use pods. Put all the ingredients, except Butter Buds™, milk and mint in a saucepan and cook until tender. Sieve to remove fibers and then puree in a food processor. Add a little more water or stock if thinning is desired. Just before serving, add the imitation butter and skim milk and sprinkle with a little finely chopped mint. Serve hot.

Serves 4

Per Serving: less than 5 mg cholesterol; 1 gm saturated fat

Irish Leek and Mussel Soup

A rich blend of mussels, cider, leeks, and hearty fish stock. Good on a cold day to warm the tummy.

4 pints mussels
1 cup fresh apple cider (not hard)
2 leeks, finely chopped (split leeks in half lengthwise to remove grit)
1 shallot, finely chopped
6 black peppercorns, crushed
3 sprigs of fennel
4 tablespoons chopped parsley
1/2 cup white wine
1/2 cup water
1/2 teaspoon Old Bay Seasoning™

3 cups fish stock
2 teaspoons flour
2 teaspoons I Can't Beleive It's Not Butter™ margarine
2 Egg Watchers™ imitation eggs
1/2 cup skim milk
3 tablespoons nonfat dry milk
Pepper
Dash cayenne
3 tablespoons Harvey's Bristol Cream™ sherry (optional)

Clean and prepare the mussels, removing beards and grit thoroughly. Any mussels even slightly open that do not snap shut when sharply tapped should be discarded. Watch out for shells filled with mud or sand—even one such shell is enough to ruin a dish.

Put cider, leeks, shallot, pepper, and herbs in pan. Cover and turn up the heat. In another pan steam the mussels in the wine, water, and Old Bay Seasoning™ for a minute or two, until they open. Discard those that do not open. Remove them from the heat and drain. Empty the mussels and their juices from shells into the cider pan. Keep the mussels warm. Add the fish stock to the pan juices. Blend the flour and margarine together and stir into the simmering stock. Continue simmering for about 10 minutes until the soup thickens and the flour is well cooked. Remove from the heat; add the imitation eggs, beaten with the skim milk and powdered skim milk. Stir well into the soup. Return to the heat and allow to simmer very gently for a few moments only. Do not boil. Test for seasoning; add optional sherry. Serve 5 to 6 mussels to each bowl of soup as a garnish.

Serves 4 to 6

Per Serving: 85 mg cholesterol; 1 gm saturated fat

Turnip, Leek, and Broccoli Soup

A rather different blend of flavors that can get you hooked.

1 large onion (preferably Spanish), peeled and diced

2 leeks, white only, washed well and chopped (slice leek lengthwise in half to remove all grit)

1 large potato, diced

1/3 cup wild rice

2 cloves garlic, thinly sliced

1/2 teaspoon ground ginger

1/4 teaspoon Tabasco™

4 cups defatted chicken stock

1 large turnip, peeled and coarse chopped

5 scallions, white and green, chopped diagonally into 1-inch pieces

1 1/2 cups broccoli florets plus 8 to 10 broccoli leaves

Freshly ground black pepper

For Garnish:

Tangerine or mandarin orange slices

Fresh tomato bits

Simmer Spanish onion, leeks, potatoes, wild rice, and garlic in stock for 8 to 10 minutes, or until vegetables are done (rice won't be cooked yet). Boil turnips until soft, drain off water, and mash lightly, keeping most pieces whole but well bruised. Add scallions, broccoli leaves and all the spices to the onions and combine with the turnips and stock. Simmer for 10 to 20 minutes. Add the florets and simmer for 3 or so more minutes, or until the broccoli turns bright green.

Serve very hot, garnished with tangerine and orange slices and tomato. Serves 6

Per Serving: 0 mg cholesterol; 0 gm saturated fat

Mulligatawny Soup

(An Indian word, *molegoo* (pepper) and *tunnee* (water))

My beautiful Italian friend Linda began living in foreign countries when she was ten. While in India, she became entranced with the food and offers this low cholesterol version of a traditional dish.

1 medium onion, very finely chopped

2 cloves garlic, minced

1/2 cup water

1/2 teaspoon mustard seed

1/2 teaspoon ground fenugreek seed (available in gourmet food stores or Indian food markets)

1/2 teaspoon ground tumeric

1/2 teaspoon ground cumin

1/2 teaspoon ground coriander seed

1/2 teaspoon black pepper

3 cups defatted chicken stock, meat stock, or vegetable stock

2 tablespoons tamarind juice (available in gourmet food stores or Indian food markets)

1 tablespoon cooked white rice

1 tablespoon cooked red lentils

Lite Salt™ to taste (optional)

Simmer the onion and garlic in small amount water until soft. Then add the spices and cook for three to five minutes. In a stock pot, heat the stock. Combine the remaining ingredients and simmer for 10 to 15 minutes. Add Lite Salt™ to taste. Serve very hot with Indian *nan* (bread).

Makes 6 servings

Per Serving: 0 mg cholesterol; 0 gm saturated fat

Hot and Sour Soup

An exotic and spicy prelude to a meal or the whole meal itself. For me, few soups are as satisfying as this one. You can vary the peppery hot oil depending on how spicy you like it.

10 ounces bean curd, (tofu) sliced into 2" x 1/2" pieces

1 ounce dried mushrooms, soaked, squeezed and stems removed (you can soak in equal parts water and sherry for more flavor)

1 ounce dry transparent noodles, soaked in water and drained and cut into 2 to 3-inch pieces

4 cups water or defatted chicken stock

3 ounces lean pork, blanched, defatted, and sliced thinly

2 tablespoons sugar

1/2 teaspoon white pepper

2 tablespoons dark soy sauce or low salt soy

6 to 10 drops China Bowl™ hot oil (found in Oriental grocery stores)

3 tablespoons red rice vinegar (or cider vinegar)

2 tablespoons chopped scallions

2 tablespoons chopped fresh coriander

2 tablespoons cornstarch mixed in 2 tablespoons cool water

4 Egg Watchers™ imitation eggs, lightly whipped

Combine all the ingredients except cornstarch and imitation eggs and heat to boiling point. Simmer for 1 to 2 minutes. Add cornstarch mixed in water to thicken. Stir over low heat as soup thickens. While simmering, slowly drizzle imitation egg in thin stream, stirring slowly with a wooden spoon to break egg steam. Serve immediately.

Makes 4 servings

Per Serving: 10 mg cholesterol; 1 gm saturated fat

Corn Soup

A variation on a traditional favorite. Sometimes I add a diced precooked potato with the corn and milk.

6 ears fresh corn, husked, silk removed (or substitute 4 10-ounce packages frozen cut corn, thawed)

1 tablespoon Weight Watchers™ margarine

2 medium tomatoes, peeled, and coarsely chopped

2 medium onions, finely chopped

1 tablespoon ground cumin

3 cloves garlic, peeled and minced

1 jalapeno pepper, seeded and minced (or 1/2 jalapeno and 1/2 teaspoon serrano for a bit more heat)

2 green peppers, seeds reserved, de-ribbed, and cubed

2 red peppers, seeds reserved, deribbed and cubed

1 teaspoon Lite Salt™ (optional)

4 cups defatted chicken stock

For Garnish:

Fresh cilantro

Strips of roasted pimiento

King Cholesterol Free™ imitation sour cream

Freshly toasted pumpkin seeds or green pepper seeds, simmered for 1 to 2 minutes in 1/4 cup water.

Cut the kernels from the ears of corn over a bowl to catch any corn milk. Then scrape the ears with the back of a knife to extract the remaining milk. The milk will act as a natural thickener for the soup.

Heat the margarine in a heavy casserole over low heat. Add the tomato, onion, and cumin. Cook, stirring, until the onion is softened, but not brown. Add the garlic and stir for about 2 minutes. Add the peppers and optional Lite Salt™. Continue stirring until the peppers are slightly limp. Add the stock and corn milk and, stirring, bring to a simmer. Cook 5 minutes, so the corn is still crunchy. Taste for seasonings.

To finish, garnish with cilantro leaves and strips of pimiento. Or add dollops of imitation sour cream, flecked with the pumpkin seeds, or sprinkle with pepper seeds. For a thicker consistency, fully incorporate the imitation sour cream and then garnish. Serve hot.

Makes 8 servings

Per Serving: Less than 1 mg cholesterol; less than 1 gm saturated fat

Recipes: More Than 200 for a Healthy Heart

Fennel Soup

A very different treat with the musky flavor of fennel.

3 large white onions, sliced thin
1/4 cup water
3 fennel bulbs, sliced thin
1 tablespoon fresh lemon juice
4 white potatoes, unpeeled and
** sliced thin**

4 cups defatted chicken stock or
** water**
For Garnish:
  Fennel leaves
  Fresh chives, chopped or left
  whole

In a Silverstone™ non-stick pan, simmer onions in 1/4 cup water for a few minutes. When softened, add fennel and lemon juice; cook for 10 minutes, adding more water if necessary. Add potatoes and stock. Bring to a boil and simmer for 30 minutes or until potatoes are tender (or microwave for 20 minutes). Soup can be pureed in a blender but it isn't necessary. Garnish with fennel and chives. Serve hot.

Makes 6 servings

Per Serving: less than 5 mg cholesterol; 0 gm saturated fat

Leek and Lentil Soup

Leeks can be substituted for any kind of onion. The soup can be pureed or left chunky.

2 cups lentils, washed, soaked in cold water for 1 hour, and drained

2 quarts defatted chicken stock or water

1 small onion, chopped

2 carrots, shredded or chopped fine

1 turnip, shredded or chopped fine

2 medium boiling potatoes, diced

4 large celery stalks, chopped fine

6 leeks, chopped (halve the leeks lengthwise to remove grit)

1 cup chopped cabbage

2 cloves garlic, minced

1/2 teaspoon dried basil

1 teaspoon fresh lemon juice

1/8 cup Harvey's Bristol Cream™ sherry

3 ripe tomatoes, chopped very fine, plus juice

For Garnish:

Chopped parsley

Very thin lemon slices

Cook the lentils in the stock in a large pot for 45 minutes or in a microwave for 25 to 30 minutes. Meanwhile, simmer the onions, carrots, optional turnips, potatoes, celery, and leeks in 1/4 cup water. Add remaining ingredients to the onion, carrot mixture except tomatoes and cook for 20 minutes or microwave for 10 to 12 minutes. Add the tomatoes, juice, and the drained lentils and simmer for 20 minutes, or until lentils are soft. Garnish and serve hot.

Serves 8

Per Serving: 0 mg cholesterol; 0 gm saturated fat

Bean and Barley Soup

This is a variation of the familiar beef and barley soup. We've omitted the beef but not the flavor. By omitting the knuckle bone, the cholesterol and saturated fat content is nearly zero. Leave in the knuckle bone and add two teaspoons of vinegar and you get extra calcium. The cholesterol and saturated fat values are with the bone.

1 large onion, coarsely chopped
2 garlic cloves, minced
2 stalks celery, including green leaves, coarsely chopped
2 carrots, grated
1/2 cup water
1 knuckle bone (must be simmered for 1 to 2 hours in advance so all fat can be thoroughly skimmed. Small amounts of meat left on bone can be used)
1/2 cup pearl barley

4 cups water or defatted beef stock (from knuckle bone)
2 teaspoons Harvey's Bristol Cream™ sherry
Pinch of nutmeg
1 cup dried lima beans, soaked for 2 to 3 hours in cold water and drained

For Garnish:
Fresh parsley, finely chopped
Lite Salt™
Freshly ground black pepper
Very ripe tomato cut in large slices

Simmer onion, garlic, celery, and carrots in 1/2 cup water for 3 to 4 minutes. Then add everything else and simmer covered over low heat for 1 1/2 hours or microwave for 50 to 70 minutes. Garnish and serve hot.

Variation: Substitute the dried lima beans with barley for a total of 1 1/2 cups of barley. Add 1 cup chopped tomatoes during the last half hour of cooking.

Serves 6 to 8

Per Serving: 15 mg cholesterol; 1 gm saturated fat

Fresh Lettuce Soup

This creamy soup can be served hot or chilled.

2 heads young lettuces
4 scallions, thinly sliced
2 teaspoons Weight Watchers™ margarine
2 cups water or defatted chicken stock
1 cup skim milk
1 bay leaf
Pinch of nutmeg

Freshly ground black pepper
4 tablespoons Better Than Cream Cheese™ imitation cream cheese, softened
For Garnish:
Chopped parsley
Nutmeg
Lemon wedges

Remove the hard stalks and any discolored outer lettuce leaves and finely grate lettuce into shreds. Melt margarine in Silverstone™ non-stick pan and cook scallions and lettuce very gently for about 15 minutes. Add stock, skim milk, and bay leaf. Simmer for about 20 minutes. Add nutmeg and pepper to taste. Remove bay leaf. Sieve.

Whip in softened cream cheese and garnish with parsley and additional nutmeg just before serving with lemon.

Serves 4

Per Serving: less than 5 mg cholesterol; less than 1 gm saturated fat

Cabbage Soup

Here is a very simple cabbage soup that is a winter favorite at my house. Canadian bacon is almost the lowest in cholesterol of all the red meats, so the cholesterol and saturated fat count are low and the flavor is high.

3 onces lean Canadian bacon, diced
6 cups water
6 black peppercorns
1 large cabbage, shredded
1 small turnip, diced
2 carrots, diced

3 to 4 medium potatoes, diced
2 bay leaves
Lite Salt™ (optional)
Freshly ground black pepper to taste
For Garnish:
    1/4 cup chopped fresh parsley

Bring Canadian bacon to a boil in the water with peppercorns and simmer for about 5 minutes. Skim off any fat. Add the vegetables and the bay leaves to the stock. Season. Simmer for about 30 minutes more until the vegetables are tender. Remove the bay leaves. Sprinkle with parsley and serve very hot.

Serves 6

Per Serving: 15 mg cholesterol; less than 1 gm saturated fat

Icy Cucumber Soup

In summer this favorite is one of the easiest, most refreshing soups. Although seen in many guises, it's easy to enjoy this version on a low cholesterol diet, thanks to imitation sour cream.

3 cucumbers
1/4 cup cooked defatted chicken
   stock, chilled
2 cups lowfat buttermilk
1/2 cup chopped fresh parsley
1/4 cup chopped fresh dill
4 scallions, chopped

2 cups King Cholesterol Free™
   imitation sour cream
1 tablespoon fresh lemon juice
Lite Salt™ (optional)
White pepper
For Garnish:
   Dill and Parsley chopped or left
   in larger pieces

Trim the ends off the cucumbers. Carefully remove the skin of one cucumber in evenly spaced, lengthwise strips with a vegetable peeler. If cucumber skin is waxed, discard all peel. Cut the cucumber crosswise into paper-thin slices and reserve in ice water. Peel the remaining 2 cucumbers, halve them lengthwise and scoop out the seeds and reserve them. Puree half the cucumbers with 1/2 teaspoon of chicken stock in a food processor. Add 1 cup of the buttermilk, 1/4 cup chopped parsley, half the dill and 2 scallions. Repeat the procedure with the remaining cucumber, stock, buttermilk, parsley, dill and scallions, but don't puree completely so there is still some texture. Gradually whisk in imitation sour cream, lemon juice, optional Lite Salt™ and pepper to taste. Cover and chill thoroughly.

Serve cold, garnished with the reserved slices of cucumber, sprigs of dill and parsley leaves. If you like cucumber seeds you can garnish with a teaspoon of the seeds you scooped out.

Variation: Watercress; Tomato and Basil; Asparagus; Zucchini; Tarragon and Parsley; Dandelion; Nasturtium; Turnip and Parsley; Broccoli Leaves; Okra and To mato. With the same basic recipe, substitute the cucumbers for any of the above vegetables. The second vegetable is the garnish. For a cold okra soup, garnish with bits of tomato; for tomato soup, garnish with basil.

Serves 4

Per Serving: 5 mg cholesterol; 1 gm saturated fat

Gazpacho

This cold Spanish, now Mexican and Tex-Mex soup should only be made with vine-ripened tomatoes. Use skins and all. Don't remove seeds from the cucumbers. Why some recipes still call for olive oil, I'll never know. My motto is "Fat in, fat on!" You just can't eat enough of this fine food to gain an ounce or raise your cholesterol.

1 large cucumber, coarsely chopped (remove skin if cucumbers are waxed)
1/4 cup tarragon vinegar or 1/4 cup cider vinegar plus 1/4 teaspoon dried tarragon
1/2 green pepper, coarsely chopped
1/2 red pepper, coarsely chopped
1 large stalk celery, chopped fine (use the leaves too)
1 large Spanish onion, coarsely chopped

3 large very ripe tomatoes, chopped
1 tablespoon fresh lemon juice
3 cups tomato juice
2 cloves garlic, minced
1/8 teaspoon cayenne or 1/4 teaspoon Tabasco™

For Garnish:
Wafer thin slices of lemon or lime
Sprig cilantro

In a blender or food processor, puree half the cucumber, vinegar, half the green and red peppers, celery, half the onion and half of the chopped tomato, lemon juice and all the garlic.

Add all of the other ingredients to soup. Mix and chill well.

Serve cold with a garnish of sliced lemon or lime floating on top. Reserved cucumber strips can be cut into leaves or slivered and floated next to lemon slices, or place pieces of fresh cilantro on top.

Serves 6

Per Serving: 0 mg cholesterol; 0 gm saturated fat

Chicken Soup Senegalese

Chicken with lots of fruit and vegetables is fun to cook and fun to eat. To garnish, cut some of the chicken into julienne strips and float on the surface with some thin wedges of peeled mango and/or papaya. For an added flourish, present the cold soup tureen nestled in a slightly larger bowl filled with cracked ice. Or serve with additional bowls of finely diced apple, banana, mango, and papaya so you can add your own mixture. Sprinkle fruit with lemon juice to avoid darkening.

1/2 chicken breast, deboned, defatted and skinned
5 cups defatted chicken stock
2 tablespoons white wine (optional)
3 1-inch carrot slices
3 1-inch celery slices
2 tablespoons chopped fresh parsley
1 teaspoon chopped fresh tarragon
2 tablespoons Weight Watchers™ margarine (optional)
1/2 onion, chopped
2 leeks, trimmed and chopped (cut lengthwise, and washed well to remove all grit)

1 clove garlic, minced
1 or 2 tablespoons curry powder
1 banana, peeled
2 tart apples, cubed
1 jalapeno pepper, minced
3 red skinned potatoes, cubed
3 tomatoes, diced
1 medium mango, cubed
1 tablespoon cayenne
Lite Salt™ (optional)
Freshly ground black pepper
4 1/2 cups defatted chicken stock
1 cup lowfat yogurt, drained in cheesecloth for 10 to 15 minutes.

Poach the chicken gently in 1 cup of stock and white wine, to which you have added the carrot and celery, parsley, and tarragon. The chicken is done when it is slightly springy to the touch (about 20 minutes) (or microwave for 10 to 15 minutes). Set it aside, moistened with some poaching liquid. When cool, cover and refrigerate. The vegetables will be al dente.

In a heavy casserole, heat 4 tablespoons water and 2 tablespoons margarine. Add the onion, leeks and garlic. Soften the vegetables and sprinkle them with the curry powder. Stir over low heat to coat vegetables evenly with curry. Add the banana, apples, jalapeno pepper, potatoes, tomatoes, mango, cayenne, and remaining stock. Stir well to combine; add optional Lite Salt™ and freshly ground pepper to taste. Simmer for about 20 minutes, or until all the vegetables are soft.

Puree the mixture in batches in a food processor, then pour into a large bowl. Cool, cover and refrigerate. To finish the soup, whisk in the drained lowfat yogurt. Dice the chicken breast and add to the soup.

Serve cold.

Serves 6 to 8

Per Serving: 10 mg cholesterol; 1 gm saturated fat

Vichyssoise

Vichyssoise never has to be made with heavy cream. Enhance this version with a dash of nutmeg. In the late summer or fall, diced raw apples or pears may be sprinkled on top. Coat the fruit with lemon juice to avoid darkening.

4 leeks, white part only, chopped very fine (halve leeks lengthwise to remove all grit)
1 large onion, chopped very fine
4 potatoes, chopped very fine
2 cups defatted chicken stock
2 cups skim milk

1/2 cup nonfat dry milk
2 teaspoons flour
1/4 teaspoon mace
1 cup finely diced cucumber
For Garnish:
   Chopped fresh chives and paprika

Simmer leeks, onion, and potatoes until soft in a small amount of water. Add stock and milk with dry milk whisked in. Simmer for 15 minutes. Add flour and mace and beat until soup thickens and is lump-free. Cool and add cucumber. Garnish. Serve cold.

Serves 4-6

Per serving: 10 mg cholesterol; 1 gm saturated fat

Beef (Meat) Stock

4 pounds total of lean beef
    shank, chuck roast and oxtail
2 pounds chicken trimmings:
    backs, necks, remove skin
Bouquet garni (tied in large
    cheesecloth) of 2 leeks,
    trimmed, cut in half
    lengthwise and washed well to
    remove any grit

1 garlic clove, cracked into
    quarters
2 onions, stuck with 2 cloves
4 large carrots, scraped
4 stalks celery
1 tablespoon vinegar
1/2 teaspoon black peppercorns

Put all the meats on a rack in a large stock pot and cover with at least 2 inches of water. Slowly bring to a boil and begin skimming off the scum that rises. Continue skimming for 15 to 20 minutes, adding 1 cup cold water halfway through. Add the bouquet garni and vinegar and gently simmer, partially covered, for 5 hours, skimming if necessary.

Strain stock by ladling it through a cheesecloth-lined strainer into a large bowl. Cool stock overnight in the refrigerator. The next day, remove any congealed fat that has collected on top of the liquid. The stock may be frozen in quart containers and, if you like, freeze 1 quart in ice cube trays (to have small amounts of stock readily available). If frozen in ice cube trays, remove when solid, stack carefully in bags, squeezing out any air. Stock may be kept frozen for 2 months.

Makes 12 cups

Per Serving: less than 5 mg cholesterol; less than 1 gm saturated fat

Chicken Stock

5 pounds stewing hen or chicken
  parts
5 carrots
4 medium onions stuck with 2
  cloves
1 large leek, split and cleaned to
  remove any grit
2 stalks celery, with top leaves

1/2 bulb unpeeled garlic
A bouquet garni (tied in
  cheesecloth) of:
3 parsley sprigs
2 thyme sprigs
2 bay leaves
1 teaspoon vinegar
1 teaspoon black peppercorns

If possible, buy a fresh stewing hen for rich flavor and do not use carcass after cooking. Remove all visible fat and skin.

Split the larger bones of the chicken with the back of a cleaver. Add chicken to a large, heavy stockpot. Cover with about 2 inches of cold water. Slowly bring liquid to a boil and skim off scum that rises with a fine mesh skimmer. Add about 1 cup cold water and skim again. Repeat this step again. Add carrots, onions (2 of them stuck with cloves), leek, celery, garlic, the bouquet garni and vinegar. Skim once more and add 1 teaspoon black peppercorns. Bring to a boil, reduce heat to a low and simmer for 3 hours, or microwave for 1 1/2 hours.

Strain stock through a cheesecloth-lined colander into a large bowl. Cool the stock and then cover it tightly and refrigerate overnight. This allows the fat in the liquid to solidify on the surface so you can spoon or pick it off and discard. The stock can be kept safely in the refrigerator 3 or 4 days. Freeze most of it in quart containers. The remainder can be frozen in ice cube trays in 2 tablespoon-size cubes, which, once frozen, can be carefully packed into freezer bags.

Makes 3 to 4 quarts

Per Serving: less than 5 mg cholesterol; less than 1 gm saturated fat

Fish Stock

3 pounds fish heads (bones and gills discarded)
1 onion, sliced
1 celery heart with leaves, cleaned and chopped
1 carrot, chopped
1 leek, cleaned and chopped
2 cloves shallots
1 tablespoon vinegar
5 cups water
1 cup white wine
Bouquet garni
Lite Salt™ (optional)

Put all ingredients in a very large, microwave safe bowl and seal airtight with plastic film. Microwave on high for 30 minutes. Strain contents into a bowl. Cool and pick off any fat or cook on stovetop for 1 1/2 hours, chill and remove fat.

The stock is ready to use as a sauce base or it can be frozen. *(See beef stock.)*
Makes 5 to 6 cups

Per Serving: less than 5 mg cholesterol; less than 1 gm saturated fat

Fresh Tomato Sauce

This sauce is wonderful on pasta. It stays fresh for about two weeks and can be frozen.

1 large onion, chopped fine
3 cloves garlic, minced
2 pounds plum tomatoes, chopped fine
2 to 3 tablespoons finely chopped fresh basil or 2 tablespoons dried basil
1/2 teaspoon sugar
Dash cayenne pepper
3 tablespoons chopped fresh oregano or 2 teaspoons dried oregano
Freshly ground black pepper

Lightly simmer onions and garlic in 1/4 inch water until soft. Add remaining ingredients and cook in covered skillet for 30 minutes. Leave chunky or, if desired, puree until smooth.
Makes 3 cups

Per Serving: 0 mg cholesterol; 0 gm saturated fat

Faux Bearnaise Sauce

Bearnaise sauce is delicious on beef and lamb. If you want a more buttery taste, add 4 1/2 ounce packages of Butter Buds™ or a few shakes of Molly McButter™ to the herb mixture as it cooks. For Butter Buds™ to work best, whip or whisk them into a teaspoon or so of warm water, or they may lump.

2 tablespoons chopped fresh
    tarragon or 3/4 teaspoon dried
    tarragon
1 tablespoon chopped fresh
    chervil leaves or 1/2
    tablespoon dried chervil
1 tablespoon finely chopped
    shallots

1/2 cup white vinegar
3 tablespoons dry white wine
1/2 cup walnut oil
Freshly ground black pepper
6 Egg Watchers™ eggs, softened
    and whisked to remove any
    lumps
1/2 cup hot water

Simmer the tarragon, chervil, shallots, vinegar, and wine until reduced to about 3 to 4 tablespoons. In a food processor, mix the oil, pepper, and cooked herb mixture. Whisk imitation eggs slowly into the hot water. Blend the oil and egg mixture and pour in a fine stream while the processor is mixing until well blended.

Makes 2 cups

Per Serving: 0 mg cholesterol; 2 gm saturated fat for each 4 ounces

Mock Hollandaise Sauce

This more than acceptable Hollandaise may be poured on asparagus, broccoli, or "eggs" Benedict. It's even good on a baked potato.

3/4 cup cool water
1 1/2 teaspoons cornstarch
2 Egg Watchers™ eggs
3 tablespoons fresh lemon juice

1/2 teaspoon Lite Salt™ (optional)
Dash of cayenne

Stir water into cornstarch a little at a time, in a non-stick pan. Bring to a boil; cook 1 minute while stirring. Remove from heat. Beat imitation eggs until light and fluffy. Beat lemon juice, optional salt, and cayenne into egg mixture. Gradually pour hot liquid into egg mixture, beating constantly. Return saucepan to heat and heat gently, beating constantly until thickened. Do not boil. Use immediately.

Makes 4 servings

Per Serving: 0 mg cholesterol; 0 gm saturated fat

Sweet Wine Sauce

This sauce may be used on fruit or on cake with fruit, or you might want to try it on duck or chicken. Fruit such as blueberries may be poached for 2 to 3 minutes in the sauce.

1 cup sugar
3 tablespoons red wine

1 teaspoon fresh lemon
1/2 cup water

Cook everything for 5 minutes. Serve cold.
Makes about 1 cup

Per Serving: 0 mg cholesterol; 0 gm saturated fat

Rouille Sauce

Use this as a savory sauce for fish and fish stews. If you wish to reduce the salt, omit some or all of the anchovies and capers.

2 new potatoes, boiled, or
  steamed 15 to 25 minutes or
  microwaved until soft
8 cloves garlic, minced
3 red peppers, roasted, peeled,
  and seeded
4 scallions, trimmed, and cut into
  3 to 4 pieces
2 tablespoons drained capers
2 chilies—jalapeno or serrano

3 anchovy fillets, rinsed and
  patted dry
1/4 cup fresh tarragon leaves
1/4 cup tightly packed fresh
  parsley leaves
Lite Salt™ (optional)
Freshly ground black pepper
2 tablespoons white wine vinegar
1 cup fish stock (recipe page 130)
1/4 cup Egg Watchers™ eggs

Place the vegetables, anchovy, and seasonings in a processor and puree. Add the vinegar, stock, and imitation eggs; then slowly dribble in the oil. Serve chilled.

Makes 2 cups

Per Serving: less than 5 mg cholesterol; 1 gm saturated fat for each 4 ounces

Tartar Sauce

Great with any fish. The United Foods Company makes a cholesterol-free tartar sauce if you wish store-bought.

2 teaspoons white vinegar
1 cup King Cholesterol Free™ imitation sour cream or Bright Day™ imitation mayonnaise
2 teaspoons Dijon mustard
2 cornichon pickles, chopped
1/3 cup finely chopped onions and scallions

1 tablespoon chopped fresh parsley
2 tablespoons chopped red pepper
1/2 teaspoon dried tarragon
1/2 teaspoon sugar
Freshly ground black pepper to taste

Mix everything well and refrigerate until serving time.
Makes about 1 1/2 cups

Per Serving: 0 mg cholesterol; 3 gm saturated fat

Ecuadorian Aji Side Sauce (or Salsa Cruda)

This sauce, traditional in Ecuador, is stirred in soups. It is also a side dish for serving with meats, rice, or over potatoes or over fish.

1 hot chili pepper with seeds removed and discarded, chopped fine
1 tomato, chopped fine
2 scallions, chopped fine

1 small onion, chopped fine
1/2 teaspoon finely chopped cilantro
1 teaspoon vinegar
1/2 teaspoon sugar

Shake all ingredients well in a closed container. Keep covered and refrigerate until 1/2 hour before serving. Serve at room temperature.
Makes about 3/4 cup

Per Serving: 0 mg cholesterol; 0 gm saturated fat

Middle Eastern Yogurt Sauce

This divine yogurt sauce is served over small amounts of well-cooked lean lamb or beef or with any grilled fish. It's so versatile you can even serve it with chilled beets or use as a dip for vegetables.

14 cup drained tahini paste (found in most markets and Oriental grocery stores)
1/2 cup fresh lemon juice
1/4 cup pinenuts
4 cloves garlic, minced, then mashed with about 1/2 teaspoon Lite Salt™ (optional) with the back of a knife

2 cups plain nonfat yogurt*
For Garnish:
1/4 cup finely chopped flat leaf parsley
1/4 cup finely chopped fresh mint
1/4 cup pinenuts

Thin tahini with lemon juice; add ground pinenuts which have first been toasted for 15 minutes in a low oven, just until golden. Cool, and reserve a teaspoon for garnish, after finely chopping them. Add garlic gradually. Slowly combine with the yogurt.

*The yogurt is creamier if first drained through a cheesecloth-lined strainer for about an hour and whisked to a smooth, thick consistency.

Serve cold.

Makes 2 1/2 to 3 cups

Per Serving: 10 mg cholesterol; 4 gm saturated fat for each 3 ounces

Dill White Sauce

This dill sauce is perfect to dress up chicken and fish. It's been used successfully for major banquets for several hundred people and for dinner just for me. The sauce also holds together well when made in big batches. It can be made in small quantities very quickly. Without the dill, it is a perfect roux, made the new low cholesterol way.

1 tablespoon I Can't Believe It's Not Butter™ margarine
3 tablespoons flour
1 cup skim milk
3 tablespoons powdered nonfat dry milk

3 large sprigs dill, chopped fine (optional)
For Garnish:
Whole dill sprigs

Melt margarine and whisk in flour. When blended, slowly pour in half the skim milk, stirring with a wooden spoon, or whisking if lumpy. Whisk in dry milk and add rest of milk, continuing to stir, until thickened. Add dill last and mix well.

Pour over chicken or fish and garnish with dill sprigs.

Makes 1 cup

Per Serving: less than 5 mg cholesterol; 1 gm saturated fat for each 4 ounces

Salsa

Great stuff! Serve on fish, or as a dip with corn chips. If you can't find chili peppers (which are nice for the color and texture), use Tabasco™.

1 large Spanish onion, chopped
2 garlic cloves
3 to 4 fresh chili peppers (add one at a time to your taste)

8 to 10 very ripe tomatoes
1 teaspoon fresh lime juice
1/2 teaspoon cumin

Chop (but don't puree) everything in a food processor. Serve cold.
Makes 6 to 8 cups.

Per Serving: 0 mg cholesterol; 0 gm saturated fat

Virgil Brown's Horseradish Sauce

This sauce is perfect with a small (3 ounce) filet or steak. It's a snap to make. Virgil did it with frozen lemonade but advises using the fresh lemon.

1 pint King Cholesterol Free™ Dressing

2 teaspoons bottled sharp horseradish, drained

2 tablespoons lemonade concentrate or

2 teaspoons sugar and 1 tablespoon fresh lemon juice

Mix well. These ingredients can be varied to taste of course. Serve cold. Makes just over 1 pint.

Per serving: 0 mg cholesterol; 3 gm saturated fat for each one ounce serving

Quick Orange Sauce

This is for duck, chicken, Cornish game hens, turkey, or pheasant. It may be cooled and served cold over cold sliced fowl, but the cornstarch breaks down if reheated. We've suggested one brand of sweet and sour sauce because it is particularly tart and tasty.

1 tablespoon cornstarch
1 cup fresh orange juice

4 tablespoons La Choy™ sweet and sour sauce
Orange slices for garnish

Blend cornstarch well into 2 to 3 tablespoons orange juice. Mix the rest of the orange juice and sweet and sour sauce. Heat in a non-stick frying pan, stirring constantly until sauce thickens. Serve immediately.

Makes about 1 cup

Per Serving: 0 mg cholesterol; 0 gm saturated fat

Raspberry (Melba) Sauce

Cooled sauce can be used over Tofutti™, non-dairy ice cream, a fresh peach half, angel food cake, and other fresh fruits. Keeps in refrigerator for two weeks.

3 cups fresh raspberries
1/2 cup sugar
2 teaspoons cornstarch
2 tablespoons water
1/2 teaspoon lemon

1/2 cup currant jelly
1/4 teaspoon cinnamon
For Garnish:
   10 to 15 perfect raspberries
   Mint leaves

Puree raspberries and sugar in a food processor. Make a paste with cornstarch and cool water. Mix everything together with remaining ingredients and cook over moderate heat, stirring continually for about 3 minutes, or until the sauce is thickened.

Makes about 2 1/2 to 3 cups

Per Serving: 0 mg cholesterol; 0 gm saturated fat

Lemon Yogurt Sauce

Ingredients can be shifted to suit your taste. Use less sugar, more or less zest, cinnamon, whatever you like. This is a topping for Tofutti™ non-dairy ice cream, fresh fruit or cake.

1 cup nonfat yogurt
1 teaspoon grated lemon rind
1/2 teaspoon grated lime rind
3 tablespoons fresh lemon juice

1/8 to 1/4 teaspoon ground
   cinnamon
1/2 cup sugar

Beat everything well in a mixer. Serve cold.
Makes 2 1/4 cups

Per Serving: 0 mg cholesterol; 1 gm saturated fat for each 4 ounces

Pasta and Rice

Pasta, noodles, spaghetti, macaroni: all are excellent for a low cholesterol, low calorie, low-fat, and high complex-carbohydrate diet. Pasta itself can have a high egg yolk content so we've included a recipe with no egg yolks. You can now buy pasta made with no yolks, or you can substitute imitation eggs for the egg yolks if you make it at home. If the label says egg noodles, obviously it has egg yolks. An unusual and wonderful way to use pasta is in ''wrapped pasta,'' which is a pasta pie crust wrapped around a filling. (Recipe page 154)

The sauce is another story, and usually where the cholesterol and saturated fat are found. If it has butter or cheese, it can raise the cholesterol and saturated fat content greatly. We've addressed that problem. These sauces gathered here, from a traditional hearty tomato sauce to a feather light, skim-milk ricotta topping, are all nearly free of fat and cholesterol. We've included several brand new sauces and have adapted old favorites. Pasta can be elegant or simple, country or uptown, Italian or Oriental. It has so many varieties and shapes, it can almost be a part of a daily diet.

Fettucini Carbonara

16 ounces egg-free fettucini or
  spaghetti (Recipe page 144)
12 ounces cooked lean ham,
  completely defatted, cubed, or
  julienned
1 1/2 cups Italian-style green
  beans cut into 1-inch pieces.
  (Italian green beans are larger,
very flat beans; or substitute
  regular green beans)
1/2 cup water
6 Egg Watchers™ eggs
3/4 cup skim milk
1/2 cup freshly grated Parmesan
  cheese
For Garnish:
1/4 cup grated Parmesan cheese

Cook fettucini al dente, and drain. Heat ham in microwave on high for
1 minute, or steam in 1 to 2 teaspoons water for 1 minute in a Silverstone™
non-stick skillet sprayed with PAM™ until hot. Heat beans in 1/2 cup boiling water over medium heat, stirring occasionally. Reduce heat, cover, and
simmer 3 minutes. Remove from heat and stir in imitation eggs which have
been blended with skim milk and Parmesan cheese. Heat gently just until
slightly thickened, about 2 minutes. Pour over pasta. Sprinkle with remaining cheese.

Serves 4 to 6

Per Serving: 55 mg cholesterol; 5 gm saturated fat

Risotto

For a one-dish meal or served with several other courses, nothing beats rice, mushroom and cognac topped with a small amount of freshly grated Parmesan cheese. This recipe does take time and effort but it's worth it for the unusual texture.

6 ounces dried wild mushrooms, such as porcini

3 tablespoons cognac

5 cups defatted meat stock, heated with 1 cup dry white wine

1 onion, chopped fine

2 cloves garlic, minced

1 tablespoon I Can't Believe It's Not Butter™

1 tablespoon olive oil

2 cups Arborio (Italian)™ rice (or any white rice)

1/2 cup finely chopped parsley

1/4 cup freshly grated Parmesan cheese

Soak the mushrooms in the cognac for 30 minutes; trim off stems, and chop mushrooms.

Heat the meat stock with the wine. Drop the mushrooms in heated stock, cover, and add the cognac marinade (optional). Reserve and set aside.

In a large non-stick pot, saute the onions and garlic in the margarine and oil for 10 minutes, until translucent. Add the rice and stir for several minutes to coat each grain.

Add ladleful of reserved stock and mushrooms, continuously stirring. When stock has been absorbed, add another ladleful. Continue adding liquid and stirring. This process will take 20 to 30 minutes until the rice is al dente, tender but chewy. The continual stirring takes time but will activate the starch in the rice so that a creamy sauce forms. Fold in the parsley and cheese. Serve hot.

Variation: Fold in briefly blanched, freshly shelled peas with the Parmesan cheese.

OR

Dissolve saffron threads in a few tablespoons of the meat stock and add along with the first ladleful of stock to the rice.

Serves 6 to 8

Per Serving: 10 mg cholesterol; 1 gm saturated fat

Pasta and Mussels

This fettucini entree is gorgeous. It needs to be served on a very large round or oval platter big enough to hold all the food for the number of people dining. The pasta is heaped in the center and the hot mussels are placed around the edge. Reserve some of the vegetables so they're not covered with sauce or bruised in the mixing and insert them all over top of the pasta. It has to be served immediately as the mussels cool rapidly. The recipe can be doubled easily, although more than double the sauce is needed.

1 pound egg-free flat pasta
1 very large onion, coarsely chopped
2 cloves garlic, minced
(The following vegetables are arbitrary, but reds and greens are needed; vary your choices with the season)
2 cups snow peas trimmed or 2 cups small broccoli florets or 10 thin asparagus spears cut into 2-inch pieces
1 cup French cut trimmed green beans, or trimmed Haricorts vertes (a French green bean that is tiny and slender) or 1 cup trimmed baby zucchini or rounds or slivers of zucchini,

or 1 cup trimmed tiny whole okra
1 red pepper, very thinly sliced, seeds reserved
1 cup fresh or canned tomatoes (leave skin on and cut in small bits)
1 cup sliced scallions
3 pounds mussels, scrubbed and rinsed well to remove beards and grit. (After rinsing for several minutes in very cold water and tapping each shell with a spoon, discard any that remain open)
For Garnish:
Chopped fresh parsley

Sauce:
1 1/2 cups skim milk ricotta cheese
1/4 cup skim milk
1/4 cup Better Than Cream Cheese™ imitation cream cheese

6 tablespoons freshly grated Parmesan cheese
1 teaspoon sherry
1 tablespoon dry white wine
Pinch of nutmeg
Lite Salt™ (optional)

Recipes: More Than 200 for a Healthy Heart

For Mussels:

Freshly ground black pepper
Few drops Tabasco™ sauce or 1 to
  2 shakes cayenne
1/2 cup white wine
1/2 cup water

1 teaspoon thyme or (2 fresh
  sprigs) or 1 teaspoon Old Bay
  Seasoning™

For Garnish:
Parsley

Boil pasta until al dente. Drain, keep hot. Simmer onions and garlic in a small amount of water in a large Silverstone™ non-stick skillet. Add all other vegetables except scallions. Add a few teaspoons more water, cover, and steam everything 20 to 30 seconds, or until the snow peas or broccoli turn bright green. Remove from heat. (You may wish to pre-cook the green beans or the baby zucchini, as they take slightly longer.) At the same time, steam mussels in the water and white wine plus the Old Bay Seasoning™ for 2 to 3 minutes, until very hot and shells open. Drain mussels but keep hot by placing them back in cooking vessel (which is hot) and cover. Now discard any that do *not* open.

Reserve 1/3 of vegetables for garnish.

Prepare sauce by blending ricotta and skim milk mixture, cheese, and sherry. Add sauce to pan with 2/3 vegetables, blending without breaking vegetables. Heat gently but don't boil.

On heated platter, heap pasta in the center and add sauce with vegetables, tossing once lightly. (You may wish to do this in separate bowl.) Quickly place wide ring of mussels in shells around pasta mound and place reserved vegetables on top of pasta, inserting colorful pieces all over. Garnish with chopped parsley. Serve immediately.

Serves 6

Per Serving: 75 mg cholesterol; 5 gm saturated fat

Fettucini

This cream-style sauce without the dairy fats is delicious and simple. Prosciutto ham can be eliminated. It is reasonably low in cholesterol but has some salt.

12 ounces egg-free narrow fettucini (or spinach fettucini)
1 tablespoon Weight Watchers™ margarine
1 1/2 cups skim milk
3 tablespoons nonfat dry milk
1/4 cup Better Than Cream Cheese™ imitation cream cheese
1 small onion, finely chopped

1/4 pound prosciutto ham, completely defatted and diced in tiny bits or julienned (optional)
1/2 cup grated Parmesan cheese
Lite Salt™ (optional)
Freshly ground black pepper
Dash of freshly grated nutmeg
For Garnish:
Paprika
Sprigs fresh basil

Cook fettucini, al dente, in boiling, unsalted water and drain. Meanwhile, prepare sauce by melting margarine in small saucepan. Add skim milk and whisk in dry milk. Add imitation cream cheese. Cook until hot, but do not boil. Keep warm. Simmer onion in a few tablespoons of water, over high heat in Silverstone™ pan, stirring often. Add prosciutto pieces and toss. Add the heated sauce, ham and onions and half of the grated cheese to the fettucine; toss until pasta is evenly coated with sauce. Season with optional Lite Salt™, pepper and nutmeg, and add most of the remaining cheese. Toss again and sprinkle the top with the rest of the cheese and paprika. Garnish each serving with a fresh basil leaf or two. Serve hot.

Serves 4

Per Serving: 45 mg cholesterol; 3 gm saturated fat

Quick Pasta Primavera

This is a simple but striking pasta and vegetable dish that is light and colorful. It can be prepared in less than 15 minutes. The recipe serves four, but it is easy to double or quadruple. Each vegetable is either grouped separately on the plate with little or no sauce, or tossed with the pasta.

2 large carrots, sliced diagonally 1/2 to 1/4 inch thick, 3 to 4 inches long or 1 yellow bell pepper sliced

1/2 cup fresh orange juice or water

1 very large white onion, cut in small wedges

20 to 30 snow peas (or 6 to 8 asparagus, 8 to 10 string beans, 8 to 20 broccoli florets, or zucchini), whole or trimmed, and cut in long strips (use whatever green vegetable is available)

Soba noodles for four (4 4x3x1/2-inch blocks are ample for four persons; soba noodles come in block style; they are curly and tend to stay together; they have no eggs and can be bought in Oriental grocery stores) or use traditional egg-free pasta for four

15 black olives

Paprika

8 tablespoons freshly grated Parmesan cheese (optional)

1 teaspoon of Parkay™ liquid margarine (optional)

Put carrots and onion wedges in boiling water or orange juice and cook until carrots are tender, about 4 to 5 minutes, or microwave for 3 minutes in a plastic bag with a smaller amount of liquid. When carrots have cooked about 3 minutes, add the soba noodles to another pot of boiling water and cook only 4 to 5 minutes until noodles are al dente (regular pasta takes 12 minutes). Drain. Add the snow peas to the vegetables the last minute, cooking covered for 2 minutes. Place drained snow peas together near the edge of a large plate. Place drained onion wedges next to them also near the edge of the plate, then, the drained carrots, and lastly the noodles on one side. In the center, put the 15 olives (or toss everything together), sprinkle noodles with optional margarine, paprika, and Parmesan cheese. Then, pepper everything. Serve hot immediately.

Serves 4

Per Serving: 10 mg cholesterol; 2 gm saturated fat

Hearty Spaghetti

Spaghetti is the easiest pasta recipe to convert to low cholesterol. Simmer the onions and garlic in water instead of fat. Incidentally, soy products that are meat substitutes may be added successfully. (Check the directions on the package.) The soy meal adds excellent texture if you wish to omit meat entirely. Use either fresh or canned tomatoes in this dish or a combination of both. Fresh tomatoes are more watery and need to be cooked longer or thickened with tomato paste or with 2 tablespoons cornstarch softened in 1 tablespoon cool water. Use all seeds and skin on the tomatoes, but be sure skin is in very small pieces.

1 very large onion, preferably Spanish, coarsely chopped

3 stalks celery with leaves, coarsely chopped

4 cloves garlic, minced

1/2 sweet red pepper, coarsely chopped; thumb off seeds to use in sauce, discard pulpy center

1/2 green pepper, coarsely chopped; thumb off seeds to use in sauce, discard pulpy center

8 large fresh mushrooms, cleaned and thickly sliced

8 fresh ripe tomatoes (6 if tomatoes are very large), finely chopped with skins left on (or 2 18-ounce cans whole tomatoes, drained and broken into small pieces)

1 6-ounce can tomato paste

2 6-ounce cans tomato sauce with peppers

Meat (optional, see below): beef, pork, pepperoni, or pork sausage

1 cup water

2 springs parsley, finely chopped

1/2 to 1 teaspoon brown sugar if tomatoes are canned, bitter or not homegrown

1/4 teaspoon fennel seed

1/4 cup red wine

3 tablespoons fresh sweet basil, chopped (or 2 teaspoons dried basil)

1 teaspoon oregano

Freshly ground black pepper

Lite Salt™ (optional)

16 ounces pasta (made without egg yolks)

Optional Meat: 1/2 pound lean beef or pork (or 1/4 pound of both). Use meat with no fat, such as lean London broil or lean pork tenderloin. Have any visible fat removed and grind remaining beef or pork coarse. The meat is browned separately without oil in a Silverstone™ non-stick pan in a small amount (2 tablespoons) of hot water. Rinse meat with more hot water in a colander to remove any remaining fat. Add the cooked meat to the sauce. If your palate yearns for Italian or spicy pork sausage, use 1/3 to 1/2 pound, remove from casing, and fry out all fat. Rinse well and drain. Be aware there will be about the same amount of cholesterol in the pork but slightly more saturated fat. Sliced Canadian bacon can be used for the meat. It is surprisingly low in cholesterol. Julienne or cut strips of 1/3 pound of Canadian bacon (or very lean ham). Heat in Silverstone™ non-stick skillet, rinse (or microwave to reheat it) before adding to sauce.

Another alternative is pepperoni. Pepperoni is much lower in cholesterol than most beef and pork and adds rich flavor. For pepperoni, coarsely chop 1/4 pound in food processor, then simmer in 1/4 cup water in Silverstone™ non-stick pan for 2 to 3 minutes. Discard liquid and pat dry before adding to sauce.

Begin cooking pasta in boiling water. If made fresh, cook for only 1 to 2 minutes. If dried, 10 to 15 minutes or until al dente. At the same time, simmer onions in small amount (2 to 3 tablespoons) water in a large Silverstone™ frying pan 3 to 4 minutes, stirring and watching carefully, adding more water if necessary. Add celery and garlic for additional minute or two. Add optional, rinsed meat and stir. Add peppers, cover, and cook for another 2 minutes. Then add all additional ingredients and spices.

If tomatoes are canned, different brands have different amounts of added water, so you may have to cook slightly longer if watery or you can whisk in 2 tablespoons cornstarch softened in 2 tablespoons water to thicken. Or you may have to add a tablespoon or two of water or tomato juice if sauce is too thick. Simmer sauce for 5 to 10 minutes (if sauce is cooked longer, say 30 minutes, cornstarch thickening isn't necessary). Tomato sauce cooked for just a short period of time has a fresher taste. Cooked for 30 minutes or more, the flavors blend and a richer taste is achieved.

Serves 4 to 6

Per Serving: 0 mg cholesterol; 0 gm saturated fat if no meat is used. (20-25 mg cholesterol per serving if Italian sausage or depending on meat—pepperoni has the least, Italian sausage the most; 2-5 gm saturated fat if meat is used)

Macaroni and Cheese Squares

Macaroni and cheese on a low-cholesterol diet? Sure! The cholesterol and saturated fat is only in the cheese and we've reduced that to a minimum: in fact, to only 25 milligrams of cholesterol and less than 2 grams of saturated fat. In devising this recipe, I made eight versions. In one I used chopped fresh mushrooms, in another chopped ripe olives. In a spicy version, chopped green chilies, corn in another. There wasn't one my family didn't like.

2 cups scalded skim milk
1/2 cup nonfat dry milk
1 cup soft bread crumbs (bread made without fat or eggs, like French bread)
2 1/2 ounce packages Butter Buds™ or several shakes Molly McButter™, whisked into 4 tablespoons warm water
2 1/2 cups cooked macaroni, very al dente, drained
2 tablespoons finely chopped onion

3/4 cup grated low cholesterol Dorman's™ Cheddar cheese or Weight Watchers™ Cheddar cheese
1 cup chopped Dorman's Lo-Chol™ cheese slices (or Dorman's Lo-Chol™ grated cheese block)
3 Egg Watchers™ eggs
For Garnish:
Paprika

Preheat oven to 375°F. In a bowl, whisk dry milk into scalded skim milk and pour over crumbs. Add remaining ingredients. Mix and place in a Silverstone™ non-stick casserole set in a pan of hot water. Sprinkle with paprika. Bake for 45 minutes. Cut into squares and serve.
Serves 4-6

Per Serving: 25 mg cholesterol; 1 gm saturated fat

Pasta with Tomatoes and Sauteed Onions

This is pasta with a flourish. You won't miss the lack of salt or fat and the lean Canadian bacon satisfies any meat hunger. It can be doubled easily. Fresh tomatoes can be watery so cornstarch thickening may be needed.

6 ounces egg-free pasta
3/4 cup coarsely chopped onion
3/4 cup chopped scallions
1 clove garlic, minced
8 to 10 large tomato wedges, peeled. If fresh, do not seed, or canned tomatoes
3 tablespoons fresh basil or 1/2 teaspoon dried basil
1/2 teaspoon vinegar
1/2 cup tomato juice

1/4 teaspoon oregano
1/8 teaspoon fennel seeds
1/2 teaspoon brown sugar (optional)
1/2 cup sliced fresh mushrooms
2 ounces Canadian bacon, fat trimmed and julienned
1 tablespoon cornstarch, mixed with 1 tablespoon tomato juice to soften

Cook pasta in boiling water until al dente. At the same time, in 1/4 inch water, simmer 1/4 cup chopped onion, 1/4 cup scallions and garlic on low heat; do not let garlic brown. Add Canadian bacon and mushrooms when onions begin to soften. Add all other ingredients. After 4 to 5 minutes, add the reserved onions and scallions. Cook 2 to 3 minutes, covered, checking to be sure there is enough liquid. Just before serving, thicken with cornstarch softened in tomato juice, stirring over higher heat. Pour sauce over drained pasta.

Serves 2

Per Serving: 85 mg cholesterol; 1 gm saturated fat

White Rice and Plantains

Fresh shucked and steamed (or microwaved in the husks) summer corn, or very sweet, starchy corn that has set for a day or two, can be served with the rice. Papaya also goes well with this tasty south-of-the-border fare.

2 cups short-grained rice
1 large Spanish onion, chopped fine
5 cups defatted chicken broth
2 cloves garlic, minced
1/2 pound ground beef (select very lean beef, usually a london broil, have all of the fat removed and have beef ground coarse by butcher or meat cutter)
2 onions, chopped fine

2 cloves garlic, minced
1 pound (fresh tomatoes or 35-ounce can plum tomatoes, drained and chopped)
1 cup raisins
1/2 cup sliced pimento-stuffed olives
1/4 cup chopped red peppers
3 ripe plantains
For Garnish:
Sliced green peppers
Picadillo sauce

Rinse the rice under cold water. Simmer onions in non-stick pan in small amount (2 to 4 teaspoons) chicken broth until soft. Add four cups of chicken broth to rice, onions, and garlic, and cook until rice is tender, 15 to 20 minutes.

In a large non-stick skillet, brown the ground meat with the onions and garlic, making sure nothing burns. (Garlic in particular picks up a bitter taste when too brown.) When onions are cooked, add tomatoes and simmer for 10 minutes. Add raisins when mixture is finished cooking; cover and let sit.

Peel the plantains, halve them lengthwise and slice into several small half-inch pieces. Simmer with small amount (1/2 cup) chicken broth. Cook until tender (about 20 minutes—add more broth as necessary), or microwave for 14 minutes. Serve all separately on the same dish, adding the picadillo in a separate dish centered on the bigger platter with the rice and plantains on each side.

Serves 4 to 6

Per Serving: 15 mg cholesterol; 3 gm saturated fat

Quick Pepper Pasta

It really is quick and the taste of chili peppers (not the real hot variety, unless you specifically want that) and roasted red peppers satisfies that "I've got to eat right now" feeling. The cholesterol and fat content include the salmon.

16 ounces egg-free tomato pasta

1 4-ounce can whole El Paso™ green chilies

1/4 cup chopped canned roasted red peppers, drained

1 cup chopped fresh or canned tomatoes (If canned, add 2 tablespoons tomato juice)

2 tablespoons freshly grated Parmesan cheese

16 pitted black olives, cut in fourths

1 cup small broccoli florets

4 slices Dorman's Lo-Chol™ cheese

1/2 teaspoon sweet basil

2 to 3 teaspoons water

For Garnish:
4 to 8 small 2 x 1/4 x 4-inch slices cooked or smoked salmon (optional)
Freshly ground black pepper

In a large pot, cook tomato pasta according to package directions until al dente. Drain and place in a large Silverstone™ pan that has a cover. Add remaining ingredients to the pan with the pasta, cover and cook over low heat until cheese is melted (about 2 to 3 minutes). Uncover and stir once or twice. Transfer to platter or plates. If using salmon, heat separately, in a non-stick skillet or microwave for 30 seconds or so, and lay the hot cut slices along side the pasta and sauce. Garnish with pepper. Serve immediately.

Serves 4

Per Serving: 20 mg cholesterol; 2 gm saturated fat

Rabbit   Paella

This is a spectacular version of paella. I'm sure the Basques never made it this way, but it is superb. Christine Schuyler devised this original master-piece. The cholesterol is higher than some low cholesterol meals but lower than one egg yolk. Because of that, we advise this meal no more than twice in a week.

4 squid, cleaned, body pouches cut crosswise into rings, head severed at the tentacles, and tentacles reserved

2 pounds mussels, cleaned and debearded, steamed in white wine, onions and herbs, cooking liquid strained and reserved. As with all mussels and clams, before cooking, discard any that won't close when tapped sharply. After cooking, discard any that don't open.

20 very large hard-shelled clams

20 small little neck clams

Both prepared as the mussels. Reserve 5 shells of each of the mussels, hard-shelled clams and little neck clams, for garnish

1 rabbit, cut into 8 pieces

3 onions, chopped

3 sweet red peppers, cored, deribbed, and chopped

3 green peppers, cored, deribbed, and chopped

2 cloves garlic, minced

2 tomatoes, peeled and chopped

1 tablespoon olive oil

1/2 teaspoon saffron, powdered, or threads that have been soaked in water to intensify their color

2 1/2 artichoke hearts, prepared from fresh artichokes, cooled and sliced or quartered

3 cups defatted chicken stock

1 pound fresh peas, shelled, blanched in water for 2 minutes and drained

1 cup white wine

Freshly ground black pepper

For Garnish:

1 bunch parsley, chopped

Preheat oven to 350°F. Measure the mussel, clam, and squid's cooking liquids. Add enough stock to be a bit less than double the amount of rice. (About 4 cups total.) Flour the rabbit and brown in a non-stick pan sprayed with PAM™ and set aside. Add the onions, peppers, garlic and after, a few minutes, the tomato. Cook gently to slightly reduce the liquid.

In a paella pan (a very large enamel, stainless steel or other kind of large cooking bowl capable of holding 6 to 8 quarts of food), add olive oil and saffron. Add rice and saute with the saffron until grains are opaque. Add cooking liquids and stock, tomato, artichoke hearts, and rabbit pieces; stir well. Bring to a boil, cover with foil and bake in preheated 350°F oven for 15 minutes or until rabbit is tender when pierced with a knife tip.

Remove pan from oven. Add squid, mussels, clams, and peas. Return pan to the oven and bake uncovered for another 5 minutes. Sprinkle with parsley and serve hot immediately directly from the paella pan, garnished with shells.

Serves 6 to 8

Per Serving: 215 mg cholesterol; 5 gm saturated fat

Wrapped Pasta

An unusual use of pasta that is rolled flat like a pie crust and filled with wonderful cheeses. No need to give up anything with this sensational stick-to-the-ribs dish.

1 1/2 cup pasta flour or white flour
1 Egg Watchers™ egg

1 1/2 tablespoon water
1 1/2 tablespoon olive oil

In a large bowl, mound flour and stir in imitation eggs, water, and oil. Mix well into a ball; knead for 10 minutes and let stand covered for about 30 minutes. Divide dough into fourths, rolling out each fourth on a lightly floured board with a flour-covered pin. Roll until very thin into a 10-inch circle, like a pie crust. Cover the four round pastas with thin dusting of flour. Let stand for 10 minutes. Boil each round separately for 1 to 2 minutes in 1 inch of water and 1 teaspoon oil in large frying pan, until al dente. Lift or slide out carefully. Drain. Spread pasta pie flat on waxed paper and fill.

Filling:

1/2 pound skim milk ricotta
1/2 cup skim milk cottage cheese
2 teaspoons grated Romano cheese

3 teaspoons grated skim milk mozzarella cheese

Puree or granulate all the cheeses or mix well in a food processor. Divide into four parts. Mound one-fourth of the cheese in the center of each pasta and wrap the pasta around it tucking in the ends. Don't worry about the shape. It can be rectangular, round, square—it doesn't matter. Set each aside.

Sauce:

1 large onion, chopped fine
2 cloves garlic, minced
1 6-ounce can tomato paste
1 19-ounce can plum tomatoes
1/2 teaspoon sugar
5 leaves fresh basil, chopped or
  1 1/2 tablespoons dried basil

2 teaspoons chopped fresh
  oregano or 1/2 teaspoons dried
  oregano
1/4 cup red wine

For Garnish:
  4 teaspoons grated skim milk
  mozzarella cheese
  Chopped parsley

Preheat oven to 400°F. For sauce, simmer onions and garlic in 1/4 inch water. Add everything else and simmer for one hour to thicken, or simmer for 10 minutes and thicken by stirring in 1 tablespoon cornstarch softened in 2 tablespoons cool tomato juice. Stir in over moderate heat and continue stirring for 1 to 2 minutes until thick.

In high sided, non-stick pasta dish pour sauce over each pasta bundle, sprinkle with 1 teaspoon mozzarella and bake for 20 minutes.

Garnish with chopped parsley.

Serves 4

Per Serving: 25 mg cholesterol; 2 gm saturated fat

Basque Paella

The Basque region of Spain originally introduced this combination of fresh seafood, rice, and spices. Most paella is heavy in fat but this recipe has little; it's better tasting without it. Lobster claws are higher in cholesterol than many other meats and some shellfish, so they can either be omitted or serve just one claw per person. (The cholesterol is calculated *with* the lobster and the sausage.) Both are wonderful for color and variety so I hate to leave them out. On an extremely low cholesterol diet, substitute a tiny cooked crab claw to keep the color and different textures in this wonderful meal.

1/4 pound Spanish sausage (optional)
2 Spanish onions, chopped fine
3 cloves garlic, minced
6 tablespoons water
4 scallions, chopped
6 steamed, cooled and cleaned artichoke hearts (home made only—not canned or pickled), left whole
1 green pepper, diced large, with seeds
1 red pepper, diced large, with seeds
2 tablespoons capers, drained
2 tablespoons green peppercorns, drained
1 teaspoon paprika
1/2 teaspoon oregano

1/2 teaspoon thyme
1/4 teaspoon cinnamon
1/2 teaspoon saffron
1/2 teaspoon Tabasco™
3 chicken breasts, defatted, deboned and skinned
3 chicken thighs, defatted and skinned, chopped in half lengthwise or through bone
6 lobster claws, left in shells (or 6 cocktail crab claws)
5 fresh tomatoes, chopped or canned tomatoes
6 clams in shell, well scrubbed
6 mussels in shell, well scrubbed
3 cups cooked rice, hot
1/2 cup fresh or frozen peas

Cook sausage thoroughly, drain fat; rinse and squeeze in paper towels and set aside. In separate non-stick pan, simmer onions and garlic in a small amount of water for a few minutes or until tender. Add spices, capers, peppercorns, peppers, cooked sausage and chicken and simmer for 15 to 20 minutes or until chicken is done. Then add tomatoes, clams, mussels, lobster, peas, and cooked artichoke. Cover and cook until lobster is just done (about 5 to 6 minutes). Remove all meat, clams, mussels, lobster. Mix everything else but artichoke bottoms (so not to break) in rice, stir well. Add rice and mixture to paella dish. Arrange meat pieces, seafood, artichoke bottoms, mussels and clams on top of rice. Serve immediately.

Serves 6 to 8

Per Serving: 100 mg cholesterol; 2 gm saturated fat

Pasta with Onion Sauce

If you're an onion freak like I am, you'll love this combination. I've used as many as six different kinds of onions adding seasonal Vidalias, or chives and shallots to the other onions. The only onion I don't like in this pasta is cooked red onion, but diced raw and sprinkled on top it's very good. This pasta can be very pale in color, almost having a fragile appearance, if you don't combine it with any of the "green" of chives, leeks, or scallions.

2 leeks, cut in half lengthwise to clean well, sliced 1/4 inch thick (include some of the green, unless you want a very pale pasta)

2 large Spanish onions, sliced and cut in chunks

4 scallions, chopped (again, if you wish the pasta pale, don't use the green part of the scallions either)

3/4 cup or 10 to 12 tiny pearl onions, peeled and left hole, if small

3 1/2-ounce packages Butter

Buds™ or several shakes Molly McButter™ (optional)

2 cups small size egg-free pasta such as bow ties, wheels, macaroni noodles, or cut linguine

2 slices Dorman's Lo-Chol™ cheese, chopped fine

1/4 cup King Cholesterol Free™ imitation sour cream

1/4 cup freshly Parmesan cheese, grated

For Garnish:
Paprika
Capers, rinsed and drained
Coarsely ground pepper

In a heavy non-stick skillet, simmer all of the onions in 1/4 inch water. When limp and clear, add optional imitation butter softened in warm water and whisked to remove lumps. Add to onions and cook for another three to four minutes. (A few drops more liquid may be necessary.) Add pasta cooked al dente, stirring well. If cauliflower is used, it will be necessary to pre-cook for three to four minutes separately. Add imitation sour cream and cheese and toss well. Heat until cheese melts. Sprinkle Parmesan cheese, but do not cook, as Parmesan can get gummy. Put in serving bowl or on individual plates and garnish with paprika, coarsely ground pepper, and capers.

Serves 4
Per Serving: 10 mg cholesterol; 8 gm saturated fat

Pasta Bows with Herbs and Sundried Tomatoes

A sensuous blend of flavors that will please you I hope as much as it pleases my family.

16 ounces small pasta bows
3 bunches chives, chopped
1 bunch fresh coriander, chopped
Fresh ground black pepper
5 bottled sundried tomatoes, patted dry and chopped
4 cloves garlic, minced
1/2 cup slivered almonds, toasted 15 minutes in a 300°F oven, then ground fine
Lite Salt™ (optional) to taste

Freshly ground black pepper to taste
2 tablespoons virgin olive oil
3/4 cup King Cholesterol Free™ imitation sour cream
For Garnish:
1/4 cup freshly grated Parmesan cheese
Blanched julienne orange rind from 1 orange—left in long strips
1/4 cup slivered black olives

Cook the pasta bows in unsalted boiling water until al dente. Be sure that thicker center of the bow is not still hard.

In a large serving bowl combine herbs, sundried tomatoes, garlic, almonds, olives, optional Lite Salt™, and pepper. Whisk in oil and imitation sour cream. Heat but don't boil. Pour sauce in a warmed bowl.

Drain pasta and pour over sauce. Gently toss to evenly distribute sauce. Sprinkle Parmesan cheese over the pasta and garnish with orange strips and olives. Grind additional pepper over dish.

Serve hot or cold.

Serves 4

Per Serving: 10 mg cholesterol; 2 gm saturated fat

Pasta Rolls

This recipe is wonderful! It is also less complicated than the usual "filled" pasta presentation like ravioli or other filled shapes.
esto:

1 cup chopped fresh basil
3 tablespoons pinenuts
2 cloves garlic, minced
1/8 teaspoon fresh ground black
   pepper

1 tablespoon virgin olive oil
2 tablespoons freshly grated
   Parmesan cheese

Combine all the above except for the oil and Parmesan cheese in a food processor and puree. Add the oil slowly and process to incorporate, then add the cheese. Once made, reserve in a bowl tightly sealed with a plate or sheet of plastic wrap lying directly on the sauce.

Makes about 1 cup.

16 ounces egg-free lasagna
   noodles
8 leeks, separated, washed and
   trimmed. Reserve the long
   tender inner green leaves.
16 ounces skim milk ricotta
   cheese
1/4 teaspoon Lite Salt™ (optional)
1/8 teaspoon ground nutmeg
1 to 2 serrano chilies, cored,
   deribbed, and minced
   (optional)

1/4 cup lowfat buttermilk
1/4 cup freshly grated Parmesan
   cheese
1/8 cup freshly grated Parmesan
   cheese
For Garnish:
   8 slices prosciutto, all of the fat
   removed
   Basil leaves

Bring a large pot of water to a boil and cook lasagna strips until al dente. Rinse each one under cold running water then gently press excess water out by running 2 fingers down each side of each noodle. Lay noodles flat.

In a pan with 1 inch of boiling water, simmer the leek greens until tender. Rinse under cold water, open each out, and lay flat on paper towels.

Finely chop the leek whites and simmer in an inch of water until tender. Sieve half of the ricotta and incorporate the leek whites, beating with a wooden spoon until the consistency is smooth. Season with optional Lite Salt™ and a pinch of nutmeg. Fold in chilies, if desired.

Combine remaining ricotta with buttermilk and 1/4 cup Parmesan cheese to make sauce.

Lay each lasagna strip flat and lay strips of leek green on top. Cover lightly with ricotta-leek mixture and then top with pesto sauce. Roll up each lasagna strip.

Preheat oven to 450°F. Lightly coat a shallow ovenproof casserole with the ricotta sauce and set each lasagna roll end up in the casserole. Set them so that they support each other, pushing them together. Make shallow incisions in each roll at the top so they will gently open to reveal the green and white interiors as they bake.

Brush remaining sauce on rolls and sprinkle with 1/8 cup Parmesan cheese. Bake on upper shelf of oven for about 15 minutes, until cheeses are golden and bubbly.

Trim prosciutto into 1-inch strips and lay about 8 strips overlapping one another. Roll up each series of 8 and open slightly to resemble a rose. Use these as garnish along with basil leaves.

Serves 4 to 6

Per Serving: 40 mg cholesterol; 7 gm saturated fat

Fried Rice

The only thing that's different in this adaption is that there are no egg yolks or lard. Fried rice varies greatly so use your imagination, but the base ingredients are nearly always the same. Strips of lean pork can be substituted for the chicken. The cholesterol stays the same but the saturated fat content is raised by 1 gram if you use pork. If you don't use meat the cholesterol and saturated fat are nearly 0.

3/4 cup rice
3 cups water (or defatted chicken stock)
1 clove garlic, minced
1/4 cup low-salt soy sauce
4 Egg Watchers™ eggs

5 scallions, chopped very fine (including green)
1 8-ounce can straw mushrooms, drained
1/3 cup baby peas

Optional meat and/or vegetables (select the ones you enjoy)

6 to 8 sliced steamed white pearl onions
1/2 cup sliced carrots
3/4 cup chopped Chinese cabbage
8 to 10 sliced Chinese eggplant pieces

3/4 cup cooked chicken or pork (slightly frozen and julienned into thin strips) skin and fat removed
6 to 8 snow peas
6 to 8 sliced water chestnuts
10 to 12 florets broccoli

Cook rice in water or stock until done and transfer to a large, covered non-stick pan. In a separate pan, lightly simmer garlic and optional onion (not scallions) in 2 to 3 teaspoons water. Add optional carrots, cabbage, eggplant, chicken, or pork. Heat the rice, add the soy sauce, and stir. In a separate non-stick pan heat imitation eggs slowly. When solid, remove and cut in strips and add the strips to the fried rice. Add straw mushrooms, scallions and baby peas and all other ingredients, such as snow peas, chestnuts, and other already cooked vegetables. Toss lightly. Serve hot.

Serves 6 to 8

Per Serving: 20 mg cholesterol; less than 1 gm saturated fat

Red Meat

In a low cholesterol diet we use meat as a condiment or side dish, serving small portions with large servings of complex carbohydrates (pasta, dried beans, corn, etc.) and vegetables with fish. At the very most, we try to eat meat or animal protein including fish and chicken only four or five times a week.

Our intention in this book isn't to limit your choice of foods but to expand it. Red meat can be a part of a low cholesterol diet. However, learning to reduce the portion to 3 to 3 1/2 ounces (about the size of a deck of cards), and cutting the number of meals with meat is helpful in reducing dietary cholesterol. For some on very low cholesterol diets, meat only once a week (or even once a month) may be the optimum amount. Red meat on a low cholesterol menu should have little fat and be prepared with no additional fat or fatty sauces. That doesn't mean it has to be bland! Lamb and other red meats like brae beef (a low fat breed), beefalo (a combination of buffalo and beef, bred to lower fat content), and the new lower fat pork, selected with little visible fat and cooked in a way that allows fat to escape, can add important variety to our eating. To defat meat, trim away all visible fat with a very sharp knife. This may mean removing the bone too. See page 61 on healthier ways to prepare hamburger.

You can even enjoy an occasional hamburger if you purchase a cut of beef with little fat, have it ground by the meat cutter. Fry without added grease in a DuPont Silverstone™ non-stick pan, or broil or grill it so that the fat runs off. In the meat loaf recipe, page 168, you'll even find the name and address of the source of a meat loaf draining pan, so you get less grease.

Lean pork is slightly lower in cholesterol than beef. If lean cuts are selected, both aren't that different from chicken, but you need to visually check the fat content of the cut.

We never recommend fatty meats on a low cholesterol diet, and we eliminate all the very high cholesterol organ meats such as brains, sweetbreads, liver, kidneys, and fatty red meat such as tongue, or prepared meat like bologna and most hot dogs. But some beef, lamb, and pork can be included and enjoyed. Of all the red meats, lean Canadian bacon is probably the lowest in saturated fat and cholesterol. There are differences of opinion on whether we need meat at all. Many vegetarians are apparently in good health with very low cholesterol levels, but strict vegetarianism isn't for everyone. Diets need careful planning.

Our recipes will help you prepare red meat with low fat, low cholesterol methods that capitalize on the taste of the meat.

Wendy Garner's Green Chili with Pork

Friends can introduce you to the most appetizing food combinations and this one has a new twist—it's green! To be sure all fat is removed, you can cool the soup and pick the fat off the top. Serve with corn bread, avocado salad vinaigrette, and red peppers.

1 large onion, chopped coarse
4 4-ounce cans of El Paso™ whole
  green chilies, coarsely chopped
1/2 Serreno chili, finely chopped
3 cloves garlic, minced
1/2 pound very lean pork, cubed
  (such as tenderloin)
2 potatoes, unpeeled and cubed

1 teaspoon chili powder
1 to 2 teaspoons cumin
1/4 teaspoon freshly ground
  black pepper
1 cup water
1/2 can white kidney beans,
  rinsed and drained (optional)

Simmer onions, fresh and canned chilies, garlic, pork, potatoes, chili powder, and cumin in 1/4 water until well cooked; about 20 minutes or microwave for 10 to 12 minutes, stirring often. Add more water if needed and stir well. Add white beans, cover and cook over low heat until beans are hot. Serve immediately.
Serves 4

Per Serving: 35 mg cholesterol; 2 gm saturated fat

Beef and Tangerines

This is Chinese in origin. The flavor of tangerine and beef is quite special.

1 pound London broil cut in
small slivers and fat removed

1/2 cup frozen tangerine juice (or
orange juice—dilute with half
water if concentrated)

1 onion, finely sliced

2 cloves garlic, minced

2 tablespoons low-salt soy sauce

1/4 teaspoon crushed dried hot
red pepper or cayenne

1/2 teaspoon ground ginger

1 tablespoon brown sugar

1 cup fresh tangerine wedges (or
1 cup canned mandarin
oranges, drained)

1 tablespoon cornstarch

1/2 teaspoon fresh lemon juice

For Garnish:

1/4 cup chopped scallions

Several strips tangerine (zest
peel)

Marinate meat overnight in tangerine juice, onion, garlic, soy, pepper, ginger and brown sugar. Cook meat and marinade in uncovered, Silverstone™ non-stick skillet. Add tangerines in the last 3 minutes of cooking. Stir but don't break them. Sauce can be thickened with cornstarch softened first in cool lemon juice and added, stirring well. Cook until thickened.

Garnish with scallions and tangerine zest just before serving.

Serves 4

Per Serving: 50 mg cholesterol; 2 gm saturated fat

Beef Stew

Beef stew needn't be omitted from any low cholesterol menu. A sure way to eliminate all the fat is to cool the meat and trim off any you couldn't remove in the preparation. Letting the flavors blend overnight also improves the flavor.

2 large onions, chopped
2 cloves garlic, minced
3/4 pound London broil cut into small 3/4-inch squares (cuts more easily if slightly frozen) and fat removed
3 celery stalks, sliced into 1-inch pieces, plus leaves, chopped
5 large carrots, trimmed and sliced
2 small potatoes, unpeeled, diced
1 green pepper, unpeeled, diced
1 tomato, unpeeled and chopped fine
2 small zucchini, trimmed and sliced

1 bay leaf
1/2 cup red wine
1 cup defatted beef stock or 1/2 cup defatted chicken stock and 1/2 cup beer
1 8-ounce can tomato sauce
1 teaspoon dried thyme
1/2 teaspoon brown sugar
Lite Salt™ to taste (optional)
Freshly ground black pepper to taste
2 tablespoons cornstarch
3 tablespoons cold water
For Garnish:
    Small sprigs parsley or chopped tomatoes

Simmer onions, garlic, and meat in a large Silverstone™ non-stick skillet. Add all vegetables, spices, and stock (except cornstarch) cover and simmer over low heat until everything is cooked (about 35-45 minutes or microwave for 15-20 minutes). Season with optional Lite Salt™ and pepper. Mix cornstarch in cold water; stir into stew. Cook over low heat until juices thicken, about 2 minutes. Remove bay leaf before serving. Serve hot, garnish with parsley or chopped tomatoes sprinkled on top.

Serves 4 to 6

Per Serving: 40 mg cholesterol; 2 gm saturated fat

Stuffed Flank Steak

Flank steak has little saturated fat or cholesterol. Here it's rolled and tied with string. After baking it's sliced. Prepared this way it is pungent and flavorful. Serve with parslied potatoes, or broiled tomatoes, peas or string beans, and perhaps a homemade applesauce. The dill pickles do add salt. You can buy the lighter salt variety, however.

1/2 cup Dijon style mustard
1 cup thinly sliced carrots
3/4 cup chopped (lite salt) dill pickles
1 medium red cabbage, cored and chopped fine
1/2 cup chopped red pepper
1 onion, finely chopped
1/4 cup chopped parsley

1 teaspoon dried thyme
1/2 teaspoon dried oregano
1 1/2 pounds flank steak, completely defatted and pounded nearly flat
1/2 cup red wine (optional)
Clean string to tie (you'll need about 16 feet of string)

Preheat oven to 350°F. Brown both sides of the flattened steak in a large Silverstone™ non-stick fry pan sprayed with PAM™ Remove and lay flat. Place several (as many as you can) 2-foot long strings side by side, 1 to 2 inches apart. Place browned steak on top of strings. Spread mustard on meat and place the carrot rounds on the mustard. Then, pile on all the other ingredients, roll up firmly but not tightly, and tie each of the strings and cut off string ends. Place roll in oven in deep pan, covered for more moist dish, uncovered for more dry, and bake for 45 minutes (or microwave for 20-30 minutes, turning when necessary). Carefully remove, cool slightly, then cut into slices with sharp, serrated knife. Remove strings. Serve immediately.

Serves 6 to 8

Per Serving: 50 mg cholesterol; 2 gm saturated fat

Meatloaf

This recipe is tasty as is but can be successfully made lower in cholesterol and saturated fat with packaged soy mixtures substituted for half of the ground meat. The cholesterol and saturated fat count is for the all-meat version. One brand of soy meat substitute is Natural Touch™ made by Worthington Foods. To me, meatloaf isn't meatloaf without ketchup. To many, meatloaf is anything but gourmet yet it's a great old standby and if we keep it in our repertoire, we need to prepare it in a healthy way. And we can. *There is even a meatloaf fat draining pan set available from H.C. Specialties at P.O. Box 2317, FDR Station, New York, NY 10150. It costs $14.* It automatically drains off all the grease into another pan, and it has a non-stick surface to boot.

1 pound London broil, all fat cut off and ground by meat cutter
2 tablespoons bread crumbs
1 tablespoon safflower oil
1 onion, chopped fine
1 stalk celery, chopped fine
1/2 teaspoon vinegar
Freshly ground black pepper

2 hard-cooked eggs, yolks discarded, whites slivered
2 to 6 tablespoons chili sauce or ketchup (optional)
Other optional spices such as a teaspoon of mustard can be added for a more spicy flavor.

Preheat oven to 375°F. Half fill 8 1/2'' x 4'' x 3'' non-stick meatloaf pan with mixture. Press a 1-inch line of the egg whites down the center and top with the remaining ingredients. Spoon chili sauce or ketchup on top. Bake for 1 hour. Drain out any fat in the pan. (The meatloaf pan mentioned above has holes in the bottom and is suspended or placed over a rack on a larger pan so all the grease or fat drains off.) Serve hot or cold.

Serves 4 to 6.

Per Serving: 50 mg cholesterol; 3 gm saturated fat

Tabbouleh and Lamb Salad

The taste of lamb, bulgur wheat, and mint is a Lebanese treat. It's lip-smacking good when the lamb is lean and precooked so it is well done—quite acceptable in a low cholesterol, low saturated fat diet. This is served cold. A meatless version is offered as a variation.

1/2 cup bulgur wheat
1/2 cup warm water
3 tablespoons lemon juice
3 tablespoons nonfat yogurt
1 tablespoon olive oil
1 clove garlic, minced
1 cup well cooked, defatted lamb breast, sliced or cubed
1 cucumber, peeled and coarsely chopped

1 ripe tomato, unpeeled, coarsely chopped
1/4 cup scallions, coarsely chopped
2 teaspoons finely chopped fresh mint or 1 teaspoon dried mint
Watercress for bed
For Garnish:
   3 tablespoons fresh parsley, finely chopped
   Freshly ground black pepper

Combine Bulgur and warm water for 15 to 30 minutes (depending on cut of the grain, some bulgur may take slightly longer). Follow the direction on the package, increasing or decreasing time as suggested. Cook if necessary (in defatted chicken stock) and cool. It should be al dente. Mix lemon juice, yogurt, olive oil and garlic and toss in cooked lamb and let stand 30 minutes. Add cucumber, tomatoes, scallions, mint, lamb, and pepper. Add bulgur wheat and stir. Place mixture on bed of watercress, sprinkle with parsley and freshly ground pepper to taste, and serve. May be kept overnight in refrigerator. Add tomatoes just before serving.

Variation: Prepare bulgur including all vegetables and spices above and cool. Add 1/2 teaspoon dried dill, 1/4 teaspoon dried oregano (double both if fresh) and chop. Add 1/2 teaspoon Lite SaltTM (optional). Sprinkle extra scallions and chopped parsley on top. Serve on lettuce.

Serves 2 to 4

Per Serving: 60 mg cholesterol; 6 gm saturated fat

Spicy Oriental Beef with Orange

This recipe tastes best when made with Szechuan peppercorns, which can be purchased at Chinese, Japanese, Filipino, Thai and other grocery stores that specialize in Oriental foods. Serve with rice, orange slices, steamed Chinese celery or snow peas.

12 ounces lean beef (such as London broil), all fat cut off, sliced thinly into 3-inch x 1/2-inch slivers (slices easier if slightly frozen)

Marinade in the following:

2 teaspoons dark soy sauce (or use the low salt variety)

2 teaspoons rice wine or sherry

1 teaspoon freshly grated ginger

1 clove garlic, minced

1 teaspoon cornstarch

Juice of 1 orange plus 1 tablespoon frozen orange concentrate

Few shakes red chilies (dried) or 2 small dried chili peppers or 8 to 10 drops China Bowl™ hot oil

1/2 teaspoon crushed Szechuan peppercorns, (or crushed black peppercorns)

1/2 cup julienned orange peel

2 teaspoons low-salt soy sauce

1 to 2 teaspoons brown sugar

2 scallions, chopped

For Garnish:

Chopped scallions

Place meat in marinade ingredients for 20 minutes. Spoon marinade over meat several times.

After meat is marinated, heat the juice of the orange and the orange concentrate. Add all of the other ingredients plus any additional water if needed, as mixture cooks down and caramelizes. If you do not want the recipe too spicy, remove the chili peppers at the proper stage of flavor for you. Fry the beef very quickly in a separate Silverstone™ non-stick fry pan, covered, for 2 minutes or so until browned on each side. Add to sauce. Add one of the chopped scallions and heat for 30 seconds, garnish with the other chopped scallion. Serve immediately.

Variation: Marinate beef (or pork) and fry quickly as directed. Add sliced mushroom cut scallions, sliced red peppers, sliced green peppers, snow peas and some julienned orange peel. Thicken sauce with cornstarch as directed and serve over Oriental noodles. The saturated fat can be higher if the noodles are the fried variety.

Serves 4

Per Serving: 55 mg cholesterol; 4 gm saturated fat

Tapa Beef

Tapa beef is a Filipino dish that is quick and easy. And quite a surprise with the sweet raw onions as a base.

4 large Spanish onions, cut in
   thin wedges
1/2 cup vinegar
1/3 cup sugar (or equivalent
   substitute)

1 pound lean beef, such as
   London broil, cut into slices
   2-inch x 1/2-inch thick (cuts
   more easily if slightly frozen)
4 tablespoons low-salt soy sauce

Preheat oven to 375°F. Marinate onions in vinegar and sugar for 20 minutes. Marinate meat in soy sauce for 10 minutes. Brown meat quickly in a Silverstone™ non-stick fry pan with a few teaspoons of the marinade and place meat (separated) in 375°F oven on cookie sheet for 15 minutes to dry it.

To serve, put a bed of the drained onions on a plate with a tablespoon of the sugar/vinegar mixture. Set hot beef on top and serve immediately.

Serves 6 to 8

Per Serving: 85 mg cholesterol; 3 gm saturated fat

Rhogan Josh Gosht

Rhogan Josh Gosht a la Linda Gasparella is a meat dish from Kashmir literally meaning red juice lamb. (The usual accompaniment of ghee, which is clarified butter, has been eliminated, but we kept the buttery flavor with Butter Buds™.) It is usually served with plain white rice.

1 pound cubed, completely
    defatted lamb
1/2 cup nonfat yogurt
3 1/2-ounce packages Butter
    Buds™
1/2 cup water

2 medium onions, chopped
2 teaspoons chopped fresh ginger
1 small tomato or 1/2 cup canned
    tomatoes
Lite Salt™ (optional)

Spice Mixture 1:
3 cardamon seeds
3 cloves
3 small pieces cassia (available in
    gourmet food departments or
    Indian food markets)

1/2 teaspoon dried turmeric
1/2 teaspoon chili powder
1 teaspoon coriander powder
1 teaspoon cumin powder

Spice Mixture 2:
1 teaspoon fenugreek leaves
    (available in gourmet food
    stores or Indian food markets)

1 teaspoon garam masala (also
    available in gourmet food
    stores or Indian food markets)
1 tablespoon finely chopped
    fresh coriander leaves (cilantro)

Mix the lamb and yogurt and Spice Mixture 1. Cover with about a half a cup of cold water in which Butter Buds™ have been whisked. Let stand for at least an hour, or overnight, in the refrigerator.

Place lamb mixture into a large Silverstone™ non-stick frying pan and cook on medium heat. Stir frequently. Chop onion, garlic, ginger, and tomato in a food processor or blender and add to above mixture. Simmer for about a half an hour or so, until the meat is quite tender. Add Spice Mixture 2 and fresh coriander. Mix well and cook for about another five minutes. If at any time the stew gets too dry, add a little water. Serve hot.

Serves 4 to 6

Per Serving: 55 mg cholesterol; 5 gm saturated fat

Canadian Bacon and Kraut

The Germans specialize in sauerkraut and my part-German heritage yearns for it occasionally. This low fat variation is perfectly splendid.

1/2 cup apple cider (be sure cider isn't hard) or apple juice
2 tablespoons brown sugar
1 teaspoon cornstarch
2 tablespoons raisins
4 tablespoons water
1/2 onion, chopped
1 apple, chopped

1/2 pound Canadian bacon, cooked and sliced
1 16-ounce can sauerkraut, drained and rinsed
1/2 cup scallions, sliced lengthwise and cut into 2-inch pieces

Blend cider, sugar, and cornstarch. Cook until thickened and add raisins. In another pan, simmer in small amount water, onion and apples until tender, 3 to 5 minutes. Heat Canadian bacon slices in separate non-stick pan for one minute. Heat sauerkraut in separate pan, or microwave for 3 minutes. Place a bed of drained sauerkraut on serving platter, put meat in center and pour sauce on top.

Garnish with scallions and serve hot.

Serves 2

Per Serving: 65 mg cholesterol; 3 gm saturated fat

Hearty Chili

There is almost no meal as hearty and satisfying as chili, especially on a cold night in front of a fireplace, served with a fruity sangria, corn bread, wrapped tortillas or soft tacos, and a crisp, green salad. Chili prepared in the Mexican or South American style makes light of the lack of tender meat. It was originally a country stew of beans, whatever meat that was available (pork, chicken, rarely beef), and probably not a lot of it, tomatoes and peppers, if they are in the garden, plus the regional chilies and whatever else the cook had on hand. We have adapted the dish to a more refined but just as earthy blend of flavors with a few surprises, such as carrots, that offer a sweeter taste and chewy texture.

2 large Spanish onions, coarsely chopped
3 cloves garlic, minced
Large carrot, shredded
1/2 pound standard cube steak, completely defatted, cut in 1/2 inch or 1/4 inch squares (it cuts easier if slightly frozen) (optional), or soy meat substitute prepared as per package directions and added to chili (or use no meat or meat substitutes)
1 to 2 green peppers, coarsely cut with seeds but not pith
3 to 5 ripe tomatoes, coarsely chopped with skin and seeds (or canned wedges)
1/4 cup vinegar

1 10- to 12-ounce can tomato paste or 1 6-ounce cans tomato sauce (the paste will add a stronger tomato taste)
1 cup water
3 15-ounce cans dark red kidney beans, rinsed and drained
1 to 2 teaspoons brown sugar
4 to 8 tablespoons chili powder
1 tablespoon cumin
1/2 teaspoon oregano
1 teaspoon sweet basil
Lite Salt™ (optional)
Freshly ground black pepper
Tabasco™ or dried chilies can be added, depending on how spicy you want it; it is quite spicy, however, without either Tabasco or dried chilies

For Garnish:
1/4 cup shredded low
cholesterol Cheddar cheese

1/2 cup shredded imitation
mozzarella cheese

Simmer onions, garlic, carrots, and meat in a small amount of water (1/4 cup). After 3 to 5 minutes, add peppers and when peppers are partially cooked, add tomatoes and all other ingredients. Cook for 15 minutes. This chili can be eaten immediately or cooked for up to an hour in a microwave oven or on top of the stove. Shorten time by one third if microwaving. Long cooking changes the flavor of the peppers, and lessens some of the nutritional value, but it is just as delicious. Ladle into bowls to serve. Place finely chopped scallions and a sprinkle of Cheddar and imitation mozzarella cheese on top of each individual bowl. Cheese can also be melted under broiler or in microwave. Serve steaming hot.

Variation: Soften corn taco shells by steaming for 2-3 minutes in colander over boiling water. Wrap lid in tea towel to keep from dripping. Fill softened corn tacos with thickened chili. (Cook down or add 2 teaspoons cornstarch in 3 teaspoons cool water, and stir in chili until thickened.)

Roll chili in tacos. Place in pyrex dish, side by side. Ladle extra chili on top and garnish with cheese. Bake covered for 1/2 hour at 375°F.

Serves 4 to 6

Per Serving: 45 mg cholesterol, if meat is used; 4 gm saturated fat

Incidently, as an option you can add a meat substitute made of soy protein. It is exceptionally good, gives a chewy consistency and it's hard to distinguish from chili made with beef, or pork, except there's no fat floating on top. These meat substitutes can be found in the packaged goods department of most grocery stores.

Paste in space on previous page

Lamb Noisettes with Rice Rings

Use just the center section of the lamb chops. Like most meat in a low cholesterol cookbook, only a small amount is used.

4 to 6 lamb loins
6 cloves garlic, crushed
2 teaspoons coarsely ground black, white, Szechuan and pink peppercorns
1/2 cup long grain rice
1/4 cup chopped flat leaf parsley
1/4 cup finely chopped chives

8 ounces fresh green beans, trimmed and cooked, than tossed with 1 teaspoon I Can't Believe It's Not Butter™ margarine
1 teaspoon fresh chopped oregano (or 1/2 teaspoon dried)

For Garnish:
Fresh unchopped chives

Buy tiny lamb loins that measure 3/4 inch thick and 1 inch wide. Trim off *all* fat, and bone so only bare lean meat circle is left.

Marinate in crushed garlic and grind the mixture of 4 different kinds of peppercorns (black, white, Szechuan, and pink) over both sides. Pat into flesh. Let marinate 6 hours, covered, in refrigerator.

While lamb is marinating, prepare long-grain rice. Rinse rice and drain. Simmer rice in 3/4 cup water. Let rice rest in its pan, lid covered with tea towel wrapped around lid to absorb excess moisture. Gently fold in chopped flat-leaf parsley and chives. Pack this rice mixture tightly into individual ring molds that have been sprayed with Pam™.

Place lamb in non-stick, heavy skillet, and brown, about 4 minutes per side. Lamb should be seared brown on both sides and medium rare inside. Allow 2 to 3 tiny loins per person. If loins are over 1 1/2 inch wide, 1 per person. Unmold rice rings onto individual plates.

To serve, surround the rice with the loin chops and intertwine with green beans, and fresh chopped oregano. Garnish with a spray of fresh chives at side.

Serves 2 to 3

Per Serving: 95 mg cholesterol; 3 gm saturated fat for 3 pieces of meat each

Poultry

For a healthy heart you don't want to simply substitute equal amounts of chicken for red meat. The cholesterol content is nearly the same though the saturated fat is lower in poultry. We advise limiting all animal flesh, including chicken and fish. But when you do have chicken or other fowl such as duck, quail, pheasant, turkey, dove or guinea hen, there are many new ways to cook and serve it, hot or cold. We've eliminated goose but not duck, because when duck is skinned and the fat removed, it is quite acceptable on a low cholesterol diet. It has cholesterol levels similar to chicken. I've found it's harder to remove all the fat on a goose. So it's not included.

If you're going to have poultry, small amounts of defatted fowl can be added to most soups and salads for flavor and variety. We've also adapted traditional roast chicken, baked stuffed turkey (see holiday eating, page 310), and fried chicken so they conform to new, low cholesterol guidelines while keeping their flavor rich and satisfying.

Roasted Chicken

Roasted chicken with no skin is marvelous. The shape is different from what we're used to seeing because the skin isn't there to keep the bird tightly contained. The smooth, skinless flesh is also whiter. Sprinkles of parsley or black pepper, red pepper flakes, or lemon slices on the bird will make it look gorgeous. The stuffing, unlike most, should be very tightly packed. The roast chicken can be served whole, surrounded with fruits and vegetables, and it can be either hot or cold. If you use a prepared bread stuffing, check the package to be sure it doesn't contain palm oil. Add to the commercial breading 1/3 cup chopped onions and 1/3 cup chopped celery and a pinch of sage. Add the water as directed on the package. Then, instead of using butter or margarine, substitute the same amount of hot water. You can also use your own favorite fruit, oyster, corn bread, or wild rice stuffing.

1 1 1/2 to 2 pounds whole chicken (if possible, a whole fryer; anything other than a roaster, as a roaster is usually too fatty)
6 prunes, moist, plump, and pitted
1/3 cup chopped onions
1/3 cup chopped celery
6 medium mushrooms, chopped
2/3 cup white French or Italian bread, broken into 1/2-inch pieces and dried
2/3 teaspoon sage
1/4 teaspoon basil

1/4 teaspoon oregano
Lite Salt™ (optional)
1/4 teaspoon freshly ground black pepper
1 small clove garlic, minced
1/4 to 1/2 cup warm water, or defatted stock for flavor; use more liquid if you need it; stuffing shouldn't be mushy, but moist

For Garnish:
Chopped parsley
Red pepper flakes
Coarse black pepper

Select the least fatty whole fryer you can (or roaster, if you can get the fat off). Pull the giblets and all fat out of the cavity, rinsing well. Carefully slip your hand between the skin and breast muscle and loosen skin. With a sharp knife or scissors, cut off every bit of skin and all the fat, leaving chicken flesh and membrane intact. (Pull off any remaining fat and scrape off or cut off fat that won't pull off.)

Preheat oven to 375°F. Mix all stuffing ingredients with warm stock or water and stuff bird cavity very tightly. Put stuffed bird on a trivet placed on a cookie sheet with raised edges and wrap whole bird and pan with foil covering but not touching bird, pinching tightly around pan, leaving little air. You can also use a covered clay pot or other roaster. Cook for 1 1/2 to 2 hours, draining fat after first half hour. Unwrap and slice. Bird will be pale but succulent. You can brown bird under broiler, but it tends to dry it out. Garnish with lots of parsley flakes, red (not hot) pepper flakes, and black pepper. Serve hot or cold.

Serves 4 to 6 depending on size of bird

Per Serving: 50 mg cholesterol; 1 gm saturated fat (80 mg cholesterol if oyster stuffing is used)

Kashi™ and Chicken

Do you ever wish you could throw a bunch of good food in a pot and about a half-hour later have the most fabulous, rich, aromatic, healthful meal that sticks to your ribs? This is it. It gives you the feeling like you remember food gave you when you were a kid. Kashi™ is a 7-grain product available in most stores. Be sure you get the kind that has to be cooked. (They have a puffed cereal version also called Kashi that doesn't require cooking that is wonderful for breakfast.) This is so easy and hearty.

1/4 cup wild rice
1 cup water
1 1 1/2 to 2 pounds frying chicken, skinned and defatted; wings and back reserved for another use or discarded; separate the thighs and legs from body and divide the breasts in 2
1 6-ounce package Kashi™ (a rice and grain mixture available in most stores)
1 10 3/4-ounce can condensed chicken and rice soup, defatted (refrigerate and skim off fat)

1 carrot, cut into 1/2-inch pieces
1 celery stalk, cut into 1/2-inch pieces
1 medium onion, cut into 1/2-inch pieces
1 elephant clove garlic or 2 to 3 regular cloves garlic, peeled and cut into 1/4-inch slices
1 cup water
Sprig parsley
For Garnish:
  Chopped parsley

Boil the wild rice in the cup of water for about five minutes, or five to ten more minutes if you want more tender rice. Add all the other ingredients and cook covered or uncovered over medium heat, keeping a low boil but not a simmer. Stir occasionally, cooking for 25 to 35 minutes, or until liquid is absorbed. If you cook uncovered, you'll have a slightly chewier texture. (You can also microwave it for 15 to 20 minutes.) Turn off the heat, cover, and let sit for 5 to 10 minutes. Serve 1 piece of chicken for each person with the Kashi nestled next to it. Sprinkle with chopped parsley. Serve hot.

Serves 4

Per Serving: 70 mg cholesterol; 2 gm saturated fat

Chicken Pot Pie

This chicken pot pie is elegant even without the usual oily bottom and side crust. You end up with more vegetables and chicken in a rich sauce. The 3- to 4-inch by 1/4-inch round of pastry crust is made separately on a cookie sheet and placed on top of the pie just before serving. Popovers made with imitation eggs and margarine are delicious with this meal.

1/2 cup finely chopped onions
1/2 cup sliced mushrooms
1/4 cup diced carrots
1 stalk celery, cut into 1/2 inch pieces
2 tablespoons finely diced scallions
1/3 cup baby fresh peas
2 tablespoons I Can't Believe It's Not Butter™ margarine
3 tablespoons flour

1 cup skim milk mixed with 1 teaspoon nonfat dry milk
1 tablespoon sweet sherry or Madeira wine
2 tablespoons dry white wine
2 cups cooked chicken, defatted, deboned, skinned, and cut into bite-sized pieces
1 tablespoon chopped parsley
Baked pie crust circles

Preheat oven to 375°F. Simmer onions, mushrooms, carrots, celery, and scallions in 1/4 cup water, until soft. Add peas during the last 2 minutes. Make a roux, recipe page 136, with melted margarine and flour adding the skim milk, slowly thickening it over low heat, whisking constantly. Add sherry, white wine and chicken. Pour into individual oven dishes covered with foil and bake for 20 minutes. Remove foil.

Top with scalloped or plain, 3- to 4-inch round wafers of pre-baked pie crust (sized to the pot pie oven dishes) which have been browned separately on a cookie sheet and placed on top just before serving. Serve each hot pie in their individual oven dishes on a very large plate with green vegetables such as green beans, asparagus or broccoli and some slices of seasonal fruit.

Serves 6

Per Serving: 40 mg cholesterol; 2 gm saturated fat

Grilled Ranch Chicken with Tofu and Watercress Sauce

Grilled chicken can be found on a low cholesterol diet, but serve just half a breast per person, add lots of vegetables, corn, baked potatoes, (or other vegetables that can be grilled outside) salad, pickles (low salt varieties), and breads so that the chicken doesn't become the major food. Sauce can be made ahead of time and kept warm on the grill in a saucepan.

4 chicken breasts, 4 to 5 ounces each, deboned, defatted, and skinned

Marinade:
1 garlic clove, minced
1/2 cup low-salt soy sauce

3 teaspoons Lea & Perrins™ Worcestershire sauce

Sauce:
1 cup tofu
1/2 cup minced onion

Small bunch of watercress

Marinate chicken in garlic, soy, and Worcestershire for 1/2 hour. Grill chicken on indoor or outdoor grill. Puree tofu, onion, and watercress in a food processor and cook for 10 minutes over high heat. To serve, pour sauce on warmed plate and place grilled chicken on sauce base.

Serves 4

Per Serving: 65 mg cholesterol; 2 gm saturated fat

Persian Sweet Chicken

Indian cooking brings us wonderful mixtures of sweet and meat. Sultana raisins are suggested here because regular raisins tend to lose flavor when they cook.

4 long carrots, trimmed

3 cups defatted chicken stock

1 small orange (try to find an orange that hasn't been waxed)

1/2 cup sultana raisins

1 small onion, chopped fine

1 teaspoon cane syrup

4 chicken breasts, 4 to 5 ounces each, deboned, defatted, and skinned

4 cups water

1/2 teaspoon Lite Salt™ (optional)

1/2 teaspoon white pepper

1 teaspoon ground poultry seasoning (or equal amounts sage, thyme, and sweet basil to make 1 teaspoon)

1 teaspoon saffron (quite expensive but always worth it)

2 1/2 cups long grain rice

Cut each carrot in half, then cut each half into four pieces lengthwise. Cook carrots until tender but firm in a small amount of stock. Drain and let cool. Remove peel from orange by cutting into long strips. Blanch peel for 1 minute in 1 cup of boiling water. Drain peel strips and let them cool. Cut peeled orange in half. Remove orange pulp from peeled halves and discard seeds. Soak raisins in the orange pulp and its juice for about five minutes. Simmer minced onion in Silverstone™ non-stick frying pan in small amount of water. Add carrots and saute over low heat. Add peel and 1 teaspoon of syrup. Add raisins and orange pulp and juice and cook for 10 to 15 minutes over a low flame. Check liquid often.

Preheat oven to 350°F. Parboil the skinless chicken breasts in 4 cups water with seasonings and saffron for 15 to 20 minutes, until slightly resistant to the touch. Drain chicken and let cool slightly. Cook rice al dente or slightly undercooked. Drain. Put half of the rice into a casserole pot. Then layer half the chicken and half the carrot, onion, raisin mixture on top of the rice. Do another layering of rice, chicken, and carrot mixture. Cover the casserole pot and bake for 20 to 30 minutes or microwave 12 to 18 minutes. Serve hot.

Serves 4

Per Serving: 70 mg cholesterol; 2 gm saturated fat

East Indian Dirty Rice and Chicken

This isn't difficult to make, although it has a lot of ingredients. Serve it with chutney, and a whole fresh garden-ripe tomato. Be sure and remove bay leaves before serving.

1/4 teaspoon ground sage
2 teaspoons paprika
1 teaspoon cayenne
1/8 teaspoon white pepper
3/4 teaspoon oregano
1/2 teaspoon dried basil or 1 teaspoon chopped fresh basil
1/2 teaspoon chili powder
3 teaspoons dried ground cumin
4 bay leaves
1 teaspoon Lea & Perrins™ Worcestershire sauce
1/2 teaspoon low-salt soy sauce
1 carrot, chopped
1 pimento, chopped
3 stalks celery, chopped
1 green fresh chili, chopped very fine (use seeds unless you want a less spicy dish)
1 cup dark raisins

2 teaspoons minced garlic
1/2 cup chopped onion
1/2 cup chopped green pepper, use seeds
1/4 cup chopped scallions
1 cup white rice
1/2 cup wild rice
4 chicken breasts, 4 to 5 ounces each, defatted, deboned, skinned and cut into bite-size pieces
3 cups defatted chicken stock or 3 cups water
1/2 cup raisins
1 cup scallions
1/2 cup green beans, cut into 1-1/2-inch pieces
For Garnish:
Chutney
Chopped or whole fresh tomato

Mix all the dry spices with the bay leaves, Worcestershire sauce, and soy sauce, and set aside. Lightly simmer all of the vegetables (except green beans and 1/2 cup scallions) in very small amount of water. When vegetables begin to soften, add spices, rices, chicken, stock, and stir. Bring to a boil in a Silverstone™ non-stick pot and lower heat, stirring occasionally. Cook for 45 minutes, turn off heat, cover and remove from burner. When rice is nearly tender, 10 to 15 minutes, add raisins, scallions, and green beans. Simmer over very low heat for 10 minutes and serve.

Serves 4

Per Serving: 65 mg cholesterol; 2 gm saturated fat

Chicken with Olive and Onion Sauce

There is salt in the olives and capers, so omit them if you're on a salt-free diet. Serve with couscous or rice.

2 large onions, sliced in thin circles

2 cloves garlic

4 chicken breasts, 4 to 5 ounces each, deboned, defatted, and skinned; or chicken pieces for four, browned in a Silverstone™ non-stick frying pan sprayed with PAM™

1 6-ounce jar salad olives, drained

3 cubed tomatoes or canned tomatoes

1/2 lemon, cut in wedges

1 teaspoon oregano

Freshly ground black pepper to taste

For Garnish:

2 teaspoons capers, rinsed lemon wedges

Simmer onions in a 1/2 inch of water in a Silverstone™ non-stick pot. Add garlic and cook for 30 seconds more, being careful not to burn garlic. When onions are soft, add all other ingredients (including chicken) and cook on top of stove for 15 to 20 minutes or until chicken is done (or microwave for 12 to 15 minutes). Serve hot on individual plates.

Garnish with capers and lemon wedges to squeeze on chicken.

Serves 4

Per Serving: 65 mg cholesterol; 2 gm saturated fat

Chicken Satay Jirachi from the Grand Hotel in Washington, D.C.

This recipe comes from an Oriental chef, Jirachi Jeslakom (leng), in Washington, D.C. The skewered chicken has a delicate peanuty flavor and is served in a light vinegar sauce. Wafer-thin cucumber slices should nearly cover the skewered chicken. It works well as an hors d'oeuvre, too.

4 slightly frozen chicken breasts, defatted, deboned, skinned, and julienned into 3-inch x

1/2-inch pieces (chicken can be julienned easier if slightly frozen)

Chicken Marinade:

1 teaspoon curry
1 tablespoon sugar
1 tablespoon Oriental 'fish sauce' (can be bought in any Oriental store)

2 cucumbers, peeled (if skin is waxed) and sliced wafer thin

Cucumbers Marinade:

1/2 cup water
1/2 cup white vinegar
1 1/2 tablespoons powdered sugar
1/3 teaspoon Lite Salt™ (optional)
Freshly ground black pepper

3 heads sliced shallots
1/2 red pepper julienned in tiny slices
2 cups unsalted roasted peanuts
1/2 cup chopped garlic

Peanut Sauce:

1 teaspoon pepper paste (can be bought in any Oriental store)
5 heads shallots, roasted
2 tablespoons lemon juice
2 tablespoons honey

1 teaspoon Lite Salt™ (optional)
Freshly ground black pepper
2 quarts defatted chicken stock
For Garnish:
Red pepper slivers

Marinate chicken and cucumbers in their separate marinade for at least 1 hour. Reserve cucumber marinade for chicken dipping.

Cook all spices and ground peanuts over low heat until thick (about 1/2 hour).

Grill (barbecue) marinated chicken on skewers; place on round platter around a center dish like spokes. Pour thickened peanut sauce over chicken. Place cucumbers over everything. Put cucumber marinade in center of dish (for dipping). Place a few more cucumbers in the dish in the center for decoration. Sprinkle red pepper slices over everything. (The peanut sauce is poured over chicken and not used as a dip as more peanut sauce will raise the saturated fat level.) Serve hot or cold.

Serves 4 to 6

Per Serving: 65 mg cholesterol; 3 gm saturated fat

Sauteed Chicken Breasts with Vinegar

Chicken and vinegar is a delightful mixture. Other fruit vinegars such as blueberry or raspberry may be used (with that same corresponding fruit as a garnish).

4 chicken breasts, 4 to 5 ounces each, deboned, defatted, and skinned; halved (to keep chicken uniformly thin, you can remove the thin fillet on each breast and reserve for another use)
1/2 cup fruit vinegar, such as blueberry or raspberry

1/4 cup defatted chicken stock or water
1/4 cup chopped shallots
1/2 teaspoon cornstarch mixed with 1 tablespoon water
Lite Salt™ (optional)
Freshly ground black pepper
For Garnish:
Fresh blueberries or raspberries

Saute the breasts in a Silverstone™ non-stick pan that has been sprayed with PAM™, until browned on one side. Turn and brown on the other side. After browning, cook chicken in same pan over medium heat. When the flesh feels springy to the touch, it is done (about 8 to 10 minutes) (or microwave for 6 to 8 minutes). Remove the breasts and keep them warm. Add vinegar, stock, and shallots to pan and reduce liquid over high heat (about 3 minutes). Stir in cornstarch and simmer, stirring constantly. This will slightly thicken the sauce and give it a glossy sheen. Season to taste.

Put the breasts on plates, strain over some sauce, and garnish with the berries. Serve hot.

Serves 4

Per Serving: 65 mg cholesterol; 2 gm saturated fat

Baked "Fried" Chicken

This chicken will be crunchy. If you use the thigh, leg, and other dark parts, it will add slightly to the cholesterol and saturated fat content. (You can, if you're really fastidious, remove the fat in the thigh parts. I do, but it isn't easy.)

1/2 cup corn meal
1/2 teaspoon flour
1/4 teaspoon oregano
1/4 teaspoon sweet basil
Freshly ground black pepper to taste

1 clove garlic, minced
1 egg white, whipped until frothy, not stiff
4 chicken breasts, 4 to 5 ounces each, deboned, defatted, and skinned

Preheat oven to 350°F. Mix dry ingredients. Add garlic to egg white. Pat chicken dry. Dip in egg white and then in dry mixture and place in baking dish on Silverstone™ non-stick sheet. Bake 40 minutes.

Serves 4

Per Serving: 65 mg cholesterol; 1 gm saturated fat

Fish

There are wonderful new ways of preparing the kind of fish we want in our diet. Even better, there is some evidence that fish two or three times a week can help reduce heart disease.

Shrimp, crab, lobster, and crayfish should be limited because, even though they are low in saturated fat, they are higher in cholesterol than meat, poultry, or fish (with shrimp and crab the highest of those four). Shrimp should be restricted to 3 or 4 ounces per month on a low cholesterol diet. Clams, mussels, scallops, and oysters are lower so we have included more of them. The cholesterol content of most shellfish isn't as high as previously thought.

Most of our fish today is so fresh and delicious we don't need sauces. But if you are a sauce lover, we have several that are scrumptious when ladled onto a plate with a nice grilled halibut, or tuna steak placed on top. We've adapted the traditional tartar sauce to make it heart-healthy, and we've invented brand new sauces, such as the Yogurt Watercress (which is also excellent on pasta). The Bright Day™ brand has a commercial tartar sauce that has no cholesterol. Plain old prepared mustard thinned with nonfat yogurt makes an excellent sauce for cold fish.

Salmon Mousse

Salmon mousse is refreshing and summery, nice on a buffet, as a luncheon main course, or as an appetizer or hors d'oeuvre.

1 envelope plain gelatin
3 tablespoons fresh lemon juice
1 shallot, chopped very fine
1 stalk celery, chopped very fine
1/2 cup boiling water
1/2 teaspoon paprika
Dash cayenne
2 teaspoons finely chopped dill
1/2 tablespoon fresh lemon zest
2 cups fresh skinned salmon, poached in white wine—10 minutes per inch of thickness;

alternatively use 1 pound highest quality smoked salmon
1/4 cup skim milk
1/4 cup Bright Day Dressing™ imitation mayonnaise, or homemade, page 98.
1 teaspoon Lite Salt™ (optional)
For Garnish:
2 to 3 sprigs fresh dill
Very small amount caviar (less than 1 teaspoon)
Lemon slices

For dip:
Imitation mayonnaise, or
Imitation sour cream, or
Nonfat yogurt flavored with lemon juice or chopped dill or

wasabi (Japanese horseradish found in Asian markets)

Soften gelatin in lemon juice. Add chopped shallot, celery, boiling water, mixing well. Add paprika, cayenne, dill, lemon zest and salmon.

Put in blender or food processor; add skim milk and imitation mayonnaise and optional salt and mix completely. Fill 4 to 6 cup mold with mixture and mold for several hours in the refrigerator. Unmold and serve on lettuce with dill, caviar, and lemon garnish. Shells can be used to serve any of the dips. Serve cold.

Serves 8 to 10 (or 1/2 cup each person)

Per Serving: 25 mg cholesterol; 1 gm saturated fat (including caviar)

Cold Glazed Salmon

Whole glazed fish is spectacular, but requires the fanciful presentation which is suggested. Any whole fish can be used that will fit comfortably on your platter.

1 large cleaned salmon (or tuna), leave head and tail attached; remove scales, fins, and entrails

1 to 2 cups wine
1 to 2 cups water

Poach salmon by simmering for 10 minutes per inch of thickness, in a mixture of half wine and half water. Cool, remove any fat on fish. Chill and serve coated with chaud-froid sauce and aspic and glazed.

Chaud-Froid Sauce for Salmon or other fish:

1 cup imitation mayonnaise page 98 or Bright Day Dressing™ imitation mayonnaise
1/2 cup canned tomato sauce or tomato ketchup
1/4 teaspoon vinegar
1 teaspoon lemon juice
3 to 4 drops Tabasco™

For Garnish:
Capers
Lemon slices
Olives
Parsley
Red pepper pieces
Whole ripe olives
Hard-cooked egg whites

Mix Chaud-Froid ingredients well and chill covered.

Aspic:

2 tablespoons gelatin

1/2 cup clear, defatted fish or chicken stock

Soften gelatin in stock, heat until clear, chill until syrupy.

Cover fish, head to tail, with chaud-froid sauce. Decorate fish with capers, lemon wafers, olive slices dipped in aspic. Glaze with aspic a layer at a time, refrigerating between layers. Serve on a large platter with ripe olives, parsley, and hard-cooked egg whites.

Serves 8 to 12 (1/2 cup each person)

Per 3 ounce Serving: 70 mg cholesterol; 2 gm saturated fat

Poached Sole with Pomegranates

For a more elaborate presentation of this zesty, tantalizing sole, the remaining Calvados mixture may be used to flavor some alternative sour cream, into which you fold additional caramelized apple slices that have been chopped. Served on the side.

1 3/4 cups fresh apple cider (unfiltered if possible)
6 shallots, peeled and minced
1 clove garlic, minced
2 pounds sole fillets
1/2 cup Calvados (apple brandy, also known as applejack)
10 mushrooms, sliced thin
4 apples, peeled, neatly cored, sliced thin lengthwise, then dropped into acidulated water to prevent darkening (3/4 cups water with 2 tablespoons fresh lemon juice)

For Garnish:
8 to 10 thin strips of orange rind
Pomegranate seeds from 1 pomegranate

Combine cider, shallots, garlic in a fish poacher or shallow pan that will also accommodate the fish. Slip fish gently into broth and slowly bring to a simmer. Cover, but check to be sure liquid doesn't boil, only simmer. The fish cooks 10 minutes per inch of thickness; it will be translucent and barely flake. Remove fish to a warm platter and cover.

Rapidly bring to a boil the cider poaching liquid. Reduce by one-half. Add in 1/4 cup of the Calvados and reduce again by one-half. (There should be about 1 1/2 cups liquid.) Poach the sliced mushrooms in this simmering liquid for 3 to 4 minutes. Remove the mushrooms and add to the warm fish, first pouring off any liquids that have accumulated on the fish platter back into the cooking broth. To the remaining liquid, add 1/4 cup Calvados. Reduce these poaching liquids until syrupy. Poach the drained apple slices in this concentrate until almost golden. Quickly arrange the sole on a warmed serving platter, lay the mushrooms and apple slices over and around the fish and decorate with the orange strips and pomegranate seeds. Spoon some poaching liquid around the fish.

Serves 6

Per Serving: 70 mg cholesterol; less than 1 gm saturated fat

Sole Fingers with Macadamia Nuts

These are thin slivers of sole crisped in a coating of bread crumbs and seasonings which includes finely chopped macadamia nuts. For an attractive garnish, wash and completely pat dry a few spinach leaves per serving or a bunch of parsley leaves. Immerse in hot oil (375°F) for a few seconds, until the leaves turn translucent. Drain off excess oil and arrange these leaves around the sauteed fish. You can also blanch the spinach leaves in boiling water, drain and arrange. The water-blanched leaves are lower in calories. Accompany with steamed long-grain rice that has been tossed with finely chopped fresh herbs.

4 fillets of sole
1 1/2 cups fresh bread crumbs
  made from French baquettes or
  French bread
2 tablespoons I Can't Believe It's
  Not Butter™ margarine
2 tablespoons olive oil
3/4 cup macadamia nuts,
  chopped or processed fine

4 egg whites, plus 2 Egg
  Watchers™ eggs, beaten until
  frothy
For Garnish:
  Lemon slices
  Chopped fresh parsley
  Freshly ground black pepper

Cut each fillet in half. Slice each half on the diagonal into strips about 1/2 inch wide. Combine breadcrumbs, margarine, oil, and nuts on a plate. Dip each piece of sole into the egg white/egg substitute mixture and then into the breadcrumb/nut combination. Pat the coating into the flesh and place each strip onto a wire rack. Let the strips rest 30 minutes so that the coating can set. This is very important.

Preheat broiler. Place the fish strips on a wire rack, set on a baking pan. Do not tightly pack the strips so that they touch—that would steam them more than brown them. Broil 1 minute each side. Drain on paper towel. Serve hot, garnished with lemon slices, chopped parsley, and freshly ground pepper.

Serves 4

Per Serving: 75 mg cholesterol; 5 gm saturated fat

Sole in Papillotte

You'll need some cooking parchment paper for this. It's fun to fix and jazzy to serve.

I Can't Believe It's Not Butter™ margarine for coating paper
4 fillets of sole, 6 ounces each
1 carrot, julienned and blanched 30 seconds in boiling water
1 celery root, julienned and blanched 30 seconds in boiling water
4 to 5 shallots, chopped fine
1/4 pound fresh Shitake mushrooms, thinly sliced and tossed with fresh lemon juice (If mushrooms are dried, reconstitute and slice)
1/3 cup dry vermouth
Lite Salt™ (optional)
Freshly ground black pepper
For Garnish:
1 sprig of thyme (lemon thyme, if available)

Sauce:
1 cup nonfat yogurt drained 45 minutes through a cheesecloth-lined strainer
1 sweet red pepper, charred in the broiler, peeled, cored and seeded over a plate to catch juices, then pureed with juices
Lite Salt™ (optional)
Freshly ground black pepper

Preheat oven to 350°F. Cut 4 pieces of parchment paper into 15-inch x 20-inch rectangles. Fold each piece in half, bending long end up. Cut out the largest half-heart shape you can from each. Unfold each "heart" and lightly coat the paper with I Can't Believe It's Not Butter™ margarine. For each sole fillet, cut it on the diagonal at the thick end.

Make a bed of one half of the carrot and one half of the celery root and a few teaspoons chopped shallots on one side of each heart-shaped piece of parchment. Sprinkle with Lite Salt™ (optional) and pepper and lay on top the trimmed end of each sole fillet. Cover each piece of fish with mushroom slices (reserve 1/4 of the mushrooms). Cover mushroom slices with the large slices of sole. Sprinkle with Lite Salt™ (optional) and pepper.

Complete each of the 4 stacks with the larger slices of sole. Top each with the remaining slices of carrot, celery root, shallot, and mushroom and the thyme sprigs and pepper. Moisten each package with the vermouth. Fold the facing half of parchment over the fish and vegetable stacks so that the edges of paper align. Crimp the edges together by making neat folds all around to seal. Place the packages on a baking sheet. Bake 10 minutes at 350°F. However, if the stack of fish and vegetables exceed 1 inch, bake following the standard rule of 10 minutes per inch of thickness of the fish.

Sauce:

Combine ingredients for the sauce. To serve, transfer lightly browned parchment packages to plates. Place any remaining sprigs of thyme to the side, and tear parchment packages open at the table to allow diners to enjoy the fragrant steam. Pass the sauce for the fish.

Serves 4

Per Serving: 80 mg cholesterol; 1 gm saturated fat

Halibut on Watercress Sauce

This is the best sauce ever—the kind you can't get enough of, and it will make your halibut an unbeatable success.

Sauce:

10 scallions, trimmed and chopped
2 green peppers, cored, seeded and chopped
2 cups defatted fish broth
2 bunches fresh watercress, stems removed
4 anchovy fillets, soaked and patted dry

2 cups plain nonfat yogurt, drained through a cheesecloth-lined strainer for 1/2 hour
Freshly ground white pepper
Lite Salt™ (optional)
4 halibut steaks, 1-inch thick

For Garnish:
Watercress sprigs
Lemon zest strips

Blanch scallions and green pepper in fish stock (or water) for 3 minutes. Remove with a slotted spoon to the bowl of a food processor. Blanch watercress for 30 seconds and remove to food processor bowl. Let broth cool for about 5 minutes, then add it to the processor along with the anchovies and process until smooth. Gently whisk the puree and yogurt together along with optional Lite Salt™ and pepper.

For the halibut, heat a Silverstone™ non-stick skillet over medium heat and add optional Lite Salt™ and pepper to each side of the fish. Plan cooking time based on 10 minutes per inch of thickness. Each side of fish should be nicely browned, yet barely done and retaining moisture in the middle.

Cut fish in half and remove the central bone. To serve, make a pool of sauce on serving plates and place halibut on top. Garnish with fresh watercress sprigs and lemon zest.

Serves 4

Per Serving: 85 mg cholesterol; 2 gm saturated fat

Pompano Poached in Chili-Lime Broth

A glamorous fish course or entree with a Latin flavor.

For poaching liquid:

3 onions, peeled and thinly sliced

4 leeks, trimmed, cleaned and julienned

2 cloves garlic, peeled and sliced

2 limes, sliced

5 hot chilies, cored, seeded, and julienned (preferably use assorted chilies for different flavors)

2 bay leaves

5 sprigs fresh thyme

2 stalks celery, chopped

2 carrots, chopped

10 peppercorns

2 teaspoons mustard seed

2 cups fish stock

2 cups white wine

1 pompano, large enough for 4 to 6 servings or about 1 1/2 to 3 pounds

1 stalk fresh coriander

1 cup imitation King Cholesterol Free™ sour cream (or nonfat yogurt)

For Garnish:

Fresh coriander springs

Thin lime slices

Variously colored sweet red, purple, green, and yellow peppers finely julienned into 2-inch long pieces

Simmer poaching liquid ingredients for 15 minutes (or microwave for 10 minutes). Strain broth into a fish poacher. Add cleaned and rinsed fish. Bring liquid to a boil, reduce heat to a very gentle simmer. Cover and cook 10 minutes per inch of thickness. Remove fish and reduce poaching liquid over high heat until syrupy. Strain. Quickly blanch fresh coriander.

Puree coriander and fish liquid. Whisk puree into imitation sour cream (or nonfat yogurt). Present fish on a bed of coriander sprigs and paper-thin lime slices, decoratively garnished with pepper slivers. Serve sauce on the side, or stream over fish before garnishing.

Serves 4 to 6

Per Serving: 60 mg cholesterol; 6 gm saturated fat

Baked Scrod with Mussels and Cheese

It's sad, but "scrod" is a terrible sounding name for such a succulent white fish. In this recipe you can have your cheese flavor and eat it too, even on a low cholesterol diet.

1 to 1 1/2 pounds scrod fillet
Olive oil to brush on fish
1 cup white wine
1 cup skim milk ricotta cheese
1 cup grated Dorman's Lo-Chol™ cheese (usually comes pre-sliced but can be purchased in block form)
2 teaspoons freshly grated Parmesan cheese
4 teaspoons honey
4 teaspoons fresh lemon juice

1 teaspoon dried tarragon or 2 teaspoon fresh, coarsely chopped
20 mussels, cleaned and debearded
1/4 cup white wine
1/2 cup water
For Garnish:
Lemon wedges
Sprigs of tarragon

Preheat broiler. Brush olive oil on fish. Heat fish in covered Silverstone™ non-stick frying pan in wine for about 10 minutes. While fish is cooking, in a separate pan, bring to a boil the 1/2 cup of wine and 1/2 cup water. Add the mussels and steam for 3 to 4 minutes. Drain and keep hot. Mix cheeses together and sprinkle on fish. Place under broiler until browned. Mix together honey, lemon, and tarragon and serve with the fish. Place five mussels on each plate or, if presented on a platter, arrange around fish. Garnish with lemon wedges and sprigs of tarragon. Serve immediately.

Serves 4

Per Serving: 90 mg cholesterol; 7 gm saturated fat

Whitefish and Salsa

Use any fish such as flounder, scrod, sole, even halibut, pompano (slightly higher in cholesterol), or bonita. It can be accompanied with a spicy (or mild) Tex-Mex salsa, which we have here, or South American aji sauce, on page 134. It is delicious whether hot or cold.

Salsa:

2 to 3 large very ripe tomatoes or 1 32-oz can drained and seeded whole tomatoes, chopped

3/4 cup scallions, chopped

1/2 medium onion, chopped

1 clove garlic, minced

1/4 teaspoon sugar (or sugar substitute to equal 1/4 teaspoon sugar)

1 teaspoon cider vinegar

1 tablespoon fresh lemon or lime juice

1 tablespoon El Paso™ canned green chilies, chopped

1 fresh or 2 dried chipotles (available at Spanish or Mexican markets), soaked in water to cover them, pureed, or a combination of fresh chilies

Freshly ground black pepper (reduce amount for milder flavor)

3/4 teaspoon parsley, chopped (reserve 1/2 teaspoon for garnish)

3/4 teaspoon cilantro, chopped (reserve 1/2 teaspoon for garnish)

4 fillets of fish

1 teaspoon cider vinegar

1 teaspoon fresh lemon or lime juice

For Garnish:

Chopped parsley

Chopped cilantro

Combine salsa ingredients and let stand for an hour or so. Heat fish with vinegar and lemon juice. Cook in a Silverstone™ non-stick pan over high heat until opaque, 10 minutes per inch of thickness. Be careful not to overcook. Serve the fish hot with salsa poured partly over the top of fish and on the plate as a spicy sauce or serve cold with salsa on the side. Garnish with chopped parsley and cilantro.

Serves 4

Per Serving: 75 mg cholesterol; less than 1 gm saturated fat
(Can be as low as 50 mg of cholesterol if halibut is used)

Tuna a la Chartreuse

A bright red-green entree. Leave off the anchovies if you don't want the salt. Chartreuse is an alcoholic beverage that adds a special taste.

1 1/2 to 1 3/4 pound tuna steak (the lighter the tuna flesh, the closer to the belly and therefore the more fat the flesh contains; purchase steaks that are a rich red color unless you prefer it lighter)
Juice of 2 lemons
1 quart boiling water
4 anchovies, soaked in water 15 minutes or until soft; halved and de-boned, then slivered
4 cloves garlic, slivered

2 heads Boston lettuce
3/4 cup peeled, chopped shallots
1 cup carrots, scraped and thinly sliced
1 cup chopped green pepper
10 leaves sorrel, deveined and shredded
4 tomatoes, cored, peeled, seeded and chopped
1/4 cup yellow Chartreuse liqueur
1/2 cup white wine
For Garnish:
1 orange, thinly sliced

Preheat oven to 325°F. To prepare tuna, place on a plate and pour lemon juice over it, moistening both sides. Let rest 15 minutes. Place in a wide colander or sieve and slowly pour boiling water over the tuna. This will remove excess oil from the fish. Pat the fish dry. Gently pry open narrow slits along the concentric circles of the flesh and ease in slivers of anchovy and garlic.

In a heavy casserole, large enough to just hold the tuna and its vegetables, place some lettuce leaves slightly overlapping on the bottom and up the sides. Scatter on half the vegetables. Place tuna on top of vegetables and sprinkle on the Chartreuse. Cover with remaining vegetables and encase all with the remaining lettuce leaves. Pour around the white wine. Cook covered in the oven for 10 minutes per inch of thickness of the entire package, about 30 minutes. Remove the fish and its vegetables. Reduce braising liquids over high heat until syrupy or about half in volume. Garnish with orange slices. Serve immediately

Serves 4

Per Serving: 75 mg cholesterol; less than 1 gm saturated fat

Broiled Fish with Lemon-Lime Topping

We've included lots of variations and they're all excellent. My favorites are (after this one) the vegetable, then the peppercorn variation. The chili and salsa are terrific whether the fish is presented cold or hot.

4 fish steaks, 1-inch thick each, such as sablefish, halibut, or grouper
Juice of 2 lemons
Juice of 2 limes
Zest of a lemon and lime, finely chopped

2 garlic cloves, minced
4 shallots, chopped fine
1 1/2 cups imitation mayonnaise (page 98) or Bright Day Dressing™ imitation mayonnaise

Marinate the fish for about 30 minutes in the combined juices and zests, garlic and shallots. Heat the broiler. Pat the fish dry, combine the marinade ingredients into the imitation mayonnaise. Place the fish steaks on the broiling rack and coat each evenly with the sauce. Place the broiler pan about 5 inches from the heat and broil for 8 to 10 minutes. Do not turn the fish. It is done when the topping is golden brown and bubbling. Serve immediately.

Serves 4

Variations to add to imitation mayonnaise:

Chili: Fold in 1/4 to 2 tablespoons chili paste, made from pureed chilies. The amount varies and depends upon the pepperiness of the chilies. Add the juice from 1/2 lime and proceed.

Green peppercorn: Use 1/2 to 1 teaspoon freshly drained and coarsely chopped green peppercorns and 2 teaspoons chopped cornichons (a type of pickle) with 1 to 2 tablespoons grainy mustard folded into the mayonnaise.

Salsa: Use fresh tomato salsa, 1/3 cup to 1 cup mayonnaise with additional chilies or peppers. Salsa is on page 136.

Vegetable: Use any vegetable puree, such as a mixture of carrots, onions, celery, and mushrooms folded into the mayonnaise.

Per Serving: 75 mg cholesterol; 6 gm saturated fat

Middle Eastern Stuffed Fish

Pomegranates add the unusual taste to this savory baked fish. If you can't find them or they're not in season, try fresh or canned cranberries or even lingonberries, which are bottled and found in most grocery store's fancy food department. Vegetables and rice make good accompaniment to the fish.

3/4 cup chopped scallions
4 cloves garlic, minced (reserve 1/4 teaspoon garlic)
Juice of 2 lemons (reserve 1/2 teaspoon lemon juice)
Lite Salt™ (optional)
Freshly ground black pepper
1 pound spinach, stemmed and washed, dried in a salad spinner and julienned
1/2 cup pinenuts, lightly toasted in a 300°F oven on a baking sheet for 10 minutes; shake every few minutes until evenly golden, then coarsely chop
1/2 cup currants (or raisins)
3 tablespoons pomegranate juice (or grenadine, cranberry, or lingonberry concentrate)

1 5-pound fish, striped bass or red snapper if you can find it, otherwise almost any fish that can be left whole; cleaned and scaled
5 carrots and 4 stalks celery, scraped and cut into 1/4-inch lengthwise pieces that will fit into your casserole
1/2 cup white wine
1 cup King Cholesterol Free™ imitation sour cream
For Garnish:
1/4 cup pomegranate seeds (or cranberries or lingonberries)
Lemon slices

Preheat oven to 350°F. Gently soften the scallions and garlic in a Silverstone™ non-stick pan in some of the lemon juice. Add optional Lite Salt™ and pepper. Remove from the heat, quickly toss in the julienned spinach, 1/4 cup of the pinenuts and all the currants (or raisins). Moisten with the pomegranate juice (or other juice). By hand, rub the rest of the lemon juice into the fish's cavity and fill with the spinach stuffing mixture. Gently skewer the fish edges and tie the opening with kitchen twine.

In a casserole dish make a bed of the flat carrots and celery strips, and pour in white wine. Lay the fish on the vegetable bed, cover and bake 10 minutes per inch of thickness measured at the thickest part. When done, the fish should barely flake at the backbone. Remove the fish from the vegetable bed and keep warm.

Puree the vegetables in the wine and cooking juices along with the remaining pinenuts and additional garlic, moistened with lemon juice. Fold in imitation sour cream to create a sauce consistency, and ladle over the fish. Sprinkle with pomegranate seeds and garnish with lemon slices. Serve immediately with vegetable and rice.

Variation: Combine 1/4 cup tahini to the sauce.

Serves 6

Per Serving: 85 mg cholesterol; 1 gm saturated fat

Wine-Poached Scallops

Scallops are delicious and this recipe can be served hot or cold as an appetizer or entree. If used as an entree, serve with fresh pineapple hunks, al dente green beans or asparagus, and cooked brown rice.

1 pound bay or sea scallops
1 cup white wine
1 teaspoon lemon juice
1 1/2-ounce package Butter
Buds™, or several shakes
Molly McButter™ (optional)

For Garnish:
Parsley

Poach scallops in a broth of white wine and lemon juice beaten into the imitation butter if you choose to use it. Cook scallops until just done (about 5 minutes) or microwave for 3 1/2 minutes, stirring after 1 and 1/2 minutes. Sprinkle with parsley. Serve hot with Tomato Sauce (page 130), Aji Sauce (page 134), or lemon wedges.

Serves 4

Per Serving: 45 mg cholesterol; less than 1 gm saturated fat

Oriental Steamed Fish

This is fun to fix and there's something beautiful, yet primitive, about serving a whole fish! Serve it hot with a green "Oriental" vegetable (snow peas, braised Chinese celery, even asparagus or haricorts verte, a French green bean which is tiny and slender) tangerines and rice.

Sauce:

1/3 cup dry sherry

1/2 cup Chinese fermented black beans (or canned, rinsed and drained black beans)

1/4 cup low-salt soy sauce

2 tablespoons sesame oil

1/4 cup fresh lemon juice

6 cloves garlic, minced

2 jalapeno peppers, seeded and finely chopped

8 scallions, trimmed, cut into 3-inch pieces and julienned

2-inch piece fresh ginger, peeled and chopped fine

4 small seabass or red snapper, gutted and cleaned but with head and tail left on (measuring about 10-12 inches in length or 1/2 to 1 pound each)

For Garnish:

Chopped parsley

1 scallion, julienned and cut into 5-inch shreds

Gently warm the sherry—do not boil—and add the beans. Turn off heat and allow beans to soften for at least 15 minutes. Add all other ingredients, except fish, and let flavors mingle while you prepare fish.

Rinse fish under running water and pat dry. Make 3 or 4 shallow slits on the sides of each fish. Place a bamboo steamer in a wok or large non-stick frying pan that contains several inches of boiling water. Put the fish on a plate that fits in the steamer, pouring the sauce over them. Be sure sauce is dribbled into slits in the fish. Put plate in steamer, cover and cook for 10 minutes per inch of thickness. Serve hot. Garnish with shredded/julienned scallion and chopped parsley.

(If you do not have a bamboo steamer and wok, choose a cooking pot that will hold your plate. Invert a small bowl in the casserole, bring several inches of water to a boil, add the plate of fish and steam as above.)

Variation: Stuff a 2 1/2 pound red snapper with equal amounts of julienned scallions (about 5) and fresh ginger. They both should be matchstick size.

Sprinkle a third of it on top. Marinate stuffed fish in 2 tablespoons low salt soy sauce and 5 tablespoons sherry for 10 minutes and steam.

Serves 4

Per Serving: 75 mg cholesterol; 1 gm saturated fat

Steamed Fish

Steaming fish is one of the best ways to preserve its natural flavors. This method can be as simple as placing a fish steak in an ordinary kitchen steamer set over boiling water or, to be a bit more elaborate, steaming a whole fish in an Oriental steamer with added seasonings.

The fish can be simply garnished with wedges of fresh citrus fruit and chopped fresh herbs, or with our mayonnaise (page 98) with additions of pounded anchovy or flecks of diced tomato or pepper. Serve with steaming, long grain white rice mixed with peeled, seeded, and cored cucumber slices. Toss with 1 tablespoon I Can't Believe It's Not Butter™.

4 fish steaks (salmon, tuna, swordfish or small halibut steak), about 1-inch thick, each 1/2 pound, or a whole red snapper (see variation)
1 teaspoon Old Bay Seasoning™
Lemon, lime, or orange wedges

Chopped fresh herbs (any mixture you like such as 1/2 teaspoon each of the following: parsley, thyme, oregano, sweet basil, etc.; mix and sprinkle on top)

Bring 2 inches of water to a boil in a pot that will accommodate the kitchen steamer that, when open, will in turn comfortably to hold the fish. Add Old Bay Seasoning™ and herbs to water. With steamer in place, lower fish onto steamer and cover. Steam 10 minutes per inch of thickness. Gently remove fish to a plate.

Serves 4

Per Serving: 100 mg cholesterol (for salmon, the highest in cholesterol of the four fish mentioned above, with halibut the lowest at 70 mg for this recipe); 1 gm saturated fat

Squid with Cellophane Noodles

Oriental cuisine has always featured squid. If you overlooked it in the past, you won't after this. It is an exciting entree.

4 squid

1/2 cup dry white wine

1/2 cup defatted fish stock, chicken stock or water

6 scallions, trimmed and cut on the diagonal

1 green pepper, chopped

2 cloves garlic, minced

1-inch fresh ginger, peeled and chopped fine

1 long hot fresh chili, seeded and chopped fine

10 cloud ear mushrooms, rinsed and soaked 30 minutes in 1/2 cup warm brandy and 1/2 cup water or enough to cover; remove stems and sliver after soaking

4 ounces cellophane noodles, soaked in hot water for 10 minutes

3 tablespoons low-salt soy sauce

For Garnish:

Chopped fresh coriander

Freshly ground black pepper

Rinse squid well under cold, running water. Hold the body pouch in one hand and the tentacles in the other. Gently pull the two apart; the viscera will come away with the tentacles. Free the tentacles just above the eyes and discard the viscera. Open the tentacles and squeeze out the bony, black-tipped beak from the center of the tentacles. Set tentacles aside after rinsing well. Locate the transparent quill or pen bone that runs the length of the body pouch and pull it out. Peel off the thin skin from the body and rinse well, removing any stray bits from the inside. Cut off the triangular fins. Cut the body into rings about 3/4 inch thick (or the body can be julienned into strips).

Bring the wine and stock to a boil, add all the squid pieces and simmer 1 1/2 to 2 minutes, stirring gently. Drain, reserving the cooking liquid. Add the scallions, green pepper, garlic, ginger, hot chili, and mushrooms to a large, non-stick skillet and moisten with some reserved cooking liquid and the mushroom soaking liquid and simmer until softened (about 3 minutes). Add noodles and remaining cooking liquid and cook for 1 minute. Add the squid and soy sauce and heat through. Arrange on a platter with tentacles forming a rosette in the center of the white noodles. Sprinkle on the snipped coriander and fresh pepper. Serve immediately.

Serves 4

Per Serving: 90 mg cholesterol; 1 gm saturated fat

Marinated Oysters

It's important not to overcook the oysters or they will be tough. Marinated oysters can be served as an hors d'oeuvre, a summer salad, served on a crinkly lettuce leaf with cold string beans and black olives, or as part of a buffet.

1 1/2 cups white wine
1/2 cup fresh lime juice
1 fresh jalapeno pepper, cored, seeded and minced
10 black peppercorns
1 1/2 teaspoons thyme
1 1/2 teaspoons coriander seeds
2 cloves garlic, minced

8 shallots, chopped
40 oysters, shucked with liquor reserved; scrub and reserve all shells
For Garnish:
1/2 cup chopped fresh parsley and coriander combined

Place all ingredients except oysters and their shells into an enameled sauce pan and gently simmer for 30 minutes or microwave for 15 to 20 minutes. Remove from heat and strain, discarding the solids. Pour this liquid over oysters in a pan and bring to a simmer. Remove from heat and pour contents of pan into a bowl. Marinate, covered and refrigerated, at least 3 hours but preferably overnight.

To serve, place a shell on each plate and heap on oysters. Spoon on marinade to moisten and sprinkle with the parsley-coriander mixture. Serve cold.

Serves 8

Per Serving: 35 mg cholesterol; less than 1 gm saturated fat

Grilled Tuna with Vegetable Julienne

Fish and vegetables go well together and are enormously satisfying. There can be lots of variations on this recipe such as pan broiling or oven cooking by tightly wrapping in foil in a 375°F oven for 15 to 20 minutes. The fish can be served with any number of baby vegetables like carrots, summer squash, cherry tomatoes—all steamed very lightly.

About 3/4-pound green beans, trimmed and julienned
4 stalks of fennel, cut into matchstick-size pieces
16 ounces fresh mushrooms trimmed and thinly sliced
Juice of 1 orange
4 tuna steaks, 1-inch thick (about 4 to 5 ounces each)
1 cup dry white wine
4 shallots, chopped fine
Dash of Pernod (an anise- or licorice-flavored liqueur)
1 cup nonfat yogurt

For Garnish:
4 oranges, peeled and cut into segments
10 anchovy fillets, boned, desalted, and patted dry to desalt (optional)
24 black olives, pitted and slivered
1/2 cup snipped Italian parsley leaves
Lite Salt™ (optional)
Freshly ground white pepper
(Olive oil for pan grilling)

If barbecuing, prepare barbecue, lighting coals. Begin cooking when the coals are uniformly covered with white ash. Grill fish for 10 minutes per inch thickness, turning once. For pan broiling, use a ridged pan sprayed with PAM™ or a Silverstone™ non-stick pan and brush olive oil on each side of fish. Cook over medium-high heat for 5 to 10 minutes covered.

Blanch the vegetables in boiling water for 1 to 2 minutes to set the color of the beans. Drain and keep warm. Meanwhile, simmer the wine and shallots over medium heat and reduce to half the volume. Add Pernod to taste, (1 to 2 teaspoons). Reduce a few more minutes, add the orange juice, and again reduce. Quickly strain. Slowly whisk in the yogurt so it doesn't separate. Add optional salt and pepper.

To serve, pool the sauce on a warm platter, add the tuna, and arrange the vegetables, orange segments, anchovies, and black olive slivers around fish. Sprinkle with parsley.

Serves 4

Per Serving: 85 mg cholesterol; 2 gm saturated fat

Seviche in Radicchio Cups

Very tangy! Very fresh! Very good!

1 1/2 pounds bay scallops
3/4 cup fresh lime (or lemon) juice
1/4 cup fresh tangerine (or orange) juice
3 fresh serrano chilies, seeded, deribbed, finely chopped
1/2 red onion, coarsely chopped
4 shallots, minced
2 tablespoons fresh ginger, peeled and chopped finely
2 heads radicchio lettuce

1 avocado, peeled, pitted, and sliced thinly lengthwise, sprinkled with lime juice to prevent darkening
2 pears, peeled, cored, and thinly sliced lengthwise, sprinkled with lime juice
4 tangerines, peeled, sectioned, and seeded
For Garnish:
Sprigs of fresh coriander
Very thin red onion slices

Marinate the scallops in combined juices of lemon and lime along with chilies, chopped onions, shallots, and ginger for about 3 hours, gently stirring occasionally. This marinade will "cook" the scallops. Carefully open 2 heads of radicchio, removing outer leaves. Mound the drained scallops and seasonings in the center and arrange slivered avocado, pears, and sectioned tangerines around the radicchio cups. Garnish with coriander and onion slices just before serving. Serve cold.

Serves 6

Per Serving: 45 mg cholesterol; 1 gm saturated fat

Grilled Swordfish in Pepper Sauce

Swordfish is a not-too-fishy-tasting, absolutely delicious saltwater fish, that some even compare it to steak! The only problem with swordfish is that it can be dry, so we've added a marvelous sauce.

2 1-pound swordfish steaks, 1-inch thick each

3 tablespoons lemon juice

2 cloves garlic, minced

5 scallions, chopped fine

2 tablespoons defatted fish or chicken stock or water

2 sweet red peppers, roasted in the broiler until lightly charred, peeled, seeded, juices reserved

2 cloves garlic, peeled

4 scallions, peeled

1/4 cup green peppercorns, rinsed, drained and chopped

1/2 cup King Cholesterol Free™ imitation sour cream at room temperature

For Garnish:

6 snowpeas, lightly blanched and cut crosswise to form diamonds

1 red pepper, lightly blanched, quartered and cut into diamond shapes

Red pepper bits and seeds

Brush the fish steaks with fresh lemon juice and let rest 10 minutes. Pat the fish dry. Pan broil or grill the steaks. If pan broiling, lightly spray a ridged saute pan or a Silverstone™ pan with PAM™. Or, alternatively, heat coals in a charcoal grill and allow to cook down until coals are uniformly covered with a white ash. The fish should cook 10 minutes per inch of thickness or until opaque.

Simmer garlic and scallions in a few tablespoons of defatted fish or chicken stock in a Silverstone™ non-stick pan until softened.

Meanwhile, combine the peppers, their juices, the garlic, scallions, peppercorns in a food processor. Quickly add in the imitation sour cream and mix. Spoon some sauce on each plate.

Remove fish from heat and carefully peel away skin and central bone. Cut each piece in half. Place each piece of fish on the sauce and decorate sauce with the diamond slivers of snowpeas and bits of red pepper and seeds.

Serves 4

Per Serving: 50 mg cholesterol; 5 gm saturated fat

Vegetables

For a healthier heart, vegetables and grains, not meat, should be the center of each meal. Most of us need to increase complex carbohydrates in our diets.

Vegetables that have complex carbohydrates include potatoes, lima beans, dried beans, corn, and peas. Dark green leafy vegetables like kale, collards and bok choy are rich in calcium. Although white asparagus (white because it hasn't emerged yet) may look pretty and be fashionable, the above-ground, darker green variety has more vitamins. As a rule of thumb, the more intense the color or the darker the color of a vegetable, the more vitamins it has. Vegetables are a mainstay in a low saturated fat, low cholesterol diet.

The microwave oven is a boon to vegetable preparation. Corn can be cooked in its husk; frozen vegetables can be heated right in the box; asparagus can be beautifully and quickly steamed in a plastic bag and with no extra liquid added; and potatoes and yams can be cooked quickly and easily. Baking potatoes can just be pricked and heated on high; other potatoes, washed but not peeled, can be placed into a plastic bag or covered dish and steamed using no additional water.

A simple microwaved baked russet potato can be topped with generous heaps of skim milk ricotta cheese or imitation sour cream. Ricotta cheese is only slightly higher in cholesterol than the imitation sour cream. Many sauces for vegetables, such as Hollandaise sauce, contain enormous amounts of cholesterol from the egg yolks. Butter skyrockets off the charts. Instead, add scallions or lightly steamed pieces of asparagus, green beans or broccoli to the potato and ricotta and you have a quick, hearty, and healthy meal.

We've included many new ideas to help you enjoy vegetables. Small amounts of margarine with spices and herbs can add to or enhance vegetables. The lowest fat margarine I've found is Weight Watchers™ in tubs and Parkay Diet Spread™. We have a delicious no-cholesterol, low saturated fat Hollandaise as well as other sauces that bring out the natural goodness of both raw and cooked vegetables.

Cauliflower Oriental Style

1 small cauliflower, cut in florets
(or left whole)
6 medium Shitake mushrooms,
sliced
8 water chestnuts, sliced in
halves or fourths
2 tablespoons cornstarch

2 tablespoons low-salt soy sauce
2 tablespoons sherry
2 tablespoons defatted chicken
stock or water
For Garnish:
1 tablespoon finely chopped
scallions

This recipe can also be made without cutting up the cauliflower. Just cut off the end so the cauliflower sits flat, steam it whole and pour the sauce on top. People can slice off their own servings, or it can be quartered and served.

Lightly simmer the whole or pieces of cauliflower in an inch of water in a covered pot. Add the mushrooms after a few minutes, adding more water if needed. Add water chestnuts. In a separate pan, make a paste with the cornstarch, soy, sherry, and stock, stirring as sauce thickens. When thick, remove from heat. Transfer drained cauliflower and vegetables to platter and pour sauce over vegetables. Sprinkle with scallions. Serve immediately.

Serves 3 to 4

Per Serving: 0 mg cholesterol; 0 gm saturated fat

Sweet-and-Sour Carrots and Onions

This is an Oriental way to serve vegetables. It is sweet and spicy. The sugar can be reduced, and all manner of other vegetables can be substituted, such as green beans, cut-up Oriental eggplant, cut Chinese celery, snow peas, and so on.

1 pound carrots, cut into sticks
6 to 8 scallions, cut into 4 to
    5-inch pieces and sliced
    lengthwise into strips
1/2 cup water
2 tablespoons cornstarch
1 teaspoon low-salt soy sauce

3 to 4 drops Chinese hot oil
1 teaspoon water
2 tablespoons brown sugar
1 pound parsnips, trimmed and
    sliced diagonally
2 tablespoons Dijon mustard

Simmer carrots in 1/2 cup water until tender; add scallions the last two minutes. Make a paste from cornstarch, soy sauce, cool water, brown sugar, and oil. With remaining pan water (or add more water in pan to make 1/2 cup), mix in cornstarch paste. Thicken over medium heat, stirring constantly and serve immediately.

Serves 4

Per Serving: 0 mg cholesterol; 0 gm saturated fat

Parsnips

Parsnips are often ignored. For that very reason parsnips are a real treat when prepared deliciously. I've taken this same recipe, omitted the chives, peppercorns, mustard and parsley; added a dash of nutmeg, pureed the parsnips and piped them onto a plate with baby carrots and other mini vegetables, for a sensational look and taste. Chives or parsley can be sprinkled on top of the decorative white mound. Cooked, sliced parsnips can also be served cold in salads.

1 teaspoon honey
3 tablespoons bourbon
1/2 teaspoon walnut oil
1/2 teaspoon green peppercorns,
  drained

2 teaspoons snipped chives
2 tablespoons chopped fresh
  parsley

Simmer parsnips in a half inch water in a covered pan for 6 to 7 minutes, or until tender, and drain. (Keep adding water as needed. Or microwave in a plastic bag for 4 minutes.) In a separate pan, cook all the other ingredients except half of the parsley and half of the chives for a few minutes. Pour over parsnips, sprinkle with reserved chives and parsley, and serve hot.

Serves 3 to 6

Per Serving: 0 mg cholesterol; less than 1 gm saturated fat

Four Onion Saute

If you're an onion lover, nearly any mix of onion flavors is glorious. I've served this with some low cholesterol white sauce, page 136, over pasta or rice, and it's wonderful. If these onions are to be the main dish, add a sprinkle of grated Parmesan cheese and chopped parsley. Some slices of canned red pimiento can adds a little color.

1/2 cup dry white wine (diluted with 1/2 cup water)
1/2 cup water
2 large sweet Vidalia onions, sliced (or 1 sweet Spanish onion, sliced)
3/4 cup tiny pearl onions
3 leeks, sliced
4 scallions, sliced in 3/4-inch diagonal pieces, including green

1/2 cup fresh or frozen early peas (smaller size than usual)
2 1/2-packages Butter Buds™, whisked in 1 tablespoon warm water to remove lumps
Lite Salt™ (optional)
Freshly ground black pepper
For Garnish:
Several slices of pimiento
1 teaspoon grated Parmesan cheese
Chopped parsley

Pour 1/4 cup white wine and 1/4 cup water in a large non-stick Dupont Silverstone™ skillet. Steam all of the onions (except the scallions) and cook until nearly soft (or cook covered in a microwave). Add the rest of the wine and water. Add the scallions, peas, and Butter Buds™. Serve immediately. If the rest of the meal is pale in color, several slices of pimiento (or red pepper) can be placed on top of the onions.

Serves 4

Per Serving: 0 mg cholesterol; 0 gm saturated fat

Zucchini with Tomatoes

Many of the herbs used in this recipe, such as lemon thyme, flat parsley, and chives, can be grown easily inside in a sunny window during the winter and moved outside to pots or a garden in the summer. Or ask the green grocer at your local market, who can probably get them for you.

4 medium zucchini
1 pint cherry tomatoes
1 teaspoon I Can't Believe It's
  Not Butter™ margarine
2 teaspoons fresh thyme, finely
  chopped
5 scallions, trimmed and chopped
1/2 teaspoon dried mustard
Freshly ground black pepper

Lite Salt™ (optional)
1/3 cup fresh lemon juice
1/2 cup King Cholesterol Free™
  imitation sour cream
For Garnish:
  Chopped fresh herbs, such as
  thyme, lemon thyme, flat
  parsley, chives, or any of the
  tiny flowers of the herbs

Slice the zucchini into 1/2-inch rounds. Halve the cherry tomatoes and gently squeeze to remove excess moisture. Reserve. Put the zucchini in a skillet and barely cover with boiling water. Reduce the heat and simmer for about 4 minutes, until the slices are still slightly crisp. Drain and return to the skillet with the margarine, spices, and lemon juice. Toss gently to mix. Add the cherry tomato halves; and cover for about 1 minute. Fold in the sour cream and toss to combine. Heat gently for about a minute more. Sprinkle the vegetables with chopped fresh herbs before serving. Serve hot.

Serves 4

Per Serving: 0 mg cholesterol; 2 gm saturated fat

Spicy Green Beans

Most Chinese restaurants serve spicy green beans but they are usually deep fried in oil. This recipe omits the oil and greasy taste yet keeps the wonderful flavors. The garlic and sugar can be doubled. The hot oil is made with red chilies and can be very pungent so use sparingly.

1 pound green beans, trimmed
1 clove garlic, minced
2 teaspoons low-salt soy sauce

4 to 8 drops China Bowl™ hot
  oil, available in Oriental
  groceries
1/2 teaspoon brown sugar
4 teaspoons water

Place green beans and garlic in 1/2 inch of water. Add the soy sauce and simmer over high heat. Be sure not to burn or scorch garlic or beans. When beans are bright green (about 2 to 3 minutes), add all other ingredients, stirring and reducing liquid. Drain and serve hot.

Serves 3 to 4

Per Serving: 0 mg cholesterol; less than 1 gm saturated fat

Beets, Yogurt, and Chives

These beets can be served hot or cold. Sour cream alternatives can be substituted for the yogurt.

4 to 5 large beets
1/2 teaspoon vinegar

For Garnish:
  Chopped fresh chives
  1/2 cup nonfat yogurt

Peel and cut beets into bite size chunks, steam in small amount of water and vinegar until tender (or cook covered in a microwave). Drain. Garnish with a dollop of yogurt on top and sprinkle with chives.

Serves 4 to 6

Per Serving: 0 mg cholesterol; 0 gm saturated fat

Easy Stuffed Mushroom and Onions

You can make these for hors d'oeuvre, an entree, or a side vegetable. This recipe is so quick and easy you'll rely on it again and again.

15 very large domestic
    mushrooms, 2 to 5 inches
    across (3 to 5 each serving
    depending on size)
1 medium onion, finely chopped
1/4 cup chopped scallions

1 teaspoon Madeira wine
    (optional)
Lite Salt™ (optional)
Freshly ground black pepper
For Garnish:
    Chopped parsley
    Freshly ground black pepper

Wash or wipe mushrooms just before preparing. Pull off end of stem, trim, and chop fine. In 1/4 inch water in a Silverstone™ pan, heat onions, scallions, Madeira, and chopped stems until onions are clear (about 4 minutes). Place empty mushroom caps upside down so they can be filled, in a non-stick frying pan. Fill each cap with onion and mushrooms. If the fillings spill over into the water, don't worry about it, you'll scoop it up later. Cover and steam (with a small amount of water—1 to 2 teaspoons) over low heat for 10 to 20 minutes. Keep checking moisture content. Since mushrooms exude water generously, you need less than you think. Scoop up any mixture in pan, pile on mushrooms, and serve hot. Sprinkle with parsley and pepper.

Serves 3 to 4

Per Serving: 0 mg cholesterol; 0 gm saturated fat

Chinese Eggplant and Garlic Sauce

Chinese vegetable dishes are traditionally cooked in oil. Instead, these vegetables are simmered in a small amount of water. The texture is firmer and there is a fresher taste. It is essential to this recipe that you use authentic Chinese eggplants, which are very long and thin and purple-white. Ask your grocer. Incidently, steaming can be achieved in several ways. Use a traditional steamer over boiling water or just take a non-stick pan, like Silverstone™, add 1/4 to 1/2 cup of water, cover and steam.

1 1/2 large Spanish onions, thinly sliced

4 cloves garlic, minced

6 Chinese eggplant, unpeeled and unseeded, thinly sliced into strips about 1/2 inch wide and 2-3 inches long

4 teaspoons low salt soy sauce

6 to 10 drops Chinese hot oil (China Brand™ is one brand)

2 tablespoons brown sugar

Freshly ground black pepper

2 tablespoons cornstarch softened in 2 tablespoons cold water

For Garnish:
5 scallions, chopped

Steam the onions and garlic, adding the eggplant after 2 to 3 minutes. Add soy sauce, hot oil, sugar, and pepper. More water may be necessary. Cook until tender over high heat, stirring often. Just before serving, drain off all the liquid and reserve. Add softened cornstarch mixture to reserved liquid, blend and pour over vegetables in pan, stirring until sauce thickens over medium heat (about 30 seconds). Dish should be quite spicy and sweet. Serve hot. Garnish by sprinkling vegetables generously with sliced scallions.

Variations: Add 1/2 cup snow peas, 1/4 cup sliced water chestnuts, or small bits diced chicken breast.

Serves 4

Per Serving: 0 mg cholesterol; less than 1 gm saturated fat
(Chicken will raise the cholesterol to about 45 mg and the saturated fat to 3 grams)

Spicy Hot Oriental Stir Phry

Almost anything fresh can go in this, but it isn't fried, so it doesn't have the usual calorie-laden fat (which is why we call it phry, so you won't think you're frying).

1/2 cup finely chopped onions
1 cup scallions, shredded, 1-inch
  long, 1/4-inch wide (reserve
  1/2 cup)
2 cloves garlic, minced
1/2 cup Shitake mushrooms
1 teaspoon brown sugar
1 teaspoon rice wine vinegar
2 teaspoons low-salt soy sauce
1/2 teaspoon freshly grated ginger
2 pounds chicken breast pieces,
  deboned, defatted, skinned,
  and diced

2 teaspoons sweet sherry
1 red pepper, sliced crosswise,
  pith discarded, seeds reserved
1/2 cup broccoli florets
1 cup snow peas
2 tablespoons cornstarch
1/2 cup fresh orange juice
1 pound tofu, drained and sliced
4 to 10 drops China Bowl™ hot
  oil
For Garnish:
  1/2 cup scallions, chopped

Place onions, scallions, garlic, and mushrooms in 1/2 inch water in a large Silverstone™ non-stick pan. Cook for 3 to 4 minutes. Add sugar, vinegar, soy sauce, and ginger. Stir to combine, than add chicken pieces and simmer for 10 to 12 minutes, stirring occasionally, until chicken is cooked (adding more water as needed). Add sherry and stir in. Add other vegetables, except snow peas, and cook covered until broccoli brightens. Add snow peas, cover and heat for 2 minutes more. Soften cornstarch in orange juice, add and heat to thicken sauce, stirring constantly. Add tofu, tossing gently so as not to break, until tofu is hot. Serve immediately. For garnish, sprinkle each serving with raw scallions.

Serve 4

Per Serving: 105 mg cholesterol; 2 gm saturated fat

Duxelles

These are best made in quantity and then frozen. Duxelles are a wonderful addition to sauces, fillings, or on their own. Excellent for filling artichokes or cabbage leaves moistened with tomato sauce, or for braised, baked or broiled vegetables, or rolled and baked chicken. You can even fill hardboiled egg halves. (Discard the yolks.) The duxelle eggs can be served hot or cold. Duxelles also make a great garnish for nearly any cooked vegetable, poultry, or fish.

16 ounces mushrooms, wiped clean, stems trimmed and finely chopped in a food processor

1/4 cup finely chopped shallots

1/4 cup finely chopped parsley

Lite Salt™ (optional)

Freshly ground black pepper

1/4 cup Madeira wine

Pinch of nutmeg

Put the mushrooms and shallots in a non-stick skillet and gently stir over medium-high heat until all moisture has evaporated. Season, add the Madeira and again cook down rapidly until the mixture is fairly dry. Use immediately, or cool and refrigerate, or freeze.

Makes 1 1/2 cups

Per Serving: 0 mg cholesterol; 0 gm saturated fat

Vegetable Tureen

This takes a little time, but it's worth it as the presentation of grape leaf-wrapped vegetables is unique.

3/4 pound Great Northern white beans, soaked overnight in water to cover by 2 inches (or boiled 10 minutes)

12 cups defatted beef stock, or water to cover the beans by 1 to 2 inches

1 bouquet garni (sprig parsley, pinch thyme, a bay leaf tied in a cheesecloth pouch)

2 carrots, scraped and trimmed

2 stalks celery, cleaned and trimmed

1 head of garlic or 8 to 12 cloves

1 cup carrot cubes, blanched in boiling water for 5 minutes, then drained under cold running water

1 1/2 cups (use 2 or 3 kinds) elbow macaroni (tomato, spinach, plain, etc.), cooked in boiling water until al dente and drained after being held under cold running water

3 Egg Watchers™ eggs, whisked

1 1/2-ounce package Butter Buds™, mixed with 2 teaspoons beef stock, or water, according to instructions or a few shakes Molly McButter™

2 teaspoons green peppercorns, rinsed, patted dry and chopped

1 tablespoon dried oregano (double if fresh)

1 tablespoon dried thyme (double if fresh)

1 teaspoon cayenne pepper

Lite Salt™ (optional)

Freshly ground black pepper

Grape leaves, rinsed and patted dry - enough to line a 6-cup loaf pan

Herbed Bright Day™ imitation mayonnaise or light tomato sauce (page 130) (Herb the mayonnaise with 1/2 teaspoon dried thyme, 1/4 teaspoon dried oregano flakes or other spices you like)

Drain the beans, place them in a large pot, and cover with the stock. Bring to a boil and skim the liquid. Add the bouquet garni, carrots, celery, and garlic and simmer covered for about an hour. The beans are done when tender. Drain them, but reserve the cooking liquid and the head of garlic. Squeeze the garlic out of its skin, mash and add to the beans. Puree the beans and garlic with some of the cooking liquid.

Preheat oven to 350°F. Combine the beans, carrots, pasta, imitation eggs, and Butter Bud™ mixture, pepper, and seasonings. Use a Silverstone™ non-stick pan; line it with the rinsed grape leaves, shiny side out. Carefully spoon in the bean mixture, pat down or rap the pan sharply on the counter to eliminate air pockets. Fold the grape leaves over the top, adding extra leaves if necessary to encase the mixture. Bake for about 45 minutes, or until a skewer inserted in the tureen comes out clean. Take the tureen out of the oven, let cool slightly, and wait it for 2 to 3 hours. Invert it onto a serving platter, slice and serve warm or cold with herbed mayonnaise or light tomato sauce.

Serves 6 to 8

Per Serving: 0 mg cholesterol; 0 gm saturated fat (2 teaspoons imitation mayonnaise will add 1 gm saturated fat)

Capponata Sicilia

The recipe traditionally called for olive oil. If you miss that flavor, add a half a teaspoon after vegetables are simmered. They won't be oily but they'll have the flavor and aroma.

1 large eggplant, cubed, leaving skin on	2 cloves garlic, minced
1 large onion, chopped	1 teaspoon sugar
3 stalks celery, chopped	2 bay leaves
4 black olives, pitted and chopped	1/2 teaspoon oregano
	2 tomatoes, chopped fine with seeds and skins
4 green olives, pitted and chopped (optional)	2 tablespoons capers, drained

Simmer all ingredients except tomatoes and capers quickly over fairly high heat in 1/4 inch water until the eggplant and onions are nearly cooked through, about 5 to 8 minutes. Add more water if necessary. Add the tomatoes and capers, cooking the moisture out of the tomatoes and serving when the liquid is reduced. Remove bay leaves before serving. Serve hot or cold.

Serves 4 to 6

Per Serving: 0 mg cholesterol; less than 1 gm saturated fat

Vegetable Couscous

Couscous is an interesting grain. You have to like or get used to the unusual texture, which is much like chopped rice. It is quite wonderful, and can be served hot as an entree or a side dish or cold as a salad. A spicy optional accompaniment is a red pepper paste. Some peppers are imported from North Africa and some from the Orient. Either will work. Thin the paste with a few tablespoons cooking liquid until a sauce-like consistency is reached. If desired, add a clove of minced garlic and a pinch of cumin to round out the flavors. Serve this at the side of the couscous in small bowls.

2 cups defatted chicken stock
1/2 teaspoon turmeric
1 teaspoon ground ginger
1/2 teaspoon cumin
1 teaspoon ground cinnamon
Lite Salt™ (optional)
1 jalapeno pepper, seeded and
    minced
1 cup diced pumpkin, peeled and
    seeded (if desired reserve the
    seeds; wash them, pat dry and
    toast on a baking sheet at
    325°F until golden—about 15
    minutes)
2 turnips, peeled and cubed
1/2 cup dried chick peas, soaked
    in water to cover overnight,
    then drained and cooked until
    tender in homemade chicken
    stock; or 1 16-ounce can

cooked chick peas, drained
    and rinsed well; in either case,
    remove the skins
20 pearl onions, peeled
12 baby zucchini, trimmed
12 baby carrots, trimmed
12 baby patty pan squash
3/4 cup julienned dates that have
    been plumped in warm stock
    for 30 minutes
1 cup peas, cooked
3 cups defatted chicken stock
1 tablespoon I Can't Believe It's
    Not Butter™ margarine
2 cups couscous
For Garnish:
    2 teaspoons grated lemon peel
    2 teaspoons grated orange peel
    1/2 cup chopped parsley

In 2 cups chicken stock, with the spices, 1 teaspoon Lite Salt™ (optional), and jalapeno, simmer the pumpkin, turnip, the chick peas, and onions for 5 minutes. If canned chick peas are used, simmer them first in the stock for 20 minutes, then continue with the pumpkin. Add the zucchini, carrots, squash, and dates and simmer another 5 minutes. Add the peas and simmer 2 minutes.

While the vegetables are simmering, bring 3 cups of chicken stock to a boil with the margarine. Pour into the couscous in a steady stream and return to a boil, stirring constantly. Simmer the grains for 2 to 3 minutes, turn off the heat, wrap the lid of the pot in a tea towel, and let the couscous stand covered for another 2 to 3 minutes. It should be al dente, but cooking time will vary depending on the age of the couscous. Turn the couscous onto a serving platter and fluff with 2 forks. Spoon the vegetables in the center and moisten well with the vegetable cooking liquid. Scatter the combined garnish ingredients over all. Serve immediately.

Serves 6 to 8

Per Serving: 0 mg cholesterol; 0 gm saturated fat

Autumnal Fresh Vegetable Stew

This has lots of vegetables and lots of flavor. Serve steaming hot with big chunks of French, brown, or black bread. It can be kept, refrigerated, for 7 days.

12 small pearl onions, peeled
3 white potatoes, unpeeled, sliced 1/4-inch thick
1 eggplant, stemmed and cubed
1/2 head cauliflower, broken into florets
2 carrots, trimmed and sliced into 2-inch pieces
20 green beans, trimmed
1/2 green pepper, cored, seeded and cut into strips
1/2 red pepper, cored, seeded and cut into strips
2 medium yellow squash, sliced
2 medium zucchini, sliced
5 stalks celery, sliced
1 long hot pepper, minced
6 cloves garlic, minced
2 cups stock or water

1/2 cup dry red wine
2 2-1/2 ounce packages of Butter Buds™ mixed according to instructions or 3 tablespoons margarine
2 bay leaves, crumbled
1 teaspoon marjoram
1 teaspoon thyme
1 teaspoon oregano
1 teaspoon Lite Salt™ (optional)
Freshly ground black pepper
1/2 pound okra, ends trimmed
1 small head cabbage, cored and cut into wedges
5 tomatoes, peeled and quartered
1 cup green peas
For Garnish:
1/4 cup chopped fresh parsley

Preheat oven to 350°F. Carefully brown the onions, potatoes, and eggplant separately in a Dupont Silverstone™ non-stick pan. Combine all vegetables except okra, cabbage, tomato wedges, and peas in a baking dish. Combine the stock, wine, Butter Buds mixture, and seasonings in a non-stick saucepan and heat for 1 minute. Pour this mixture over the vegetables, cover tightly, and bake for 40 minutes. Uncover and add the okra, tomato, and cabbage and stir gently. Add more stock or wine if necessary, cover and bake an additional 20 minutes. Add the peas and bake a final 5 minutes or until tender. Taste and correct the seasonings. Sprinkle with parsley and serve hot.

Serves 6 to 8

Per Serving: 0 mg cholesterol; 0 gm saturated fat
(Less than 1 gram saturated fat if margarine is used)

Grape Leaves Stuffed with Wild Rice and Vegetables

Stuffed grape leaves take time to make, but they are worth it. Serve as an hors d'oeuvre, an entree, or an accompaniment. This is exciting, exotic, spicy and delicious food.

1 cup wild rice
1 cup fresh peas
1/2 cup finely chopped sweet red pepper
1/2 cup finely chopped purple bell pepper, (green, if your store doesn't have purple)
5 scallions, finely chopped
1/2 cup chopped fresh mint
2 tablespoons virgin olive oil

1/2 cup fresh lemon juice
6 cloves garlic, peeled and sliced in half
1 18 to 22-ounce jar grape leaves
Lite Salt™ (optional)
Freshly ground black pepper
For Garnish:
Several lemon and lime wedges
6 to 8 fresh mint sprigs

Rinse the rice, drain and simmer, covered, in 3 cups water for about 1 hour. Let the rice rest 10 minutes off the heat with the lid wrapped in a tea towel. The towel will keep the condensed water from dripping back onto the rice. Blanch peas in boiling water for 2 minutes and drain. Blanch the peppers and drain. Blanch scallions and drain. Toss the cooked rice with the vegetables and fresh mint, olive oil, lemon juice, 6 garlic cloves (optional), Lite Salt, and pepper. Let rest 1 hour for the flavors to blend. Remove garlic.

To assemble, rinse grape leaves and pat dry. Put leaf shiny side down. Place about a tablespoon of rice mixture on each leaf. Fold the bottom up over the filling, then flap each side over and roll up into neat bundles. Serve cold or at room temperature. Garnish with lemon and lime wedges and sprigs of mint.

Makes 20 to 30 stuffed leaves

Per Serving: 0 mg cholesterol; less than 1 gm saturated fat

Phyllo Triangles of Leeks and Duxelles

This is a spectacular hors d'oeuvre, main course, or vegetable. Margarine produces flakier results and is a little easier to handle than the Butter Buds™ mixture. But Butter Buds™ has no fat. If using Butter Buds™, use double sheets of phyllo and bake a bit longer. If you're making them for hors d'oeuvre, cut phyllo pastry smaller to make bite-size pieces. If making the smaller triangles, bake just 8 to 10 minutes until crisp and golden.

5 leeks, trimmed, halved and quartered, rinsed of sand and chopped; blanched 5 minutes, rinsed and patted dry

1 cup duxelles (made from 16 ounces of mushrooms) (recipe page 225)

1 hot chili, trimmed and chopped fine

1 clove garlic, minced

3 ounces farmer's cheese, sieved

1/2 Egg Watchers™ egg, lightly whisked

1 tablespoon finely chopped fresh mint

3 tablespoons I Can't Believe It's Not Butter™ margarine, melted or 1 1/2-ounce package Butter Buds™, mixed according to instructions

6 to 12 sheets phyllo

1/2 cup Bright Day™ imitation mayonnaise

Drops sesame oil

1/8 teaspoon chopped coriander

1/2 teaspoon freshly grated ginger

For Garnish:

Numerous Enoki mushrooms

Sprigs herbs

Sprigs parsley

Preheat the oven to 350°F. Spray a baking sheet with PAM™; cut parchment to fit the sheet and spray PAM™ on the paper. Alternatively use a non-sticking baking sheet. Combine the leeks, duxelles, chili, garlic, cheese, 1/2 imitation egg and mint. Cut sheets of phyllo lengthwise into sixths. Trim edges if dry. Keep unused sheets under plastic wrap.

Use 1 sheet thickness for each batch of 6 pastries. Brush gently with margarine, or very lightly brush 2 sheets thickness with imitation butter mixture. Allow about 1/2-inch border at the bottom of lengthwise strips. Spoon on 1 (generous) teaspoon filling. Carefully fold the border over the filling, then begin folding like a flag into triangles, left, then right. Continue until there is about 1 inch of dough left; fold that in half and neatly tuck under the final fold. Arrange on baking sheet and bake the pastries 15 to 20 minutes or until crisp and golden. Place on a platter with sprigs of Enoki. Serve hot.

Makes 6 triangles serving 6

Per serving of one duxelle: less than 5 mg cholesterol; 1 gm saturated fat

Sweet Maple-Baked Acorn or other Squash with Seeds

This is a simple, delicious way to prepare the many wonderful kinds of squash available in the summer and fall. If you're restricting sugar, use margarine instead of maple syrup. Vicki Wenger gave me this recipe.

2 acorn squash, cut in half, seeds not removed
4 teaspoons maple syrup

1 1/2-ounce package Butter Buds™ or Molly McButter™ (optional)

Preheat oven to 375°F. Cut the squash in half if it is large; otherwise cook whole. Place face down on a tray and bake for 45 minutes or in a microwave on high for 7 to 10 minutes, rotating once halfway through the cooking if microwave is not equipped with a carousel.

When cooked, spoon out seeds and rinse seeds in colander to remove pith. Replace 1 teaspoon of seeds in each half and add 1 to 2 teaspoons maple syrup. If you want to have a buttery flavor, sprinkle on Molly McButter™ or Butter Buds™ in syrup. Brown under broiler 1 to 2 minutes if you wish.

Variation: Add microwaved Canadian bacon slivers on top or toss with maple syrup in a non-stick pan.

Serves 4

Per Serving: 0 mg cholesterol; 0 gm saturated fat (The variation with Canadian bacon slivers can change the cholesterol to 10 mg if 8 tiny strips (1/8″ x 1/8″ x 2″) and the saturated fat content to just under 1 gram.)

Phyllo-wrapped Vegetables

Phyllo-wrapped vegetables are a delicious and showy presentation. It takes some preparation, however. You can buy phyllo already prepared in the frozen section of the grocery store.

12 sheets phyllo

1/2 cup I Can't Believe It's Not Butter™ margarine, melted

4 asparagus spears: Snap off tough ends and, using a vegetable peeler, gently remove outer skin. Cut into 1-inch pieces. Blanch in boiling water a few minutes, until color of the tips is bright green. Refresh under cold running water and pat dry.

6 snow peas: Snap off ends and pull away strings. Blanch in boiling water for 30 seconds, until bright green. Refresh under cold running water and pat dry. Chop.

6 baby carrots or daikon - a root vegetable found in the fresh vegetable department or in Oriental markets. Scrape and trim. If the carrots are slim, blanch them whole; if not, cut them into 1/2-inch slivers and blanch in boiling water. Refresh under cold running water and pat dry. Handle daikon slivers in the same fashion.

6 scallions: Trim and then blanch in boiling water for about 30 seconds. Refresh under cold running water and pat dry. Cut into pieces. Pepper strips that have been cored, seeded, and julienned may be handled similarly.

8 broccoli florets: Peel stems with a vegetable peeler, then blanch in boiling water for about 3 minutes. Refresh under cold running water and pat dry. Chop.

For Garnish:
  20 Enoki mushrooms
  Bunch parsley or dill
  1/2 cup imitation mayonnaise
  (page 98) or Bright Day™

imitation mayonnaise
3 to 4 drops sesame oil
1/8 teaspoon chopped coriander
1/2 teaspoon freshly grated
ginger

Preheat oven to 350°F. For each 6 vegetable bouquets, lay out 1 sheet phyllo and cut into 6 squares. Brush each square with I Can't Believe It's Not Butter™. Lay several blanched vegetables on the phyllo, 3/4 on the center of the dough, and 1/4 overhanging. Fold dough up to cover the bottoms, then 1 side, over the vegetables. Carefully roll up the vegetables in the dough and moisten the last edge with a bit more margarine to seal.

Lay all assembled vegetable packages on a cookie sheet lined with parchment, or use a non-stick pan. Bake 350°F for 12 minutes or until pastry is golden.

For added garnish, tuck in trimmed Enoki mushrooms or tiny sprigs of fresh herbs or parsley.

Serve with imitation mayonnaise (page 98) seasoned with a few drops of sesame oil, 1/8 teaspoon fresh chopped coriander, and 1/2 teaspoon freshly grated ginger.

Serves 8 to 10

Per Serving: 0 mg cholesterol; 1 gm saturated fat

Turnips and Onions

Turnips are one of those vegetables we don't use often enough. This recipe can be mashed or pureed and piped on a plate and filled with other vegetables, wild rice, even chutney or kumquats, whatever is fun and interesting.

2 pounds turnips, trimmed and peeled, sliced in 1-inch pieces
1 large white onion, cut in small strips
1 cup water
2 teaspoons nonfat dry milk
1/2 cup skim milk

1/4 cup Better Than Cream Cheese™ imitation cream cheese
2 tablespoons freshly grated Parmesan cheese
Several (2 to 3) slices Dorman's Lo-Chol™ cheese, slivered thin
For Garnish:
Chopped chives

Simmer turnips and onions in a covered pan with small amount water. Cook 20 to 30 minutes, until tender, adding more water when needed. (Or microwave in a plastic bag or covered bowl with a small amount of water for 15 to 18 minutes.)

Whip the dry milk into the skim milk and heat. Add the imitation cream cheese, the Parmesan cheese, and the low cholesterol cheese slivers. Heat until just melted. Transfer vegetables to serving platter, add cheeses on top, and brown under broiler.

Serve immediately.

Serves 6

Per Serving: less than 5 mg cholesterol; 1 gm saturated fat

Breads

Bread is an ideal way to include grain and fiber, both important in a low cholesterol diet. Many are made without either egg yolks or fat, making them even better from our standpoint!

Many south-of-the-border breads are wonderful but are made with lard, so they aren't included. Bagels traditionally aren't made with butter and eggs, and we've included a topped bagel sandwich. Breads like banana nut or zucchini bread can be easily adapted by omitting the butter and substituting low saturated oil or margarine, and egg breads such as Challah can be made with egg substitutes. Included also are several traditional sandwiches—like BLT's and grilled cheese—normally high in cholesterol because of the cheese, bacon and mayonnaise—but we offer tips on making them in a healthier way.

Oat Bran Muffins are example of an ideal way to include much needed grains and carbohydrates in your diet. Oat bran is recommended as daily fare on low cholesterol diets. We have wonderful oat bran muffin and oat bran cookie recipes.

Toppings and spreads for bread vary widely, with butter being extremely high in cholesterol and saturated fat. Margarines also vary in saturated fat content. Substitute fats are being developed, but in the meantime, check the labels on margarine or spreads for lowest saturated fat content. (Weight Watchers™ and Parkey Diet™ are the brands we've found to be the lowest at this time.)

French Bread

Always a classic bread, this is perfect for a low cholesterol diet. Other ingredients can be added to the batter, such as chopped Greek olives (salty), chopped onions, garlic, even dill. If you like a margarine spread, try the diet varieties which are usually whipped with air and water. Remember, if you pile too much on hot bread or toast, it'll wind up soggy.

2 envelopes dry yeast
2 1/2 cups lukewarm water

6 to 7 cups flour
1 teaspoon Puritan™ oil

Add yeast to water, mixing to blend and let sit about 5 minutes or until dissolved completely. Add flour and knead for at least 10 minutes on floured bread board. Place kneaded dough in large, lightly oiled bowl, covering with tea towel. Place in a warm spot (not oven). Let rise for 2 to 3 hours, punch down, and knead. Let rise again for 1 hour. Punch down and make two loaves on lightly floured board; let rise for 20 minutes. Put dough lightly oiled bread pans, cover and let rise for 1 hour. Score top.

Preheat oven to 425°F. Bake for 30 minutes. Remove from pan and cool on a wire rack.

Serves 6 to 8

Per Serving: 0 mg cholesterol; 0 gm saturated fat

Peppery Corn Bread

This irresistible combination of flavors is originally from the Southwest. It makes enough for one loaf and also makes excellent muffins. For cocktail servings, use miniature, gem-sized muffin tins. For miniatures, bake only for about 20 minutes. Just before baking, lightly sprinkle on Parmesan. Once slightly cooled, they can be split open and filled with a spread.

1 cup all purpose flour
1 cup corn meal, preferably stone milled
2 teaspoons double-acting baking powder
1/2 teaspoon baking soda
1/2 tablespoon Lite Salt™ (optional)
1 cup buttermilk mixed with 1 teaspoon red pepper flakes about 15 minutes before making this recipe
1 egg white, whisked until frothy

2 Egg Watchers™ eggs, whisked until foamy
3/4 cup green pepper, cored, seeded, chopped and lightly dusted with a little flour
3/4 cup fresh or canned kernels, chopped and lightly dusted with a little flour
Freshly ground black pepper
2 tablespoons melted, Weight Watchers™ margarine
1/4 cup grated Dorman's Lo-Chol™ cheese (optional)

Preheat oven to 400°F. Sift dry ingredients together. Quickly stir in combined liquid ingredients and fold in vegetable pieces and optional cheese.

Pour into a 4″ x 4″ x 8″ Silverstone™ non-stick loaf pan that has been lightly oiled. Bake 45 minutes, or until a cake tester comes out clean. Let the bread rest 5 minutes. Remove from pan and cool on a wire rack.

Per Serving: 1 mg cholesterol; less than 1 gm saturated fat

Karen Dubek's Oat Bran Muffins

Oat bran daily is highly recommended for those on a low cholesterol diet. Studies have shown oat bran may lower cholesterol by helping the body get rid of some of the excess. This recipe is the best, and it's an easy way to eat oat bran. (Mothers™ is the name of one brand of oat bran and the one I use. Quaker Oats distributes it.)

2 1/2 cups oat bran	1/4 cup brown sugar
2 teaspoons baking powder	1 Egg Watchers™ egg
1/4 teaspoon baking soda	1 cup skim milk
1/2 cup raisins	2 tablespoons Puritan™ oil

Preheat oven to 425°F. Mix dry ingredients together in one bowl and liquid ingredients in another. Blend. Avoid overmixing. Bake in non-stick muffin tins for 15 minutes. Remove from pan and cool on a wire rack. Store in covered container. May be frozen.

Makes 12 large or 18 small muffins.

Per Serving: 0 mg cholesterol; 1 gm saturated fat for 2 muffins

Bagel Layer from Sue Wydler

Bagels are always fun to eat, and this topping is delicious.

1 1/2 cups skim milk cottage
cheese
1/4 cup chopped radishes
2 tablespoons chopped pimientos
1/2 cup chopped celery
1/4 cup chopped green pepper

2 tablespoons chopped parsley
1 clove garlic, minced
1/2 cup finely chopped scallions
Freshly ground black pepper
6 to 8 bagels, split

Preheat broiler. Mash the cottage cheese and beat in remaining ingredients. Spread on bagels and toast under broiler for 10 minutes. Watch them in case your broiler works overtime! If bagels are extra thick, toast them for a few minutes before adding topping.

Serves 6 to 8

Per Serving: 10 mg cholesterol; 1 gm saturated fat

Bacon, Lettuce, and Tomato Sandwich

There's no reason to give up old favorites on a low cholesterol diet. If you use bacon, just pick off all the fat and substitute a mayonnaise spread made without egg yolks (like Bright Day™) or Hain™, or our recipe on page 98.

2 slices bread for each sandwich,
toasted
Bright Day™ or Hain™ imitation
mayonnaise
2 to 3 bread-size romaine or
iceberg lettuce leaves

2 to 3 very ripe tomatoes, thinly
sliced
1 1/8-inch x 3-inch slice Canadian
bacon, julienned, or bacon
cooked in microwave wrapped
in paper towel and defatted
(fat trimmed off) after cooking

Prepare sandwiches by lightly spreading imitation mayonnaise on a slice of toast. Layer lettuce, tomato, and bacon, and top with the other piece of toast. Cut in half or fourths to serve.

Per Serving: 10 mg cholesterol; 1 gm saturated fat

Grilled Cheese Sandwich

Grilled cheese on a low cholesterol, low saturated fat diet? You bet! Substitute Dorman's Lo-Chol™ for regular cheese. It melts beautifully and keeps its taste, which is something like Muenster. The cholesterol and saturated fat doesn't include the Canadian bacon option, which would raise the cholesterol about 15 milligrams and the saturated fat by 2 grams.

Bread for sandwiches
1 to 2 slices Dorman's Lo-Chol™
  cheese
Optional additions:
Slice of sweet red or green bell
  pepper
Slice of tomato

Slice of roasted red pepper
Slice of onion
1 thin slice Canadian Bacon
Cut up pieces pepperoncini
  peppers
Cut up pieces El Paso™ canned
  green mild whole chilies

Method 1: Microwave
Toast bread in regular toaster. Mound selected fillings on toast and cover with second slice of cheese. Microwave on high for 1 to 2 minutes or broil until cheese melts.

Method 2: Dry Fry
Place bread slice in Silverstone™ non-stick pan on stove top. Mound selected fillings on bread and cover with second slice of cheese. Cover pan and cook on medium heat. Watch bottom of bread carefully; when nicely browned, cover with second slice. Turn and toast other side.

Variation: The photograph on page 191 shows a plain grilled cheese sandwich served with a fourth cucumber, grapes, avocado slices, black olives and Greek string cheese served on cactus leaves (which can be eaten). Add 15 mg cholesterol and 1 gm saturated fat for the ounce of cheese.

Per Serving: 15 mg cholesterol; 2 gm saturated fat

Cucumber Sandwiches
Kathy McLain

Yes, this simple mixture of flavors and textures was popular in the Victorian era. Tiny pieces of onion and chopped fresh parsley or mint can also be added. These came from an old fashioned friend.

Bread for sandwiches
Bright Day™ imitation
  mayonnaise
Cucumber, thinly sliced
Lite Salt™ (optional)

White pepper
For Garnish:
  Grated onion
  Chopped parsley or mint

Slice the crust off of white bread, spread with Bright Day™ (imitation mayonnaise) and thin slices of peeled or strip-peeled cucumber. Season and garnish. If you have a small, round cookie cutter, press into bread making about 3 to 4 rounds per slice. Make smaller rounds to cover (optional). If you don't have a round cookie cutter, place round of cucumber between whole slices of bread spread with Bright Day™. Trim edges and cut into 4 pieces, either diagonally into triangles or lengthwise into fingers.

Cholesterol and saturated fat are estimated for six 2-inch round sandwiches.

Per Serving: 0 mg cholesterol; less than 1 gm saturated fat

Desserts and Sorbets

There are many special and wonderful desserts that have no butter or cream, as you'll see here. We haven't eliminated all fats or sugar, and we have adapted several traditional recipes (like Oatmeal Cookies) but with no egg yolks and no butter.

If you have a weight problem, it is probably preferable to get more of your calories from vegetables, breads, or fruits. If you tend to overeat sweets, we hope these recipes can help you still enjoy dessert. Of course, fresh fruit is the ideal dessert. A small amount of Grand Marnier™, Kirsch, or other liqueur can make fruit a very special finish to any meal.

Incredible Chewy Oat Bran Raisin Cookies

Eating large amounts of oat bran daily has been shown to help *lower* cholesterol. These oat bran cookies are scrumptious, easy to prepare and make eating oat bran daily easy. I'm never sure I'll like anything with ''healthful,'' ''germ,'' ''bran,'' or ''fiber'' in it (actually I'm used to hearing about fiber now). I vary the recipe by adding chopped walnuts, or by pressing in the center of the uncooked dollops of cookie dough with half a walnut just before they go in the oven. You can also eliminate the raisins and nuts and substitute a half a cup of chopped cranberries. I've tried other berries, but they just collapse.

I've also made these plain with no raisins or nuts, and they're still excellent. If you like more molasses flavor, use 1/4 cup brown sugar instead of the white, although I think the little bit of white sugar is better. The walnut oil gives the cookies a mellow flavor. Walnut oil is one of the lowest in saturated fat. Kids love these cookies.

1 cup walnut oil
1 cup maple syrup
1/2 cup honey
1/2 cup sugar
2 teaspoons vanilla
2 Egg Watchers™ eggs
1 fresh egg white

2 cups white flour
2 cups Mothers™ oat bran
2 teaspoons baking powder
1/2 teaspoon Lite Salt™ (optional)
Variations:
    1/2 cup raisins and 1/2 cup
    chopped walnuts

Preheat oven to 350°F. Mix well the walnut oil, maple syrup, honey, sugar, vanilla, egg substitutes, and egg white. In a separate bowl, mix well the oat bran, white flour, and baking powder. Add the liquid ingredients, blending well. Let stand 15 minutes. Mixture will rise slightly. Fold in raisins or raisins and nuts. Spoon by tablespoonfuls on an ungreased, non-stick cookie sheet and bake for 20 minutes or until done. Remove from cookie sheet immediately when taken from oven and place hot in an air tight plastic bag or cookie jar. Serve hot from the oven or cold.

Makes 36 cookies.

Per Serving: 0 mg cholesterol; 1 gm saturated fat for 5 cookies

Brandy Snap Cookies and Cigars

These cookies can be made in lots of fun shapes.

4 tablespoons I Can't Believe It's
 Not Butter™ margarine
1/4 cup sugar
2 tablespoons dark molasses
1/2 teaspoon ground ginger

1/2 teaspoon ground cinnamon
Pinch of Lite Salt™ (optional)
1 teaspoon grated orange rind
1/4 cup flour, sifted
1 tablespoon brandy

For the cookies:

Preheat the oven to 325°F. Line baking sheets with parchment paper and very lightly brush with oil or use a non-stick cooking pan sprayed in PAM™.

Combine the margarine, sugar, molasses and spices, optional Lite Salt, and orange rind; bring to a boil and immediately remove from the heat. Let cool slightly. Whisk in the flour; add the brandy, and continue to whisk until the mixture is smooth.

Drop the mixture onto the prepared baking sheets, 1 to 2 tablespoons for each cookie. Then gently smooth into 1 1/2-inch circles with the back of a spoon. Only prepare 3 to 4 cookies at a time if you are going to shape them. Bake for about 10 minutes, until golden. Remove the cookies to a wire rack to cool and continue cooking the remainder of the batter.

For Brandy Snap Cups:

Ideal for sorbets and fresh fruits topped with fruit puree.

Before mixing batter, spray with PAM™ the outside of small custard cups and invert them on the counter. As soon as brandy snaps are baked, immediately drape a snap over a cup, and gently pinch edges to form pleats. If a cookie becomes hard, return it to the oven for a few seconds to soften and then continue. Once the cups have firmed, they can be stored in an airtight container.

For Cigars:

Have a long wooden spoon handle ready. As cookies are done, quickly wrap each one around the handle, let sit and then slide off. These can be embellished by melting a few ounces of chopped dark chocolate and adding a teaspoon of brandy. Once the cigars are set, dip one end of each cigar into the chocolate and set on wax paper or a rack to dry. If chocolate is used, add 1 gram of saturated fat for each 3 cookies.

Makes 12 to 18 cookies

Per Serving: 0 mg cholesterol; 1 gm saturated fat

Raisin Cake Cookies

Many other fruits can be substituted for the raisins, such as dried apricots, dried dates, dried sour cherries, dried figs, candied lemon rinds, and so on.

1/3 cup walnut oil
1 cup white sugar
1 Egg Watchers™ egg
1/2 teaspoon vanilla
1/2 cup skim milk, whisked with
   2 tablespoons nonfat dry milk
1 cup flour

1/4 cup oat bran
1 tablespoon baking powder
1/2 teaspoon vanilla
1 cup raisins (or currants,
   sultanas, or muscats. Currants
   aren't quite as sweet as raisins
   or muscats.)

Preheat oven to 350°F. Cream oil and sugar together; stir in imitation egg. Add vanilla, skim milk, and stir. Sift flour and oat bran with baking powder. Add to liquids and mix well. Stir in raisins. Spoon batter in 2-inch dollops on lightly oiled non-stick cookie sheet, or half fill non-stick cupcake molds. Bake for 12 to 15 minutes. Cool on a rack.

Makes 1 to 2 dozen cookies.

Per Serving: 0 mg cholesterol; 1 gm saturated fat

Angel Food Cake

Angel food cakes can be served in a variety of ways—with fruits, chocolate (which has some saturated fat), liqueur, sauces. It is a versatile, beautiful dessert, good for a picnic or a wedding. You'll need the non-stick hollow tube cake pan but non-stick loaf pans are alternatives.

1 1/4 cups superfine sugar
1 1/4 cups sifted cake flour
1 1/4 cups large egg whites at room temperature (They should be from eggs several days old.)

1/2 teaspoon fresh lemon juice
1 teaspoon cream of tartar
1/4 teaspoon Lite Salt™(optional)
1 teaspoon vanilla extract
1 teaspoon almond extract

Preheat the oven to 325°F and place the rack in the lower third of the oven. Sift the sugar. Sift the flour twice until no lumps remain. For the third sifting of the flour, sift 1/2 cup of the sugar with the flour. Put egg whites and lemon juice into a very clean, dry bowl and beat gently for 2 minutes to break them up. Sift over the whites the cream of tartar and optional salt. Beat until whites form soft peaks.

Begin whipping in 3/4 cup sugar a little at a time with a flat wire spatula. When the 3/4 cup sugar has been incorporated, sprinkle about 1/3 cup of flour-sugar mixture over whites and incorporate with the spatula quickly and gently. Repeat until flour and sugar are incorporated. With a few quick folds add almond and vanilla extracts.

Pour batter into ungreased, very clean, non-stick, 2-quart angel cake tube pan. Run a spatula through batter to eliminate air holes. Bake at 325°F for 1 hour.

When baked, the cake will have slightly pulled away from the sides of the pan, and a toothpick inserted in the cake will come out clean. Remove cake from oven and turn upside down on the counter to let it cool in pan.

To remove from pan, run a thin plastic spatula around the edges of pan and ease the cake out. Gently rub surface with your fingertips to remove stray crumbs.

Cut into wedges and serve with fresh or macerated berries, raspberry sauce (recipe page 138), sorbet, or drizzle a glaze over the cake.

Variation:

A whipped topping can be added to the cake. If it's non-dairy from the grocery freezer, check for palm or coconut oil.

Makes 1 angel food cake.

Per Serving: 0 mg cholesterol; 0 gm saturated fat

Rice Pudding

I'll bet every little kid has had rice pudding and loved it. This recipe evokes those memories.

2 cups skim milk
2 tablespoons nonfat dry milk
1 3/4 cups hot cooked rice
1/4 cup sugar
1/2 teaspoon cinnamon
1 teaspoon vanilla

1/8 teaspoon ground nutmeg, (optional)
2 Egg Watchers™ eggs mixed with 2 tablespoons skim milk
1/2 cup dark raisins
For Garnish:
Ground nutmeg

Bring skim milk to a boil in a saucepan. Whisk in nonfat dry milk. Add rice, sugar, cinnamon, vanilla, and nutmeg and stir well. Cook over low heat about 1 minute, stirring frequently. Remove from burner. Very slowly add imitation eggs to hot rice mixture, stirring rapidly. Add raisins. Pour into individual dishes. Sprinkle with nutmeg. Serve warm or chilled.

Serves 4

Per Serving: 0 mg cholesterol; 2 gm saturated fat

Oatmeal Cookies

Here's a low cholesterol cookie that's absolutely delicious when you want a snack. Oat bran is recommended daily on a low cholesterol, diet and this is one of my favorite ways to eat it.

1/2 cup walnut oil
1/2 cup brown sugar
1/4 cup honey
1 Egg Watchers™ egg
2 tablespoons nonfat dry milk
1 tablespoon skim milk
1/2 teaspoon vanilla
1/2 cup pureed fresh apples or
   applesauce
1 cup all purpose flour

1/4 cup Mother's Oat Bran™
1/2 teaspoon double-acting
   baking powder
1/2 teaspoon baking soda
1/4 teaspoon nutmeg
1/2 teaspoon cinnamon
1-1/4 cups uncooked rolled oats
1/2 cup raisins
1/3 cup chopped walnuts
   (optional)

Preheat oven to 400°F. Beat oil, sugar, honey, imitation egg, and dry milk that has been whisked into the skim milk. Stir in vanilla and apple puree. In a separate bowl, sift together flour, oat bran, baking powder, baking soda, nutmeg, cinnamon. Stir together flour mixture and rolled oats and mix in liquids, raisins and nuts, and blend well. Drop dough by teaspoonfuls on a lightly oiled cookie sheet, or PAM™-sprayed non-stick sheet, each a few inches apart. Bake in 400°F oven for 10 to 12 minutes or until edges are lightly browned. Transfer to a rack to cool.

Makes 12 to 18 cookies.

Per Serving: 0 mg cholesterol; 1 gm saturated fat in 3 cookies

Papaya-Mango Sorbet

Sorbets are easy to make, refreshing, and because they're not cooked their vitamins are preserved. They're popular in the summer, or with rich winter soups, or between courses during a formal meal. This one is a tropical gem.

1/2 cup water
1/4 cup white wine
1/4 cup sugar
1/4 cup lime juice
2 ripe papayas, peeled, halved,
    seeds scooped out and roughly
    chopped

2 ripe mangos, peeled, pulp cut
    away from the pit
For Garnish:
    Mint leaves

Boil the water, wine, sugar, and lime juice for 5 minutes and cool. In the bowl of a food processor, puree the fruit until smooth. Pour in the cooled syrup and process to combine.

Freezing Sorbet: Pour the puree into a metal pan and freeze until puree is frozen, about 2 inches in, all around the sides of the pan (approximately 2 hours). Remove from freezer; break up with a fork into chunks; and puree in the processor until smooth. Return the puree to the metal pan and then to the freezer. Freeze. Repeat the processing and freezing 3 more times, until the sorbet is smooth. Otherwise, freeze in an ice cream freezer.

Serves 4 to 6

Per Serving: 0 mg cholesterol; 2 gm saturated fat

Lemon-Lime   Sorbet

Mouth-tingling lemon and lime sorbet is growing in popularity. This can also be frozen in trays, stirring every hour or so until the contents of the tray are frozen. Serve, if you like, in lemon or lime shells that have been halved with the pulp scooped out. Cut 1/4 inch off bottom so shell will stand. Fruit can be cut for larger servings by removing top third and scooping or laying lemon or lime sideways. Fill with the sorbet and refreeze until set.

1/2 cup hot water
2/3 cup honey
2 teaspoons lemon and/or lime
   zest

1 1/2 cups fresh lime juice
1 1/2 cups fresh lemon juice
For Garnish:
   Candied lemon and lime peel

Combine hot water with honey and stir to dissolve. Add in the zest and let cool. Stir in the juices. Add to an ice cream freezer and squeeze according to manufacturer's instructions. Place in the refrigerator/freezer until needed. To serve, scoop into serving bowls or scooped out limes and lemons and garnish with candied lime and lemon peel.

Variation: Champagne Sorbet
Reduce the amount of citrus juice to 2 cups
Add 1 cup of icy champagne
Reduce the amount of honey or sugar to 1/4 cup
Serves 4 to 6

Per Serving: 0 mg cholesterol; 0 gm saturated fat

Mocha Creme Sorbet

This sorbet is as mouth watering and as rich as a coffee and chocolate soda but without the cholesterol.

1/4 cup sugar
1/2 cup cocoa
1 cup dark coffee (instant, brewed, decaffeinated or expresso)

2 cups skim milk
1/4 cup Kahlua™
4 tablespoons Kahlua™
For Garnish:
    Shavings of milk chocolate

Sift together sugar and cocoa. Gradually stir in coffee and pour into a Dupont Silverstone™ non-stick pan and stir over low heat until sugar mixture is dissolved. Stir in skim milk and Kahlua™.

Freezing Sorbet: Pour puree into a metal pan and freeze until puree is frozen about 2 inches in, all around the sides of the pan, approximately 2 hours. Break up partially frozen mixture with a fork and puree in the processor until smooth. Add 4 tablespoons Kahlua™ and blend. Return puree to the metal pan and then to the freezer. Freeze and break up with a fork and blend in a processor 3 more times, until the sorbet is smooth. Alternatively, freeze in an ice cream maker.

To serve, allow to soften a few minutes at room temperature, form into scoops and serve in chilled glasses. Garnish with one shaving of chocolate. (Chocolate does have some saturated fat.)

Serves 4 to 6

Per Serving: 0 mg cholesterol; 2 gm saturated fat

Fresh Fruit in Meringue

This is a spectacular yet simple dessert. Make the meringue ahead of time and fill just before serving. Don't try it on a humid day. Be aware the sugar content (in the meringue) is higher than most of our recipes, about four tablespoons per person.

6 egg whites, room temperature
(break open and separate just
before making)
2 cups sugar

1/2 teaspoon cinnamon
1 1/2 teaspoon vanilla
1/2 teaspoon vinegar
1/3 teaspoon cream of tartar

Meringue:
1 cup blueberries
1 cup strawberries, stems
removed and sliced
1 cup honeydew melon balls

1 cup sliced peaches, skin left on
For Garnish:
Mint leaves

Filling:
Preheat oven to 275°F. Beat egg whites with a whisk in an absolutely clean bowl until foamy. Add cinnamon, vinegar and cream of tartar and whisk until well incorporated. Switch to electric beaters and beat on high, stirring often, until egg whites form soft peaks. Beat in sugar, 2 tablespoons at a time, blending completely after each addition of sugar. Beat until peaks are stiff.

In a PAM™ sprayed non-stick spring pan. (If yours isn't non-stick, oil well with safflower oil and flour liberally.) Fill the bottom and sides with 3/4 of the egg white mixture, hollowing out the center and smoothing the inside with a spatula to form a shell for filling. Make bottom 1/2 inch and sides 1 inch thick. Gently flatten the top circle. (Make sure the meringue is high on the sides.) You can line the inside of the sides of your spring-form pan with smooth foil (that has been oiled and floured) if you want a slightly higher shell.

On a separate non-stick cookie sheet, spray with PAM™ and make a circle of rosettes with the remaining 1/4 of the egg white mixture. (Or spoon off 'kisses' which connect to each other.) Make the circle the same size as the meringue shell because you're going to place it on top of the shell after baking. Bake both for about 1 hour and 15 minutes. Turn off the oven and leave meringue inside for an additional 15 minutes after baking. Remove from oven and cool away from drafts.

Just before serving, remove meringue from spring pan, and place on serving dish. Lightly crush down center where filling is to go. Place rosette or kisses circle on top and fill with fruit. Place fruit in meringue carefully, a little of this, a little of that. Serve immediately.

Variation: Marinate fruit in champagne or kirsch for 15 minutes before filling. Drain fruit for 5 minutes in colander to be sure little moisture is left. Nonsaturated fat whipped topping can also be used. Pass it after the meringue has been cut and served on individual plates.

Serves 8

Per serving: 0 mg cholesterol; 0 gm saturated fat (If whipped topping is used, add 1 gm saturated fat for each 2 ounces.)

Cranberry Sorbet

Cranberries are identified with Thanksgiving. This tart sorbet can be used anytime: summer, winter, spring, and also at Thanksgiving.

4 cups cranberries	1/2 teaspoon grated lemon rind
1 3/4 cups sugar	1/8 teaspoon cinnamon
1 3/4 cups water	2 egg whites, stiffly beaten
1 tablespoon grated orange rind	

Heat cranberries and sugar in 1 3/4 cups water until bursting. Drain. Chop fine in blender or food processor. Add grated rind and cinnamon and blend again for a few seconds. Fold in egg whites. Freeze in an ice cream maker according to manufacturer's directions or use our directions on page 000.

Serves 8

Per Serving: 0 mg cholesterol; 0 gm saturated fat

Blackberry Sorbet

Everyone has favorite fruits. Mine are blackberries, boysenberries, and raspberries. This recipe can be made with any of the three, or a mixture.

1 pound ripe blackberries
1/3 cup sugar
1/2 cup water
1 teaspoon lemon juice
1/4 teaspoon cinnamon
2 egg whites, stiffly beaten

2 teaspoons Kirsch or Creme de
    Cassis (made from
    blackberries) (optional)
For Garnish:
    Whole perfect berries

Mash and sieve the berries, reserving a few for garnish. Boil the sugar and water together for 5 minutes to make a syrup. When cool, add syrup, lemon juice and cinnamon to the berry puree. Fold the stiffly beaten egg whites into the sorbet, and partially freeze. Add the Kirsch or Creme de Cassis and finish freezing.

Serves 4

Per Serving: 0 mg cholesterol; 0 gm saturated fat

Baked Apples and Brown Sugar

Baked apples are easy and lush additions to breakfast, brunch, and lunch or as a dinner dessert. For dessert you can serve with Vanilla Tofutti™, a non-dairy ice cream.

1 cup brown sugar
2 teaspoons lemon juice
2 teaspoons water
1/4 cup raisins
1 teaspoon cinnamon

1/4 cup chopped walnuts
1 teaspoon lemon juice
4 large firm Rome apples, cored
    but not peeled

Preheat oven to 350°F. Mix sugar, lemon juice, water, raisins, cinnamon, and walnuts. Fill core with mixture, sprinkle rest of mixture in lemon juice and add to apples. It may spill over into baking dish. Bake for 1 hour.

Serve hot, or cover and refrigerate, and serve cold.

Serves 4

Per Serving: 0 mg cholesterol; less than 1 gm saturated fat

Savory Basil Sorbet

This sorbet is a good accompaniment for chilled first-course soups, cold fish, or to cleanse the palate between the first and main courses. This sorbet also tastes good made with 1 cup finely chopped cilantro and 1 cup finely chopped parsley substituted for the basil. It is very unusual.

1 teaspoon Lite Salt™ (optional)
1/4 cup sugar
1 cup cold water
Juice of 1 lemon
2 cups fresh basil leaves, rinsed, patted dry, and finely chopped
1/2 jalapeno or serrano chili (depending on degree of heat
desired), seeded, deribbed, and minced
3 scallions, trimmed and finely chopped
For Garnish:
Small basil leaves

Dissolve the optional Lite Salt™ and sugar in the water and lemon juice. Add the chopped basil, jalapeno and scallions, and puree in a food processor. Pour into an ice cream maker. Freeze according to manufacturer's instructions. Garnish with the reserved leaves.

Makes 3 1/2 cups

Per Serving: 0 mg cholesterol; 0 gm saturated fat

Poached Pears in Red Wine

To me pears should be a subtle, even gentle dessert. This has a nice added sophistication with the sauce. You'll need parchment paper to create it.

6 firm Bosc pears with stems
Bowl of water with the juice of 2
   fresh lemons squeezed in
1 bottle (750 ml) of dry red wine
1 1/2 cups sugar

1 vanilla bean, split
3 sprigs of fresh basil
For Garnish:
   Mint leaves

Peel pears but leave stems on. Place them in the lemon water as they are peeled to prevent discoloration. Heat wine and sugar to a simmer in a glass or enamel pan large enough to hold the pears and stir to dissolve sugar. Add vanilla bean and basil. Remove pears from water and add to the wine syrup. Cover pan with a trimmed piece of parchment paper to keep pears submerged and then cover with lid. Simmer slowly for about 20 minutes, turning once or twice. To test for doneness: a knife tip piercing a pear in the bottom should feel slight resistance.

Remove the pears and set them upright in a bowl. Discard the vanilla bean and basil sprigs. Moisten pears with a bit of the poaching liquid and boil down the remaining liquid by about a third. Pour over the pears and chill thoroughly.

To serve, arrange on plates with a bit of the wine sauce. Put a mint leaf or two under each pear.

Serves 6.

Per Serving: 0 mg cholesterol; 0 gm saturated fat

Orange Amaretto Sorbet

The color of this sorbet is light. You may want to use berries or another fruit to set it off.

4 cups orange juice
1/4 cup superfine sugar
1 tablespoon fresh lemon juice
1 teaspoon orange flower water
2 tablespoons Amaretto

For Garnish:
Strip candied orange peel or strips orange zest
Berries

Heat 1 cup orange juice with sugar and stir to dissolve. Let cool. Add remaining orange juice and other ingredients and freeze in an ice cream maker according to manufacturer's directions or use the directions on page 251. Strip zest or orange peel on top of each serving and add a few berries on top.

Serves 4 to 6

Per Serving: 0 mg cholesterol; 0 gm saturated fat

Bananas Flambeed

Banana desserts are perfect with anything, and are especially good with French, Polynesian, and Mexican food. In Mexico and South America, bananas are used as a side dish with steak, and plantains, a banana-like vegetable, are served with a variety of meals. I like cooked bananas in the winter. They're nurturing with their translucent, lush sweetness.

1/4 cup golden raisins
1/4 cup slivered dates
1/2 cup cognac
1/2 cup brown sugar or 1/2 cup
  wild honey (preferred)
1/4 teaspoon cinnamon
1/4 teaspoon ground cardamon

1/4 teaspoon minced ginger
1 teaspoon I Can't Believe It's
  Not Butter™
4 bananas, peeled and cut in half
  lengthwise, sprinkled with the
  juice of 1 lemon so they keep
  their color

Soak the raisins and dates in cognac for 1 hour while stirring, melt the sugar or honey for 1 hour in a large, non-stick skillet with the spices, ginger, and margarine.

Add the bananas and the drained raisins and dates. Shake the pan over high heat until the bananas are just tender when pierced with a knife (about 4 minutes). Add the 1/2 cup soaking cognac and carefully ignite. Continue shaking the pan until the flame dies. Serve immediately, spooning the pan juices over the fruit.

This recipe also works extremely well with cored, peeled apple or pear slices, or with peeled orange, tangerine, or grapefruit segments.

Serves 4

Per Serving: 0 mg cholesterol; 0 gm saturated fat

Scottish Fruit Whip

There are many old-fashioned baked fruit dishes. One is known as a whip—a combination of fruit and egg whites. In the summer, fresh berries of any kind are perfect, but in winter any type of dried fruit or a mixture of fruits, softened in water, cognac, wine, or even port is also wonderful. The pecans have more saturated fat than the walnuts. This whip is from Scotland, the ancestral home of Malcolm Forbes, who very nicely endorsed this book, and we thank him.

1 1/2 cups fruit, if dried, soaked in 1/2 cup cognac for one hour; if fresh, simply rinse and pat dry
1/2 cup brown sugar, sieved
1/2 teaspoon cinnamon
1/2 teaspoon grated orange zest
1/3 cup chopped walnuts or pecans (optional)
6 egg whites

1/2 teaspoon orange flower water (found in the spice dept)
1 teaspoon vanilla
1 teaspoon margarine
3 teaspoons superfine sugar

For Garnish:
1/2 teaspoon freshly grated nutmeg
King Cholesterol Free™ imitation sour cream

Preheat oven to 350°F. If using dried fruit, soak until very soft, about one hour, then drain and chop finely. If using fresh fruit such as peaches or apples, peel, pit and slice thin. Simply leave small berries whole. Toss fruit with sugar, spices, orange zest, and optional nuts. Whip egg whites until foamy and incorporate orange flower water and vanilla and, from the marinade, 3 teaspoons cognac (or add 3 teaspoons cognac). Continue whipping until the egg whites are firm. Fold the egg white mixture and fruit together and pour into a souffle dish—about 2 quarts—that has been lightly coated with margarine and then lightly dusted with superfine sugar.

Bake until lightly browned for about 20 minutes, but start to check after 15 minutes. Serve with imitation sour cream and grate fresh nutmeg over each serving.

Serves 4 to 6.

Per Serving: 0 mg cholesterol; 1 gm saturated fat

Tapioca Pudding with Fruit

I love tapioca. It's one of the winter snacks I always whip up just for myself. Everyone else gets to it before I do no matter where I hide it.

1 cup pearl tapioca
1 cup water
1 cup skim milk
2 tablespoons nonfat dry milk
   (whipped into the skim milk)
1/2 teaspoon cinnamon
Grated rind of 1 lemon
3/4 cup sugar

4 Egg Watchers™ eggs
4 egg whites, stiffly beaten
1 teaspoon vanilla
For Garnish:
   1 cup fresh strawberries,
   blueberries, raspberries or
   other berries (optional)

Preheat oven to 350°F. Soak tapioca in water according to directions on package, which vary depending on size of tapioca. Add water, dry milk, cinnamon and lemon rind. Add sugar. Cook over low heat in double boiler for 3 hours. Check water often. Mix beaten imitation eggs and fold in egg whites. Add vanilla. Bake for 15 minutes. Serve with optional fresh fruit.

Serves 4

Per Serving: less than 5 mg cholesterol; 2 gm saturated fat

Plum Pudding

Plum pudding is a family favorite at Christmas. It has so many ingredients, you can make minor changes to suit your tastes, and it won't matter. A simple lowfat hard sauce can be made by blending 1/4 cup margarine with 3/4 cup powdered sugar with a few drops of vanilla, rum, or brandy stirred in. Serve with hard sauce.

8 tablespoons Weight Watchers™ margarine, beaten until soft

1 cup brown sugar, firmly packed

1/2 cup flour

1/4 teaspoon cinnamon

1/8 teaspoon cardamon

1/8 teaspoon allspice

1/8 teaspoon cloves

Grated zest of 1 lemon (1/2 teaspoon)

2 teaspoons ground almond paste or marzipan

1 cup oat bran or 1-1/2 cups bread crumbs or 1/2 cup oat bran and 3/4 cup bread crumbs

1/4 cup apple cider

1/8 cup rum

1/8 cup brandy

2 Egg Watchers™ eggs

1/3 cup moist (dried) currants (moisten in 1/4 cup cognac)

1/3 cup raisins

1/3 cup sultana or muscat raisins

1/4 cup chopped, glazed citrus peel (orange and lemon)

1/4 cup chopped, pitted dates

2 ounces candied, chopped cherries

2 ounces candied, chopped pineapple

Preheat oven to 350°F. Stir all ingredients into margarine, starting with the sugar and flour. Add spices, oat bran and or bread crumbs, and all liquids. Then add glazed and candied fruits, pack firmly in pudding mold and cover with foil. Bake in oven for 30 minutes.

It will keep for two to three weeks if well covered and refrigerated. It can then be steamed just before serving.

Steam in oven or on top of stove, placing pudding container on trivet in larger container. Fill with water halfway up mold; don't let water come too close to the edge or it may bubble into pudding. Cover larger container and steam 1 hour, replacing water when needed.

Serves 10 to 12

Per Serving: Less than 1 mg cholesterol; less than 1 gm saturated fat

Cheese Cake
Terri Frantz

With the new alternatives to cream cheeses, you can make outstanding cheese cake. This one is incredible. Terri loves sweets.

3 Egg Watchers™ eggs
1 pound Better Than Cream Cheese™ non-dairy cream cheese
1/2 cup plus 2 teaspoons sugar
1 teaspoon lemon

1 teaspoon vanilla
Zest of 1 lemon, grated
1/4 cup flour
1/4 teaspoon cinnamon
Graham crust, pressed into non-stick spring pan

Preheat oven to 375°F. Mix everything well (except crust) and pour into crust. Bake for 20 minutes in 8-inch spring pan. Cool to room temperature. Frost with the following:

1 1/2 cups King Cholesterol Free™ imitation sour cream

1/2 teaspoon vanilla
2 tablespoons sugar

Mix well and spread on top. Refrigerate until serving time. Remove from spring pan and serve. (*See below crust for cholesterol and saturated fat content.*)

Graham Cracker Crust

1 1/2-ounce package Butter Buds™
1 1/2 cups graham cracker crumbs, crushed or ground, plus 2 tablespoons reserved for garnish

1 teaspoon cinnamon
Scant 1/2 cup powdered sugar
2 tablespoons I Can't Believe It's Not Butter™

Sprinkle Butter Buds™ over crumbs and toss well. Stir in cinnamon and sugar and blend in softened margarine. Chill before filling if it is not to be baked. If you're using it for cheesecake, pat in cheesecake mixture and bake. Sprinkle extra graham cracker crumbs on top of filling.

Serves 6 to 8

Per Serving: less than 5 mg cholesterol; 5 gm saturated fat (cheese cake and crust)

Eggnog

No need to give up eggnog on a low cholesterol diet. We can't promise fewer calories in this recipe, but there's almost no cholesterol. (A regular recipe would have 200 to 500 mg of cholesterol per 1 1/2 cups.) It can also be made without the liquor.

8 Egg Watchers™ eggs
4 cups vanilla Tofutti™
4 cups very cold skim milk
2 tablespoons nonfat dry milk
4 egg whites, very cold
1 teaspoon vanilla

1 cup 80-proof whiskey
1 cup 80-proof rum, light or dark
4 tablespoons sugar
For Garnish:
  Grated nutmeg

Beat imitation eggs until frothy (2 minutes). Beat in Tofutti™, and then skim milk, vanilla, whiskey, and rum. Beat egg whites until stiff, gradually adding sugar. Fold egg whites into imitation egg mixture and sprinkle with nutmeg.

Serves 8 to 10

Per Serving: less than 5 mg cholesterol; 1 gm saturated fat for 1/2 cup

Breakfast

Your body has probably become used to a certain amount of food in the morning that is right for you. Respect what it is telling you and only eat that much, (unless you're a compulsive overeater in the morning, then you may wish to revise your habits).

Scientists are interested in oat bran in particular and oatmeal eaten regularly. They think it is helpful in lowering cholesterol. Oatmeal or oat bran muffins might be the best way to begin the day. Personally, I always start by drinking a glass of freshly squeezed orange or grapefruit juice with an oat bran muffin or oat bran cold cereal with skim milk. In the winter I may have hot oat bran or oatmeal, with some skim milk and a bit of brown sugar, and some raisins or fresh berries if I can find them. On Saturday I vary it and have just fruit and juice and a toasted English muffin with Polaners All Fruit Preserves™ or perhaps half a grapefruit and toast. I keep it simple and quick except on Saturday or Sunday when I let go and have cholesterol-free omelettes, waffles, maybe Morningstar Farms Breakfast Patties™, "the works."

When you want to have meat for breakfast, Canadian bacon is one of the lowest in cholesterol of the red meats, at about 40 mgs cholesterol per 3 ounces. If you eat red meat in the morning, you could skip meat for the rest of the day to keep a low cholesterol diet.

One brand of sausage substitute already mentioned is excellent. That is Morningstar™ "sausage" links and "sausage" patties. The fat content is moderate but they can be cooked in the microwave on paper towels to soak it up. They brown well in a non-stick skillet too.

But I'm not kidding, these soy products are darned good. And when you're hungry on a cold winter morning, and the waffles are hot off the griddle, and everything is swimming in pure maple syrup, I defy you to tell the difference.

Recipes: More Than 200 for a Healthy Heart

Oatmeal and Apples

This is so simple to make I hate to call it a recipe. On "no time to fuss" days, I dump everything in together: apples, raisins, oatmeal, water, and brown sugar, and microwave or boil it in a non-stick pot, stirring once or twice, throw in some oat bran, sprinkle nutmeg on top, and eat on the run. It can also be prepared ahead and kept cold for another day. If I run out of brown sugar, I use maple syrup. If I'm low on oats, I use more oat bran.

1 Granny Smith apple, cored and
   diced
1 cup oatmeal
2 tablespoons raisins
1/8 teaspoon cinnamon

2 teaspoons liquid brown sugar
2 cups water
2 teaspoons oat bran
1 cup skim milk

Place apple in a shallow dish and microwave on high for 3 to 4 minutes, or cook on stove top with a few teaspoons of water for 6 to 7 minutes, covered over low heat. Simultaneously, cook oatmeal, raisins, cinnamon and sugar on stove in Dupont Silverstone™ pot, in water. After 5 to 6 minutes, add nearly cooked apples, stir and cook for 2 to 3 minutes more. Apples will mash up just slightly. Sprinkle with oat bran. Serve with skim milk or eat as is.

Serves 2

Per Serving: 0 mg cholesterol; 0 gm saturated fat

Huevos Rancheros, Muy Locos

We call these eggs "locos" (crazy), because they're scrambled instead of the usual fried as you can't get a whole egg yolk look with the non-cholesterol egg substitutes. Doesn't matter, tastes the same and is excellent.

8 8-inch flour tortillas
1/4 cup chopped onions
2 tablespoons water
1/4 cup chopped canned El
Paso™ green chilies
8 Egg Watchers™ eggs
2 cups salsa, warmed (recipe
page 136)

1/4 cup King Cholesterol Free™
imitation sour cream
For Garnish:
1/2 cup finely cut scallions
Black and green olives, chopped
Diced tomatoes.

Heat flour tortillas in the oven, covered with a damp towel and with foil crimped at the edges, so they don't dry out. In a large non-stick skillet sprayed with PAM™, simmer the onions and chilies and 2 tablespoons water. Add imitation eggs, stir, and heat until done. On warmed plates, put one or two warmed flat tortillas and place the scrambled eggs and onions, and chilies mixture in center. Top with salsa and dollop with small spoon of imitation sour cream. Sprinkle everything with scallions, olives, and diced tomatoes and serve hot.

Serves 4

Per Serving: 0 mg cholesterol; 1 gm saturated fat

Omelettes

It's great to have a delicious egg-based meal with no cholesterol, and all manner of omelettes or scrambled eggs can be made without it. We've suggested a few sauces and toppings, but you may use your favorite, adapted to reduce fat and cholesterol. A few drops of Worcestershire, a teaspoon of imitation sour cream, or a teaspoon of skim milk ricotta cheese may liven up your omelettes.

8 Egg Watchers™ eggs
3 tablespoons skim milk or 2
   tablespoons Better Than
   Cream Cheese™ imitation
   cream cheese
Few drops Tabasco™ or a shake
   or two of cayenne pepper
1 to 2 teaspoons freshly grated
   Parmesan cheese

Lite Salt™ (optional)
Freshly ground white pepper
4 egg whites, whipped stiff
1 cup sauce from recipes that
   follow
For Garnish:
   Parsley

Fold imitation eggs and all other ingredients into stiffly beaten egg whites. Pour in heated Silverstone™ non-stick skillet sprayed with PAM™, cook over medium heat, lifting bottom often to be sure it doesn't burn. Turn out onto hot plates and pour sauce on top or fold inside. Garnish with parsley and serve.

Serves 4

Per Serving: 20 to 30 mg cholesterol (depending on cheese, but 30 is the highest); 3 gm saturated fat

Variations:
Spanish

3/4 cup chopped sweet Spanish
   or Vidalia onion
1 large cooked potato, slice
1/4 cup water
1/2 green pepper, chopped

1/2 red pepper, chopped
1/2 garlic clove, finely chopped
1 fresh tomato, cubed
1 teaspoon cornstarch mixed with
   1 teaspoon water

Simmer chopped onions and potatoes in small amount of water until soft; add green and red pepper, garlic, and fresh tomato. Simmer everything for 3 to 4 minutes. Drain off excess water or thicken with 1 teaspoon cornstarch in 1 teaspoon cool water. Pour hot sauce into center of omelette and fold over, reserving a little for garnish.

Per Serving: 0 mg cholesterol; 1 gm saturated fat

Mexican

3/4 cup chopped sweet Spanish
   or Vidalia onion
1/2 clove garlic, minced
1 to 2 fresh chilies, chopped (if
   very hot, use only 1/2 of one
   and discard veins and seeds)
1 teaspoon chili powder
2 teaspoons tomato paste
1/4 cup water

1 fresh tomato, cubed
1 teaspoon cornstarch mixed with
   1 teaspoon cool water
For Garnish:
   Chopped red and green
   peppers
   Sliced green chili peppers
   Chopped chives or chopped
   scallions

Simmer onions, garlic, chili peppers, and chili powder in tomato paste and water until soft. Add the cubed fresh tomato. Thicken sauce with softened cornstarch, stir well, and pour over top of omelette. Garnish with red and green peppers and slice of green chili pepper. Sprinkle with chopped raw scallions or chives.

Serves 4

Mushroom

**20 to 30, (about 1-1/2 pounds)
mushrooms, sliced**
1/3 cup chopped scallions
**2 1/2-ounce package Butter
Buds™ or several shakes Molly
McButter™**

1 teaspoon warm water
Lite Salt™ (optional)
Freshly ground black pepper

Steam mushrooms and scallions in 1/4 cup water. (Don't use too much water as mushrooms leach water.) Whisk imitation butter in warm water and add to mushrooms, cooking mixture until mushrooms are done (about 5 minutes). Season and pour over omelette.

Serves 4

Per Serving: 0 mg cholesterol; less than 1 gm saturated fat (any of the above)

Cheese

For a cheese omelette, there are several low cholesterol cheeses—Dorman's Lo-Chol™, skim milk ricotta, skim milk cottage cheese, pot cheese, and skim milk farmer's cheese—to name a few that can be melted atop the omelette, and placed under a broiler. Some Cheddars are also low in cholesterol, but they are hard to find and not low enough for regular use. Weight Watchers™ natural, Cheddar-like cheese is one you can use, though the cholesterol content is not given on the package. The fat is about half of regular Cheddar.

Serves 4

Per Serving: 10 mg cholesterol; 1 gm saturated fat (not including the Cheddar)

Spicy Fresh Corn Pancakes

These little cakes are delicious served with tomato salsa as an hors d'oeuvre or as an accompaniment to other foods.

2 cups fresh shucked corn (3 to 4 ears corn)
1/2 cup skim milk
1/2 cup sieved farmer's cheese
2 Egg Watchers™ eggs, beaten until frothy
1 jalapeno pepper, chopped
4 scallions, chopped

Freshly ground black pepper
Lite Salt™ (optional)
1 teaspoon grated lime rind (optional)
6 tablespoons self-rising white flour or self-rising cornflour (depending on desired degree of corn flavor), sifted

Cut the kernels from the ears of corn. Combine the kernels and milk from the corn with the skim milk, cheese, imitation eggs, pepper and scallions, seasonings, optional lime rind and mix well. Sift the flour over the mixture and stir to combine gently. Heat a heavy Silverstone™ non-stick pan. When hot, drop the batter onto the skillet by tablespoons. Cook until the surface of the batter bubbles all over, then flip the pancakes and brown the other side.

Serves 4 (8 to 12 pancakes).

Per Serving: 10 mg cholesterol; 1 gm saturated fat

Waffles

Waffles are my favorite food. They aren't low in fat, however, If you want a buttery flavor, add a few shakes of Butter Buds™ or Molly McButter™.

2 cups flour
2 teaspoons baking powder
2 Egg Watchers™ eggs
2 tablespoons sugar
5 tablespoons walnut oil
2 cups skim milk

1/4 cup nonfat dry milk, whisked
   into 1/2 cup of the skim milk
   above
2 fresh egg whites, stiffly beaten
Chopped walnuts (optional)
For Garnish:
   Maple syrup
   Fresh fruit

Sift flour and baking powder twice. Beat imitation eggs and add sugar, oil, milk, and dry milk mixture. Mix lightly as overbeating will toughen waffles. Fold in egg whites.

Batter can be refrigerated but gently mix before using. To fry, spoon batter on a Silverstone™ non-stick waffle iron sprayed with PAM™.

Remove when golden brown. Serve hot with maple syrup and fruit.
Serves 2 to 3

Per Serving: 0 mg cholesterol; 1 gm saturated fat

Griddlecakes

These cakes will be delicate and brown with no fat when cooked on a non-stick griddle coated with Dupont Silverstone™. Serve hot with maple or blueberry syrup, made with blueberries poached briefly in maple syrup. Add a pinch of cinnamon. For a chewier texture, substitute 1/4 cup oat bran for 1/2 cup of the flour.

1 1/2 cups flour
1 teaspoon baking soda
1 teaspoon sugar
1 teaspoon grated orange rind
1 Egg Watchers™ egg, lightly beaten

1 1/2 cups lowfat buttermilk
2 tablespoons melted Weight Watchers™ margarine
For Garnish:
Maple or blueberry syrup
Pinch of cinnamon

Sift ingredients together well. Combine liquids and whisk. Add liquids to dry mixture and stir to keep lumps from forming.

Heat the griddle until it is hot and spoon on the batter and lower the heat. If necessary, smooth the batter to even it out with the back of the spoon. When little bubbles form, turn the cakes to cook the other side. Serve hot.

Variation: Substitute buckwheat flour for half the flour and increase the baking soda to 2 teaspoons.

Serves 4 to 6. (Makes 8 to 12 griddlecakes)

Per Serving: 3 mg cholesterol; 1 gm saturated fat

French Toast

This French toast is perfect. No need to give it up on a low cholesterol diet. The Dupont Silverstone™ skillet eliminates the need for oil but you may wish to spray the pan with PAM™. The imitation butter imparts a buttery flavor.

2 Egg Watchers™ eggs, lightly beaten
1 fresh egg white, lightly beaten
1 teaspoon maple syrup
1 teaspoon skim milk
2 tablespoons nonfat dry milk

2 1/2-ounce-packages Butter Buds™ or a few sprinkles Molly McButter™ (optional)
6 slices white or brown bread
For Garnish:
Fruit syrup or maple syrup or powdered sugar
Fresh fruit

Beat imitation eggs, egg white, syrup, milk, dry milk, and Butter Buds™ or Molly McButter™ until smooth. Dip bread in imitation egg mixture and fry in hot non-stick skillet until brown on each side.

Serve with maple or fruit syrup or sprinkle with powdered sugar. Fresh fruit or berries may be served on the side.

Serves 2 to 4

Per Serving: 0 mg cholesterol; 0 gm saturated fat

CHAPTER NINE

Cholesterol and Saturated Fat Content of Over 500 Foods

• Eggs • Milk, Cream and Ice Cream • Cheese • Beef • Lamb
• Pork • Poultry • Luncheon Meats, Prepared Meats and Sausages
• Fish • Shellfish • Animal Fats • Margarines • Fish Oils
• Vegetable Oils • Salad Dressing • Breads • Selected Foods

*L*ooking at the headings of the following charts, you will see next to each Product, the Total Fat, Saturated Fat, Monounsaturated Fat, Polyunsaturated Fat and at the far right, Cholesterol. All of the fats are fatty acids and are listed in grams (g). Cholesterol is listed in milligrams (mg).

When you look under the total fat column for the chicken egg you will see it is 9.26 which is the addition of the three fats. Saturated fat numbers are important. Scanning down the Saturated Fat column, "chicken eggs, dried yolks only" stand out as having the most saturated fat, a product you want to stay away from. The cholesterol value of that product is an astronomical 2928, clearly one to avoid. The two columns that are the most important for heart health are saturated fat and cholesterol. You want them both to be comparatively low.

The other two fats, monounsaturated and polyunsaturated (as well as the total fat content) are of interest to those who are dieting, who may wish to raise or lower their polyunsaturated or monounsaturated fats, or who might just wish to know what the figures are. For instance, you might want to select a nut that has little saturated fat. You'll find walnuts very low, almonds and pecans higher. The charts enable you to make comparisons.

Values for meat and poultry are based on both cooked and raw weights; fish is all raw weight. There are minor differences between cooked and raw weight.

Eggs

Eggs top the list of products most implicated in raising cholesterol levels in the United States. Egg yolks prepared in mousses, sauces like Hollandaise, sponge cakes, mayonnaises, some mustards and many other dishes, negatively affect our diets and our heart health. The Department of Agriculture has recently revised the egg cholesterol figures upward to the astronomically high figure of 1,602 milligrams of cholesterol for each three and one half ounces of yolk. That is about 200 to 400 milligrams per egg yolk depending on the size of the egg. The total amount of daily ingested cholesterol shouldn't top 300, with 250 being the target amount. You can see how one egg alone can exceed more than the recommended intake for the entire 24-hour day.

This might surprise you—turkey eggs are 933 milligrams of cholesterol for three and one half ounces of whole egg; duck eggs are 884. Quail eggs also come in at 844. Eggs are also high in saturated fat. Obviously, one quail egg, because of its size, is less than any other if eaten on a per egg basis. A couple of eggs—scrambled or fried in butter or with cheese—can easily give you one meal well over a thousand milligrams of cholesterol. Conversely, eggs are an easy way to reduce cholesterol because frozen egg substitutes made with fresh egg white are excellent and simple replacements as shown in many of our recipes.

Cholesterol and Fatty Acid Content of Eggs

(2 chicken eggs equal about 3 1/2 ounces)

Product	Total Fat	Saturated Fat	Mono-unsaturated Fat	Poly-unsaturated Fat	Cholesterol
	g	*g*	*g*	*g*	*mg*
Chicken egg (1 egg)	4.6	1.7	2.2	0.7	275
Chicken egg (3 1/2 oz)	9.26	3.35	4.46	1.45	548
Chicken egg white	0.0	0.0	0.0	0.0	0
Chicken, yolks	27.33	9.89	13.16	4.28	1602
Chicken eggs, dried, whole	34.7	12.56	16.71	5.43	1918
Chicken eggs, dried yolks only	50.83	18.4	24.47	7.96	2928
Duck egg	12.64	3.68	6.52	1.22	884
Goose egg	11.02	3.60	5.75	1.67	N/A
Quail egg	9.2	3.56	4.32	1.32	844
Turkey egg	9.86	3.63	4.57	1.66	933
Egg substitute	10.6	1.93	2.43	6.24	2

g = gram
mg = milligram
Amount in 3 1/2 ounces unless otherwise noted (2 chicken eggs equal about 3 1/2 ounces)

N/A = Not Available
TR = trace (less than 0.05 grams per 100 grams of food)

Milk, Cream, and Ice Cream

We can still enjoy dairy products and have healthy hearts if we become knowledgeable consumers. There is a big difference in the cholesterol of whole milk and skim, 14 milligrams for 3 1/2 ounces of whole, 2 milligrams for skim milk. The highest cholesterol milk products outside of cheese are: cream, cream cheese, whipping cream, condensed whole milk, dry whole milk, and ice cream. Low fat yogurt, skim milk, ice milk (versus ice cream) and dry skim milk are all quite low and can be used often.

Some coffee whiteners have no cholesterol but are often very high in saturated fat (as is non-dairy whipped cream) because they contain palm or coconut oil, heavily used in this country. One brand of imitation sour cream, King Low Cholesterol™ contains coconut oil; another brand made by the same company has no coconut oil. It's called King Cholesterol Free™. Also, buttermilk can be made with whole milk or skim milk. Check the label. Milk products and dairy substitutes need not be eliminated but should be used carefully and with knowledge.

Cholesterol and Fatty Acid Content of Milk, Cream, and Ice Cream

Product	Total Fat	Saturated Fat	Mono-unsaturated Fat	Poly-unsaturated Fat	Cholesterol
	g	g	g	g	mg
Buttermilk (whole milk)	2.20	1.30	.60	.10	9
Coffee cream, light	18.32	12.02	5.58	.72	66
Coffee cream, medium, 2.5% fat	23.71	15.56	7.22	.93	88
Coffee whitener, powdered	33.50	32.52	.97	.01	0
Coffee whitener, liquid	9.53	1.94	7.56	.03	0
Cream, half and half		7.16	3.32	.43	37
Dessert topping, powdered	37.70	36.65	.60	.45	0
Eggnog	19.00	11.30	5.70	.90	149
Ice cream, French vanilla	11.67	7.81	3.86	.57	89
Ice cream, vanilla		8.90	4.10	.50	59
Ice milk	2.50	1.64	.76	.10	8
Milk, buffalo		4.60	1.72	.15	19
Milk, chocolate, skim	1.90	1.24	.59	.07	7
Milk, chocolate, whole	5.91	2.10	.99	.12	12
Milk, whole (3.7% fat - most milk is 4% fat but the government (USDA) only gives the figures for 3.7% and 3.3%)	3.48	2.28	1.06	.14	14
Imitation milk	3.22	3.04	.18	.01	TR

Cholesterol and Saturated Fat Content of Over 500 Foods

Cholesterol and Fatty Acid Content of Milk, Cream, and Ice Cream

Product	Total Fat	Saturated Fat	Mono-unsaturated Fat	Poly-unsaturated Fat	Cholesterol
	g	g	g	g	mg
Milk, 2%, low fat	1.03	1.20	.56	.07	8
Milk, 1%, low fat	1.01	.66	.31	.04	4
Milk, skim (some skim milk is actually 1% fat—check all labels)	0.143	.117	.019	.007	2
Buttermilk	0.83	.55	.25	.03	4
Dry milk, whole	25.32	16.74	7.92	.66	97
Dry milk, skim, calcium reduced	0.155	.124	.024	.007	2
Condensed, sweetened whole milk	7.04	5.49	1.21	.34	34
Evaporated whole milk	7.17	4.59	2.34	.24	29
Milk, condensed whole	8.26	5.49	2.43	.34	34
Milk, dried, nonfat	0.73	.50	.20	.03	20
Milk, evaporated, skim	0.18	.121	.062	.006	4
Milk, goat	3.93	2.67	1.11	.15	11
Milk, human	4.17	2.01	1.66	.50	14
Milk, malted	8.05	4.24	2.59	1.22	20
Milk, sheep	6.63	4.60	1.72	.31	N/A
Milk, skim	.60	.40	.20	TR	5
Shake, vanilla, thick	2.88	1.89	.88	.11	12
Sherbet (made with dairy products)	4.04	1.23	.24	.07	7
Sour cream	19.88	13.05	6.05	.78	44
Sour cream, imitation (with coconut)	20.09	17.79	2.24	.06	0
Sour cream, imitation (without corn oil)	N/A	3.00	N/A	N/A	0
Whey	.341	.23	.10	.011	2
Whipped cream, pressurized	20.25	13.83	6.42	.82	76
Whipping cream, heavy, unwhipped	35.07	23.03	10.69	1.37	137
Whipping cream, light, unwhipped	29.31	17.34	9.29	.88	111
Yogurt, lowfat	1.47	1.00	.43	.04	6
Yogurt, plain	3.06	2.10	.89	.07	13
Yogurt, skim	.17	.116	.049	.005	2

g = gram
mg = milligram
Amount in 3 1/2 ounces unless otherwise noted

N/A = Not Available
TR = trace (less than 0.05 grams per 100 grams of food

Cheese

Cheese, a staple of many American diets, varies greatly in cholesterol, saturated fat, and salt content. Those with high saturated fat are Cheddar, American processed, Gruyere, Fontina, Provolone, Swiss, and Gouda. At the high end in cholesterol are Port du Salut, Gruyere, Brie (wouldn't you know), Fontina, American processed, Muenster, Swiss, Tilsit, Cheshire, Romano, Colby, and any of the fancy dessert and triple creme cheeses.

We are so accustomed to relying on cheese for pastas, vegetables, and sauces that it's one of the hardest areas in which to modify our saturated fat and cholesterol intake. On the other hand, it can be a simple area in which to make massive reductions in unhealthy fat and cholesterol intakes on a daily basis. Here are some tips that may help you to select which cheese to serve if your family really craves it and just can't give it up.

On the low side (for both cholesterol and saturated fat) are low-fat cottage cheeses, but be aware that we tend to eat greater amounts of it than other cheeses. Even then, low fat or nonfat cottage cheese is one of the least "dangerous" cheeses.

• Part skim ricotta cheese is also very low in cholesterol.

• Skim milk mozzarella is also relatively low in cholesterol. The very low cholesterol cheese slices like Dorman's Lo-Chol™ are suitable for nibbling if purchased in the brick style and cut into chunks.

• Provolone is lower in cholesterol, but it is higher in saturated fat. It is still the lowest in cholesterol of the cheeses, according to figures available from the government (USDA).

• Bleu cheese at 75 grams of cholesterol, and Camembert at 72 are also somewhat lower than most.

• Grated cheeses like Parmesan are lower in cholesterol but have a higher salt content. Romano is higher in cholesterol than Parmesan. Because we usually use less cheese that we sprinkle on dishes, Parmesan and the other grated cheeses are good cheese choices. We can also reduce the quantity of these cheeses more easily.

Cholesterol and Fatty Acid Content of Cheese

Product	Total Fat	Saturated Fat	Mono-unsaturated Fat	Poly-unsaturated Fat	Cholesterol
	g	g	g	g	mg
American cheese	8.9	5.6	2.5	0.3	27
Bleu cheese	8.2	5.3	2.2	0.2	21
Brie	N/A	N/A	N/A	N/A	33
Camembert	6.9	4.3	2.0	0.2	20
Cheddar	9.4	6.0	2.7	0.3	30
Cheshire	N/A	N/A	N/A	N/A	43
Colby	9.3	6.7	3.0	0.3	31
Cottage cheese, creamed 3 1/2 oz	4.27	2.85	1.28	.14	15
Cottage cheese, dry curd 3 1/2 oz	0.45	.27	.11	.07	7
Cottage cheese, low fat 2% 3 1/2 oz	1.5	1.22	.22	.06	8
Cottage cheese, low fat 1% 3 1/2 oz	0.96	.64	.29	.03	4
Edam	8.0	5.8	2.0	TR	29
Feta	6.4	4.9	1.5	TR	29
Fontina	9.8	6.4	2.9	.65	38
Gouda	8.4	5.8	2.5	TR	38
Gruyere	9.6	6.3	3.3	.05	36
Limburger	8.3	5.5	2.8	TR	30
Monterey Jack	N/A	N/A	N/A	N/A	N/A
Mozzarella, low moisture	7.6	5.1	2.3	.2	29
Mozzarella, made with part skim	4.5	2.9	1.3	TR	16
Muenster	8.5	5.4	2.5	0.2	27
Neufchatel	7.1	4.9	2.2	TR	25
Parmesan, grated	7.9	5.4	2.5	TR	22
Port du Salut	8.6	5.5	3.1	TR	41
Provolone	7.6	5.6	2.0	TR	23
Ricotta, part skim	2.2	1.4	0.7	0.1	9
Ricotta, whole milk	3.9	2.7	1.2	TR	17
Romano	N/A	N/A	N/A	N/A	33
Roquefort	9.2	6.4	2.8	.04	30
Swiss	7.8	5.0	2.1	0.3	26
Tilsit	8.2	3.0	2.3	0.2	34
American cheese, pasteurized and processed	9.8	6.5	2.9	0.3	31
American pimiento cheese	9.8	6.5	2.9	0.3	31

g = gram
mg = milligram
Amount in just over 1 ounce unless otherwise noted

N/A = Not Available
TR = trace (less than 0.05 grams per 100 grams of food)

Beef

The cholesterol figures for beef are similar to turkey, chicken, lamb, pork, and some fish. The saturated fat content in beef is usually higher than in fish or fowl. As in other animals, the cholesterol count of beef brains, kidneys, sweetbreads, and liver are extraordinarily high and not recommended for regular consumption.

Most lean beef, especially select grade cuts instead of prime or choice grade, is only moderately high in cholesterol and the saturated fat content of many cuts such as top round, pot roast, rib eye and the organ meats is quite low.

Cholesterol is in both the muscle and the fat of meat in almost equal amounts. Trim away all visible fat and roast, broil, grill or heat it so the remaining fat drips away.

When purchasing or ordering franks, sausage, and hamburger, be aware that the fat content may vary greatly depending upon the amount of the added fat. Beef can be enjoyed in a low cholesterol diet but it definitely shouldn't be eaten on a daily basis. One nine-ounce serving of lean chuck roast has all the cholesterol (250-300 grams) recommended daily. Veal is even higher than beef in cholesterol.

Cholesterol and Fatty Acid Content of Beef

Product	Total Fat	Saturated Fat	Mono-unsaturated Fat	Poly-unsaturated Fat	Cholesterol
	g	g	g	g	mg
Beef bologna	26.88	12.07	13.80	1.01	58
Beef heart	4.3	1.68	1.25	1.37	193
Beef hot dog	27.05	12.05	13.62	1.38	61
Beef kidneys	2.57	1.09	.74	.74	387
Beef liver	6.31	2.82	1.69	1.80	482
Beef round	14.89	6.75	7.38	.76	84
Bottom round	12.99	5.66	6.74	.59	96
Brains	10.03	3.74	3.98	2.31	1995
Brisket corned beef, braised	16.23	6.34	9.22	.67	98
Chuck	22.13	10.43	10.80	.90	73
Eye of round	12.79	5.83	6.43	.53	73
Flank steak (cooked)	14.28	6.63	7.16	.49	72
Ground (fried)	15.34	6.94	7.74	.66	95
Ground	27.00	10.80	11.60	1.00	85
Lunch meat	24.30	11.18	12.25	.87	64
Pastrami	25.88	10.42	14.47	.99	93
Pot roast	8.72	3.79	4.53	.40	101
Rib eye	10.38	4.93	5.10	.35	80
Ribs, whole	27.01	12.70	13.45	1.06	86
Short ribs	38.21	17.80	18.88	1.53	94
Sirloin	16.61	7.67	8.24	.73	90
Summer sausage	3.53	1.65	1.68	.20	41
Sweetbreads	N/A	N/A	N/A	N/A	294
T-Bone, choice lean	7.20	3.20	3.40	.30	60
Tenderloin	25.08	11.74	12.23	1.11	88
Tip round	13.34	6.09	6.65	.60	83
Tongue	19.18	8.93	9.47	.78	107
Top loin	16.73	7.79	8.25	.69	79
Top round	7.45	3.36	3.70	.40	85
Tripe (chitlins)	3.41	2.03	1.31	.07	95

g = gram
mg = milligram
Amount in 3 1/2 ounces unless otherwise noted

N/A = Not Available
TR = trace (less than 0.05 grams per 100 grams of food)

Lamb

Lamb is about the same as beef in cholesterol, with the exception of chops, which are higher but slightly lower in saturated fat than a comparable cut of beef. Unfortunately, mutton isn't readily available in America to add variety to our diets. If you are a lamb eater, lean mutton is lower in cholesterol and saturated fat than lamb. It is flavorful and slightly chewier than most meat available here, so enjoy it occasionally on your next trip to Europe or other countries.

Lamb in general should be eaten sparingly on a low cholesterol, low saturated fat diet. Make sure the cut is visibly lean and cook it fairly well. Leg of lamb, butterflied (the bone cut out), marinated for a few hours, and then grilled outdoors until medium-well-done and sliced thinly on the bias is an ideal way to prepare lamb.

Cholesterol and Fatty Acid Content of Lamb

Product	Total Fat	Saturated Fat	Mono-unsaturated Fat	Poly-unsaturated Fat	Cholesterol
	g	g	g	g	mg
Lamb chops, arm, some fat	20.00	9.20	8.00	1.20	102
Lamb chops, arm, lean	10.00	4.40	4.00	.60	90
Leg, some fat	13.00	5.60	4.90	.80	78
Leg, lean	8.00	3.20	2.90	.50	86
Loin, some fat	17.00	7.90	6.90	1.00	80
Loin, lean	7.00	3.30	3.10	.50	77
Rib, some fat	26.00	12.10	10.60	1.50	77
Rib, lean	9.00	4.20	4.00	.60	66

g = gram
mg = milligram
Amount in 3 1/2 ounces unless otherwise noted

N/A = Not Available
TR = trace (less than 0.05 grams per 100 grams of food)

Pork

Pork can fool you. Many think of pork as being very high in cholesterol and saturated fat. For daily fare a pork meal gives us more saturated fat and cholesterol than we want in a low cholesterol, low saturated-fat diet, as does all red meat. But lean pork isn't higher in fat and cholesterol than beef. In fact, extra lean cured ham has only 30 milligrams of cholesterol and 1.60 grams of saturated fat per 3 ounces, the lowest of all red meats and lower than chicken and some fish (according to USDA figures). Canadian bacon at 58 milligrams of cholesterol is still low; lean pimiento loaf is low and so is cooked lean pork shoulder. This is compared to a lean cut of beef which has 75 milligrams for 3 ounces (as does skinless chicken).

When buying pork, look out for marbling and excess fat. Buy lean cuts such as a tenderloin and have excess fat removed. Remove all fat when selecting chops and make your own sausage with tenderloin and no fat, or use Puritan™ oil. Again, the average cut of pork isn't much different than beef or chicken in cholesterol content but the saturated fat content is somewhat higher.

As in beef, the organ meats, liver, brains, etc., are the highest in cholesterol. Spareribs are fairly high as are some picnic shoulders. But pork need not be eliminated. Some cuts of pork such as salt pork, fat back, and bacon do have a high saturated fat content.

Pork is a nutritious, high protein food that can be enjoyed on a low cholesterol diet especially when properly selected and prepared. Remember, fatty pork or any fatty meat isn't heart healthy. Certainly, if you're trying to lose weight, tenderloin with only 2.23 grams of total fat in 3 1/2 ounces is a much better choice than even lean ribs with 21.78 grams of fat.

Cholesterol and Fatty Acid Content of Pork

Product	Total Fat	Saturated Fat	Mono-unsaturated Fat	Poly-unsaturated Fat	Cholesterol
	g	g	g	g	mg
Fat back	89.49	32.17	41.91	10.41	57
Pork belly	49.68	19.33	24.70	5.65	72
Pork loin	11.93	4.49	5.86	1.58	93
Ham, lean	4.90	1.88	2.45	.57	68
Loin, lean	6.82	2.61	3.42	.79	60
Rib (lean and fat, cooked)	21.78	8.44	10.85	2.49	64
Center ribs (lean and fat, cooked)	24.57	9.51	12.08	2.98	93
Tenderloin	2.23	.85	1.12	.26	65
Picnic/shoulder	11.18	4.21	5.49	1.48	114
Bratwurst	24.25	9.32	12.19	2.74	60
Spareribs, cooked	29.44	11.76	14.17	3.51	121
Sausage, Italian, cooked	24.26	9.03	11.95	3.28	78
Fresh sausage, cooked	28.52	10.81	13.90	3.81	83
Brains, cooked	5.34	2.15	1.72	1.47	2552
Chitterlings, cooked	27.00	10.10	9.68	7.22	143
Pork ears, cooked	N/A	N/A	N/A	N/A	90
Pigs feet, cooked	11.44	4.28	5.81	1.35	100
Heart, cooked	3.82	1.34	1.18	1.30	221

Cholesterol and Fatty Acid Content of Pork

Product	Total Fat	Saturated Fat	Mono-unsaturated Fat	Poly-unsaturated Fat	Cholesterol
	g	*g*	*g*	*g*	*mg*
Kidneys, cooked	2.37	1.04	1.07	.26	319
Liver, cooked	2.56	1.17	.52	.87	355
Tongue, cooked	17.17	6.45	8.79	1.93	146
Ham, cured, extra lean	4.51	1.60	2.47	.44	30
Breakfast strips	34.82	12.77	16.40	5.65	105
Braunschweiger	24.54	10.90	14.91	3.74	85
Salt pork	76.72	29.38	37.94	9.40	86
Canadian bacon	7.64	2.84	4.04	.81	58
Minced ham	19.22	7.18	9.57	2.47	70
Head cheese	14.69	4.94	8.10	1.65	87
Liverwurst	26.52	10.59	13.33	2.60	158
Pimento loaf	20.02	7.85	9.60	2.57	37
Polish sausage	29.93	10.33	13.52	3.08	70
Salami	31.63	11.89	16.00	3.74	N/A
Link sausage, cooked	24.72	11.32	14.64	3.76	68
Cooked shoulder, (bought pre-cooked)	20.07	7.95	9.78	2.34	53

g = gram
mg = milligram
Amount in 3 1/2 ounces unless otherwise noted

N/A = Not Available
TR = trace (less than 0.05 grams per 100 grams of food)

Poultry

Chicken, turkey, duck, goose, squab, guinea hen, and other fowl are all excellent meat protein in our diet. Poultry, however, isn't really a substitute for lean red meat because the cholesterol is about the same, even when the skin is removed. Beef and pork have more saturated fat than most fowl, but not much more.

Chicken and turkey skin are high in saturated fat, topped by duck and presumably goose skin. (Fat figures for goose skin aren't available.) All of the poultry organ meat such as liver, are very high in cholesterol (although low in saturated fat). Poultry livers run over 450 milligrams for 3 1/2 ounces of turkey liver, over 500 for duck, and 400 plus for chicken. The cholesterol count for goose liver is unavailable, unfortunately, but is probably 600 plus because butter or fat is often added to blend it. Frying poultry in butter raises the cholesterol and saturated fat content even higher. Eating the birds broiled or baked without skin makes sense in a low cholesterol, low fat diet. Even the Kentucky Fried Chicken™ people are testing a broiled skinless chicken because more and more people just don't want that fatty unhealthy skin.

Three ounces of duck flesh without skin has 75 grams of cholesterol; guinea hen 63, and light meat chicken is 74 (lean beef has 75.) These are good choices for a low cholesterol diet. Use your own eye to judge the amount of fat on fowl. Many chicken and chicken parts are advertised as having little or no fat. A quick look at the package, or while examining a roaster, reveals this too often is untrue. Cut or pick it all off before cooking for less cholesterol and saturated fat.

Cholesterol and Fatty Acid Content of Poultry

Product	Total Fat	Saturated Fat	Mono-unsaturated Fat	Poly-unsaturated Fat	Cholesterol
	g	g	g	g	mg
Fried chicken, broiler	13.66	4.16	5.99	3.51	112
Baked chicken, broiler	15.8	4.61	7.09	4.10	87
Roasted chicken	19.1	3.79	5.34	9.97	88
Stewed chicken, fryer	5.77	1.84	2.39	1.54	83
Chicken skin	29.43	9.08	13.54	6.81	109
Chicken giblets	2.94	1.49	1.19	.26	393
Chicken gizzard	3.51	1.20	1.09	1.22	130
Chicken heart, raw	6.24	2.66	2.37	2.71	136
Chicken heart, fried	6.57	2.26	2.01	2.30	242
Chicken liver, raw	2.89	1.30	.95	.64	435
Chicken liver, simmered	4.08	1.84	1.34	.90	631
Chicken, light meat with skin, fried	10.81	3.32	4.80	2.69	87
Chicken, dark meat with skin, fried	16.96	4.95	7.85	4.43	89
Chicken, light meat with skin, stewed	8.84	2.80	3.92	2.12	74
Chicken, dark meat with skin, roasted	14.05	4.37	6.19	3.49	91
Chicken, light meat without skin, roasted	3.79	1.27	1.54	.98	85
Chicken, dark meat without skin, roasted	8.48	2.66	3.56	2.26	93
Chicken, stewing, stewed	9.98	3.10	4.05	2.83	83
Chicken, capon, roasted	10.51	3.28	4.71	2.52	103
Duck, flesh and skin, roasted	26.22	9.67	12.70	3.65	84
Duck, flesh only, roasted	4.61	2.32	1.54	.75	77
Duck liver	2.78	1.44	.71	.63	515
Wild duck, breast, without skin	3.11	1.32	1.21	.58	N/A

Cholesterol and Fatty Acid Content of Poultry

Product	Total Fat g	Saturated Fat g	Mono-unsaturated Fat g	Poly-unsaturated Fat g	Cholesterol mg
Goose, flesh and skin, roasted	19.64	6.87	10.25	2.52	91
Goose, without skin, roasted	10.44	4.56	4.34	1.54	96
Goose liver	2.66	1.49	.81	.26	650
Guinea hen	N/A	N/A	N/A	N/A	63
Pheasant	8.2	2.70	4.32	1.18	N/A
Quail	10.34	3.38	4.18	2.78	N/A
Squab (pigeon)	21.22	8.43	9.72	3.07	N/A
Squab, breast meat, without skin	2.97	1.18	1.61	.18	90
Turkey, roasted with skin	8.24	2.77	3.05	2.42	95
Turkey, skin only, cooked	36.32	10.34	16.90	9.08	113
Turkey giblets, cooked	3.85	1.54	1.15	1.16	418
Turkey gizzard, cooked	2.99	1.11	.76	1.12	232
Turkey heart, cooked	3.41	1.75	1.19	.47	226
Turkey liver, cooked	3.45	1.88	.59	1.06	626
Turkey neck without skin	5.35	2.44	.73	2.18	122
Turkey, light meat with skin, roasted	7.14	2.34	2.84	2.01	76
Turkey, dark meat with skin, roasted	7.16	3.45	3.65	.02	89
Turkey, white meat without skin, roasted	0.51	.38	.12	.01	86
Turkey, dark meat without skin, roasted	2.09	1.45	.93	.01	112
Chicken franks	10.68	5.54	1.10	4.04	101
Chicken roll	4.01	2.02	.39	1.60	50
Goose pate	N/A	N/A	N/A	N/A	750
Turkey loaf	0.91	.48	.15	.28	41
Turkey franks	N/A	N/A	N/A	N/A	107

g = gram
mg = milligram
Amount in 3 1/2 ounces unless otherwise noted

N/A = Not Available
TR = trace (less than 0.05 grams per 100 grams of food)

Luncheon Meats, Prepared Meats, and Sausages

Some of the prepared meats—so-called luncheon meats and sausages—are very high in cholesterol and saturated fats, usually because of the added fat (which is generally between 40 to 70 percent). As an example, with over 32 grams of saturated fat in 3 1/2 ounces of blood sausage, 27 grams in hot dogs, 31 grams in liver sausage, and 27 in Thuringer, you can easily see by the numbers that the saturated fat content is astronomical. Add that to the

Cholesterol and Saturated Fat Content of Over 500 Foods

already high cholesterol count in these very same foods, and you know that these items are usually too high for most people to have regularly for a healthy heart and arteries. Many of these foods, like hot dogs and bologna, are practically staples in some diets, and their consumption should be reduced or eliminated in low cholesterol diets.

Cholesterol and Fatty Acid Content of Luncheon Meats, Prepared Meats and Sausages

Product	Total Fat g	Saturated Fat g	Mono-unsaturated Fat g	Poly-unsaturated Fat g	Cholesterol mg
Beerwurst or beer salami (beef)	27.11	12.00	N/A	N/A	56
Beer salami (pork)	17.62	6.28	N/A	N/A	59
Blood sausage	32.68	13.37	N/A	N/A	120
Bologna (beef)	25.99	11.66	N/A	N/A	56
Bologna (pork)	18.78	6.88	N/A	N/A	59
Braunschweiger or liver sausage	31.55	10.90	N/A	N/A	156
Chicken roll	6.58	2.02	N/A	N/A	50
Corned beef	6.09	6.68	N/A	N/A	43
Frankfurter, beef	27.47	11.96	N/A	N/A	48
Frankfurter, pork	22.16	10.76	N/A	N/A	50
Frankfurter, chicken	18.06	5.54	N/A	N/A	101
Frankfurter, turkey	N/A	N/A	N/A	N/A	107
Ham, chopped, canned	17.5	6.28	N/A	N/A	49
Ham, sliced	4.45	1.62	N/A	N/A	47
Head cheese	14.69	4.94	N/A	N/A	81
Italian or pork link sausage	24.3	9.07	N/A	N/A	78
Kielbasa	25.93	9.91	N/A	N/A	67
Knockwurst	25.93	10.20	N/A	N/A	58
Pate fois gras	N/A	N/A	N/A	N/A	150
Pepperoni	5.79	2.29	N/A	N/A	46
Pimiento loaf	20.02	7.85	N/A	N/A	37
Salami, beef or pork	19.21	8.09	N/A	N/A	65
Thuringer, beef or pork	27.05	12.03	N/A	N/A	68
Turkey roll	6.12	2.04	N/A	N/A	55
Vienna sausage	23.51	9.29	N/A	N/A	52

g = gram
mg = milligram
Amount in 3 1/2 ounces unless otherwise noted

N/A = Not Available
TR = trace (less than 0.05 grams per 100 grams of food)

Fish

There is much new information available about fish; it appears fish is helpful for healthy hearts in a low cholesterol, low saturated fat diet. If you examine cholesterol counts and saturated fat content in fish, you'll see they differ considerably.

Caviar or fish eggs tops the list; it is also high in saturated fat. Another fish fairly high in cholesterol is eel. Moderately high are striped bass, herring, yellow perch, pike, salmon, most smelt, plaice, pollock, and catfish. They are all about the same as lean beef and chicken; however the saturated fat content is much lower, which makes them healthier. Fish lowest in cholesterol are cod, yellow tail, rockfish, halibut, mullet, sprat, swordfish, tuna, and whiting.

Diets in general all contain more animal (fish and poultry too), protein than we probably need. Having fish three times a day would not be helpful and could be harmful. Replacing fish for meat and poultry meals can help lower your cholesterol and saturated fat intake, so it is suggested that you vary the fish, both for the variety of nutrients and just for the fun of experiencing new foods.

Cholesterol and Fatty Acid Content of Fish

Product	Total Fat	Saturated Fat	Mono-unsaturated Fat	Poly-unsaturated Fat	Cholesterol
	g	g	g	g	mg
Anchovy, European	4.8	1.3	1.2	1.6	N/A
Bass, freshwater	2.0	.4	.7	.7	59
Bass, striped	2.3	.5	.7	.8	80
Bluefish	6.5	1.4	2.9	1.6	59
Carp	5.6	1.1	2.3	1.4	67
Catfish, brown bullhead	2.7	.6	1.0	.8	75
Catfish, channel	4.3	1.0	1.6	1.0	58
Caviar	93.9	.1	N/A	N/A	150
Cod, Atlantic	.7	.1	.1	.3	43
Cod, Pacific	.6	.1	.1	.2	37
Croaker, Atlantic	3.2	1.1	1.2	.5	61
Dogfish, spiny	10.2	2.2	4.2	2.7	52
Dolphin	.7	.2	.1	.2	N/A
Eel	18.8	3.5	10.9	1.4	108
Flounder, yellowtail	1.0	.2	.3	.3	46
Grouper	1.3	.3	.1	.2	49
Haddock	.7	.1	.1	.2	63

Cholesterol and Fatty Acid Content of Fish

Product	Total Fat	Saturated Fat	Mono-unsaturated Fat	Poly-unsaturated Fat	Cholesterol
	g	g	g	g	mg
Halibut, Greenland	13.8	2.4	8.4	1.4	46
Halibut, Pacific	2.3	.3	.8	.7	32
Herring, Atlantic	9.0	2.0	3.7	2.1	60
Herring, Pacific	13.9	3.3	6.9	2.4	77
Herring, round	4.4	1.3	.8	1.5	28
Mackerel, king	13.0	2.5	5.9	3.2	53
Mullet, striped	3.7	1.2	1.1	1.1	49
Mullet, unspecified	4.4	.3	1.3	1.5	34
Ocean perch	1.6	.3	.6	.5	42
Perch, white	2.5	.6	.9	.7	80
Perch, yellow	.9	.2	.1	.4	90
Pike, northern	.7	.1	.1	.2	39
Pike, walleye	1.2	.2	.5	.5	86
Plaice, European	1.5	.3	.5	.4	70
Pollock	1.0	.1	.1	.5	71
Pompano, Florida	9.5	3.5	2.6	1.4	50
Rockfish, Canary	1.8	.4	.5	.6	34
Sablefish	15.3	3.2	8.1	2.0	49
Salmon, chum (coho similar)	6.6	1.5	2.9	1.5	74
Salmon, canned	5.4	1.2	2.4	1.4	60
Sea bass	1.5	.4	.3	.5	41
Seatrout, sand	2.3	.7	.8	.4	N/A
Seatrout, spotted	1.7	.5	.4	.3	N/A
Shark	1.9	.3	.4	.8	44
Sheepshead	2.4	.6	.7	.5	N/A
Smelt, pond	.7	.2	.1	.3	72
Smelt, rainbow	2.6	.5	.7	.9	70
Smelt, sweet	4.6	1.6	1.2	1.0	25
Snapper, red	1.2	.2	.2	.4	N/A
Sole, European	1.2	.3	.4	.2	50
Sprat	5.8	1.4	2.0	1.5	38
Sturgeon, Atlantic	6.0	1.2	1.7	2.1	N/A
Sturgeon, common	3.3	.8	1.6	.2	N/A
Sunfish, pumpkinseed	.7	.1	.1	.2	67
Swordfish	2.1	.6	.8	.2	39
Trout, Arctic char	7.7	1.6	.8	.9	N/A
Trout, brook	2.7	.7	.8	.9	68
Trout, lake	9.7	1.7	3.6	3.4	48
Trout, rainbow	3.4	.6	1.0	1.2	57
Tuna, albacore	4.9	1.2	1.1	1.8	54
Tuna, bluefin	6.6	1.7	2.2	2.0	38
Tuna, canned	7.0	1.4	1.9	3.1	55
Tuna, skipjack	1.9	.7	.4	.6	47
Whitefish, lake	6.0	.9	2.0	2.2	60

Cholesterol and Fatty Acid Content of Fish

Product	Total Fat	Saturated Fat	Mono-unsaturated Fat	Poly-unsaturated Fat	Cholesterol
	g	*g*	*g*	*g*	*mg*
Whiting, European	.5	.1	.1	.1	31
Wolffish, Atlantic	2.4	.4	.8	.8	N/A

g = gram
mg = milligram
N/A = Not Available
TR = trace (less than 0.05 grams per 100 grams of food)
Amount in 3 1/2 ounces of raw fish unless otherwise noted (fish is raw)
*Some USDA figures only given for raw product. Certain forms of cooking—broiling, microwaving, grilling, steaming—reduces the fats. (Note that caviar is usually raw.)

Shellfish

Shellfish (crustaceans) and mollusk cholesterol figures have recently been lowered. There have even been rumors that there are different kinds of cholesterol in ingested food and the cholesterol in shellfish isn't as bad as the cholesterol in animals. From what *we* know, the fish and shellfish cholesterol is just as harmful as any other ingested cholesterol. The difference is that there is almost no saturated fat in most shellfish.

Shrimp, lobster, crayfish, crab, and conch are somewhat high in cholesterol. But Dungeness crab, Japanese shrimp, scallops, clams, mussels and oysters are moderate to low.

Salt content may also be high in shellfish, as some partially prepared shrimp and lobsters are salted just after being caught. Usually the astronomically high cholesterol associated with shellfish dishes has a close connection with the sauce as in lobster Thermidor which is heavy in cheese; or the preparation of oysters Rockefeller made with bacon; or shrimp scampi which has large amounts of butter. Crab may also have butter or mayonnaise garnishing it. Eliminating shellfish isn't necessary, but eating it judiciously, as with all animal protein, is advised.

Cholesterol and Saturated Fat Content of Over 500 Foods

Cholesterol and Fatty Acid Content of Shellfish

Product	Total Fat	Saturated Fat	Mono-unsaturated Fat	Poly-unsaturated Fat	Cholesterol
	g	*g*	*g*	*g*	*mg*
Crab, Alaska King	.8	.1	.1	.3	N/A
Crab, blue	1.3	.2	.2	.5	78
Crab, Dungeness	1.0	.1	.2	.3	59
Crab, queen	1.1	.1	.2	.4	127
Crayfish, unspecified	1.4	.3	.4	.3	158
Lobster, European	.8	.1	.2	.2	129
Lobster, northern	.9	.2	.2	.2	95
Shrimp, Atlantic brown	1.5	.3	.3	.5	142
Shrimp, Atlantic white	1.5	.2	.2	.2	182
Shrimp, Japanese (kuruma) prawn	2.5	.5	.5	1.0	58
Shrimp, northern	1.5	.2	.3	.6	125
Shrimp, other	1.3	.4	.3	.3	128
Shrimp, unspecified	1.1	.2	.1	.4	147
Spiny lobster, Caribbean	1.4	.2	.2	.6	140
Spiny lobster, southern rock	1.0	.1	.2	.3	N/A
Abalone, New Zealand	1.0	.2	.2	.2	N/A
Abalone, South African	1.1	.3	.2	.2	N/A
Clam, hardshell	.6	TR	TR	.1	31
Conch, unspecified	2.7	.6	.1	.1	141
Mussel, blue	2.2	.4	.4	.5	38
Octopus, common	1.0	.3	.1	.3	N/A
Oyster, eastern	2.5	.6	.2	.7	47
Periwinkle, common	3.3	.6	.6	1.1	101
Scallop, Atlantic deepsea	.8	.1	N/A	.2	37
Scallop, unspecified	.8	.1	.1	.3	45
Squid, Atlantic	1.2	.3	.1	.5	N/A
Squid, short-finned	2.0	.4	.4	.7	N/A
Squid, unspecified	1.1	.3	.1	.4	N/A

g = gram
mg = milligram
Amount in 3 1/2 ounces raw fish unless otherwise noted

N/A = Not Available
TR = trace (less than 0.05 grams per 100 grams of food)

Animal Fats

The saturated fat and cholesterol content of the most commonly used animal fat, such as butter and lard, is easy to compare, with butter being higher in both cholesterol and saturated fat than pig fat (lard).

Butter oil, such as that used for dipping with lobster, is astronomically high in cholesterol at 556 for 3 1/2 ounces. Butter itself isn't much better. Except for tallow or mutton (lamb) fat, which few of us eat separately as a spread, butter and butter oil are also the highest in saturated fat.

Pig fat, like cracklin, which is a crispy, fried—usually Southern—side dish and sometimes sold like potato chips in packages, is fairly high in saturated fat. The lowest saturated animal fats are goose fat and turkey and chicken fat, however because of their cholesterol content they are still too high to consume regularly and should be eliminated on a low-cholesterol diet.

Cholesterol and Fatty Acid Content of Animal Fats

Product	Total Fat	Saturated Fat	Mono-unsaturated Fat	Poly-unsaturated Fat	Cholesterol
	g	*g*	*g*	*g*	*mg*
Animal fat (beef tallow)	95.6	49.8	41.8	4.0	109
Butter	76.9	50.5	23.4	3.0	219
Butter oil	94.3	61.9	28.7	3.7	256
Chicken fat	95.4	29.8	44.7	20.9	85
Duck fat	95.4	33.2	49.3	12.9	100
Goose fat	95.4	27.7	56.7	11.0	100
Pig fat (lard)	95.5	39.2	45.1	11.2	95
Sheep fat (mutton tallow)	95.7	47.3	40.6	7.8	102
Turkey fat	95.4	29.4	42.9	23.1	102

g = gram
mg = milligram
Amount in 3 1/2 ounces unless otherwise noted

N/A = Not Available
TR = trace (less than 0.05 grams per 100 grams of food)

Cholesterol and Saturated Fat Content of Over 500 Foods

In looking at the values listed for different margarines, you will see that they all have no cholesterol and are very similar in each one's amount of saturated fat, (unless they contain, palm or coconut oil, two oils to avoid). For spreading on bread, the best margarines are probably those that say 'diet' or 'less fat', which are spreads whipped with air and water. You think you're getting more than you are, which is terrific! The saturated fat content of those imitation margarines or diet margarines is half of regular margarine. Pourable margarines are also a good choice because you can control the amount you use more precisely.

People often ask what hydrogenation means. That's the hardening process to make a stick of margarine stay solid. It also means it is more saturated, which happens in the hydrogenation process. Some oils, safflower for instance, clearly have less saturated fat. Finally, in reading margarine labels, check the salt content. Some diet spreads are higher than they need to be. A word of caution: using diet spreads on hot bread or popcorn can make them soggy, because of the water content. On the plus side, adding spices and flavoring to these water-whipped products makes a particularly delicious and light spread. On the plus, plus side, they are considerably lower in calories, since fat has the single highest amount of calories of all the food we eat.

Cholesterol and Fatty Acid Content of Margarines, Imitation Margarines, and Spreads

Product	Total Fat	Saturated Fat	Mono-unsaturated Fat	Poly-unsaturated Fat	Cholesterol
	g	g	g	g	mg
Corn margarine (hard, hydrogenated)	77.0	13.2	45.8	18.0	0
Safflower, soybean and cottonseed (hard, hydrogenated)	77.0	13.3	23.0	40.7	0
Soybean, corn and cotton-seed (hard, hydrogenated)	76.9	19.8	32.0	25.1	0
Soybean and palm (hard, hydrogenated)	76.9	17.5	31.2	28.2	0
Corn (tub, hydrogenated)	76.9	14.1	31.6	31.2	0
Safflower (tub, hydrogenated)	76.9	9.2	23.2	44.5	0

Cholesterol and Fatty Acid Content of Margarines, Imitation Margarines, and Spreads

Product	Total Fat	Saturated Fat	Mono-unsaturated Fat	Poly-unsaturated Fat	Cholesterol
	g	g	g	g	mg
Soybean (tub, hydrogenated)	76.9	13.5	36.4	26.8	0
Soybean and cottonseed (tub, hydrogenated)	76.9	16.5	31.3	29.1	0
Soybean and cottonseed (liquid)	77.1	13.2	28.1	35.8	0
Imitation margarine, corn hydrogenated 40% fat	37.2	6.4	14.5	16.3	0
Imitation margarine, soybean, 40% fat, hydrogenated	37.0	6.5	16.7	13.8	0
Spread, soybean and cottonseed, 60% fat	58.0	12.0	38.9	7.1	0
Shortening, soybean	95.5	27.2	54.2	14.1	0
Shortening, with palm and coconut	94.5	91.3	2.2	1.0	0

g = gram
mg = milligram
Amount in 3 1/2 ounces unless otherwise noted

N/A = Not Available
TR = trace (less than 0.05 grams per 100 grams of food)

Fish Oils

Something to be aware of when considering additional fish oils in the diet is that the added cholesterol could be detrimental. There is no current evidence that ingesting fish oil will help your arteries or heart.

Cholesterol and Fatty Acid Content of Fish Oils

Product	Total Fat	Saturated Fat	Mono-unsaturated Fat	Poly-unsaturated Fat	Cholesterol
	g	g	g	g	mg
Cod liver oil	77.7	51.2	25.8	0.7	570
Herring oil	77.0	60.3	16.1	0.6	766
Salmon oil	70.6	39.7	29.9	1.0	485

g = gram
mg = milligram
Amount in 3 1/2 ounces unless otherwise noted

N/A = Not Available
TR = trace (less than 0.05 grams per 100 grams of food)

Vegetable Oils

The saturated fat content of margarines and bread spreads varies greatly depending on whether they are made of corn oil, corn oil and soybean oil, whether they are mixtures of cottonseed oil or they come in sticks, tubs, pourable form. Are they hydrogenated, with palm oil or safflower oil, or imitation margarine, or whipped with water? The Department of Agriculture has tested 47 different margarine mixtures. We've listed just a few to give you an idea of the ratio of saturated, monounsaturated and polyunsaturated fats. We have omitted margarines with lard or animal fat, as they're high in cholesterol and should be eliminated anyway.

Because we use oil in our diet regularly, often in salads, this is one area in which we can easily select a low saturated fat oil such as rapeseed (Puritan™), safflower, or walnut oil. Eliminate palm oil, palm kernel oil, nutmeg butter, and especially coconut oil. Palm oil is "hidden" in thousands of foods like potato chips, corn chips, taco shells, cookies, crackers, popcorn, cake mixes, pastries, coffee cakes, dairy whips, etc.

Oil that is cooked may change chemical components or makeup, especially oil that is thermostatically controlled and kept at very high temperatures and perhaps burned or contains burned food particles. Consumption of too much oil and fat may be implicated in some kinds of cancer; however the connection is not clear.

Reducing oils in our diet is one clear way to cut saturated fat and overall fat consumption. Eliminate most added oil from cooking, select low saturated fats and oils, or just reduce the amount of oil and you'll have a heart healthy diet and may lose weight, too.

Cholesterol and Fatty Acid Content of Vegetable Oils

Product	Total Fat	Saturated Fat	Mono-unsaturated Fat	Poly-unsaturated Fat	Cholesterol
	g	g	g	g	mg
Almond oil	95.5	8.2	69.9	17.4	0
Cocoa butter	95.6	59.7	32.9	3.0	0
Coconut oil	94.1	86.5	5.8	1.8	0
Corn oil	95.6	12.7	24.2	58.7	0
Cottonseed oil	95.6	25.9	17.8	51.9	0
Grape seed oil	95.6	9.6	16.1	69.9	0
Hazelnut oil	95.6	7.4	78.0	10.2	0
Linseed oil	95.6	9.4	20.2	66.0	0
Nutmeg butter	138.0	90.0	48	0	0
Olive oil	95.6	13.5	73.7	8.4	0
Palm oil	95.6	49.3	37.0	9.3	0
Palm kernel oil	93.4	81.4	11.4	1.6	0
Peanut oil	95.1	16.9	46.2	32.0	0
Poppy seed oil	95.6	13.5	19.7	62.4	0

Cholesterol and Fatty Acid Content of Vegetable Oils

Product	Total Fat	Saturated Fat	Mono-unsaturated Fat	Poly-unsaturated Fat	Cholesterol
	g	g	g	g	mg
Rapeseed oil	95.6	5.4	66.4	23.8	0
Rice bran oil	94.0	19.7	39.3	35.0	0
Safflower oil	95.6	6.1	75.3	14.2	0
Sesame oil	81.4	14.2	39.7	41.7	0
Soybean oil	86.5	14.9	43.0	37.6	0
Sunflower oil	95.3	10.1	19.5	65.7	0
Tomato seed oil	105.8	19.7	22.8	53.1	0
Walnut oil	95.2	9.1	22.8	63.3	0
Wheat germ	95.6	18.8	15.1	61.7	0

g = gram
mg = milligram
Amount in 3 1/2 ounces unless otherwise noted

N/A = Not Available
TR = trace (less than 0.05 grams per 100 grams of food)

Salad Dressings

Salad dressings, sandwich spreads and the like vary greatly depending upon the ingredients. Plain vinegar with spices has no fat and no cholesterol. Some sandwich spreads have 76 milligrams of cholesterol and nearly 6 grams of saturated fat, almost one third of the daily recommended allowance (nearly one half if you are a small person). Three and one half ounces of regular mayonnaise has 59 milligrams of cholesterol and almost 12 grams of fat, the whole day's recommendation of saturated fats for a person who weighs 100 pounds. You can see how mayonnaise used in both the lunch sandwich and macaroni salad and also in the dinner fish sauce can deliver more saturated fat than we want.

Salad dressings with cheese, (although the cholesterol value is unavailable), can be astronomical in both cholesterol, saturated fat and total fat intake. If you choose to have a blue cheese dressing on a salad, you could make it a larger salad than usual, use deliberate amounts of cheese and make the salad the whole meal. If you have a blue cheese dressing salad, a small piece of meat and asparagus with Hollandaise sauce, baked potato with butter, plus any dairy product dessert, and cream in your coffee, your cholesterol intake would be about 500 milligrams (or more depending on portion sizes) of cholesterol and about 20 to 25 grams of saturated fat, in one meal, nearly double the recommendations for a whole day. And that's a fairly common restaurant meal. You can see how easy it is to get more than you want or need.

Oils vary greatly in their saturates. See our oils charts on page 303 for a closer comparison. Diet salad dressings are an easy way to cut down on calories and unwanted saturated fats and cholesterol.

Cholesterol and Fatty Acid Content of Salad Dressings

Product	Total Fat	Saturated Fat	Mono-unsaturated Fat	Poly-unsaturated Fat	Cholesterol
	g	g	g	g	mg
Regular mayonnaise (with yolks and soybean oil)	75.70	11.80	22.60	41.30	59
Imitation mayonnaise (with no egg yolks—the only ones available presently are Bright Day™ and Hains™)	45.60	7.50	10.50	27.60	0
Thousand Island dressing (regular)	29.5	6.0	1.3	19.8	N/A
Thousand Island dressing (low calorie)	10.20	1.60	2.40	6.20	15
Sandwich spreads	32.50	5.10	7.40	20.00	76
Blue Cheese Salad Dressing	50.00	9.9	12.3	27.8	N/A
French Dressing (regular)	39.2	9.5	8.0	21.7	0
French Dressing (low calorie)	5.6	0.8	1.4	3.4	6
Italian (regular)	46.2	7.0	11.2	28.0	0
Italian (low calorie)	31.3	1.3	2.0		0
Oil and Vinegar	48	9.1	14.8	24.1	0
Vinegar	0	0	0	0	0

g = gram
mg = milligram
Amount in 3 1/2 ounces unless otherwise noted

N/A = Not Available
TR = trAce (less than 0.05 grams per 100 grams of food)

Salad dressings without cheese, bacon fat, or egg yolks have no cholesterol and vary in fatty acids depending upon the types of oils.

Breads

Bread is a super staple. It has the grain, fiber, and bulk necessary (and without the fat in most cases) to be included on a low cholesterol diet. Some breads do have egg yolks, lard, or butter, and these should be reduced or omitted. Most modern-day breads are low in fat and excellent for low cholesterol diets. We have listed some of the breads used most often so you have an idea of the ingredients. If there are eggs in the bread and you are making it, Egg Watchers™ is a good substitute. With most bread, the only problem is the butter you put on it! And you should know that commercial bread often has more salt than what is considered healthy, so read the labels.

Usual Cholesterol and Fat Content of Breads, Muffins, Scones, Popovers, etc.

Usually contains no eggs and low fat	Usually contains no eggs but has high fat	Usually contains a few eggs and some fat	Usually contains lots of eggs and moderate to high fat
			Applesauce bread
Bagels	Corn pone		Banana bread (usually many eggs)
Boston brown bread	Croissants (sometimes no eggs; the fat is usually butter)	Blueberry muffins	Batterbread
Bran bread	Doughnuts	Bran muffins	Bread sticks
Buttermilk biscuits (buttermilk is lowfat)	English muffins (usually no eggs, but check label)	Coffee cake (sometimes no eggs)	Brenenstich
Caramel buns (can contain butter)	Garlic bread	Corn breads	Brioche
Cinnamon rolls (can contain butter)	Hush puppies	Crescents	Cheese bread
Corn bread (some of them)	Orange bread	Date bread	Challah
Crackers (most have no eggs; check label for palm oil)	Sweet potato bread biscuits	French toast	Coffee cake
Crumpets	Tea biscuits	Gluten bread	Croissants (sometimes no eggs; always high fat)
English muffins		Orange bread	Hush puppies (sometimes no eggs)

Cholesterol and Saturated Fat Content of Over 500 Foods

Usually contains no eggs and low fat	Usually contains no eggs but has high fat	Usually contains a few eggs and some fat	Usually contains lots of eggs and moderate to high fat
French bread		Pumpkin bread	Popovers
Hoecake		Refrigerator rolls	Sally Lunn
Indian flat bread		Rice muffins	Scones and Scotch scones
Irish potato cakes		Strudel	Spoon bread
Irish soda bread			Sponge bread
Jalapeno corn bread			Stollen
Melba toast			Vienna pastry
Matzos			Zucchini bread
Milwaukee rye			(usually many eggs)
Norwegian rye			Zwieback
Oatmeal bread			
Parker House rolls			
Pita bread			
Pizza dough			
Pretzels (can contain palm oil or butter)			
Raisin bread			
Rye crisps			
Rye rolls			
Salt-rising bread (has 1 tablespoon or more salt [usually] per loaf)			
Soda biscuits			
Sourdough (usually no eggs)			
Tortillas			
Vienna rolls			
Wheat berry bread			
White bread			
Whole wheat or whole grain bread			

Selected Foods

These values will give you an idea of certain comparisons you might not have otherwise known.

Cholesterol and Fatty Acid Content of Selected Foods

Product	Total Fat	Saturated Fat	Mono-unsaturated Fat	Poly-unsaturated Fat	Cholesterol
	g	*g*	*g*	*g*	*mg*
Corn	3.9	TR	N/A	N/A	0
Crackers	12.0	3.0	N/A	N/A	0
Black walnuts	56.6	3.6	12.7	27.5	0
Doughnuts, with eggs, 1 doughnut	13.4	6.0	5.8	3.5	13
Filberts	62.4	3.0	N/A	N/A	0
Graham crackers, 2 crackers	1.3	.3	N/A	N/A	0
Hickory nuts		64.4	7.0	32.6	21.90
Lima beans, dry	1.4	.3	.1	.7	0
Lentils, dry	1.2	.2	.2	.5	0
Oats	9.0	2.0	N/A	N/A	0
Peanuts	47.5	10.0	N/A	N/A	0
Peanut butter	50.0	9.0	29.9	8.6	0
Pecans	71.2	5.0			0
Pizza with cheese,1 piece	4.0	2.1	1.2	0.5	13
Popcorn	5.0	1.0			
Potatoes, French fried, 10 pieces	8.3	3.4	4.0	0.5	6
Potatoes, mashed with margarine	4.3	2.0	N/A	N/A	0
Potato chips	39.8	10.0	N/A	N/A	0
Potato sticks	36.4	9.0	N/A	N/A	0
Pound cake, 1 slice	10.0	5.9	3.0	0.6	68
Pumpkin & squash seeds	15.7	1.0			0
Saltine crackers, 4	9.0	0.3	0.5	0.4	3
Seaweed	7.7	2.6			0
Soybean seeds	4.5	.5	.5	2.5	0
Soybean soup (miso)	4.6	1.0			0
Sunflower seeds	47.3	6.0			0
Walnuts	61.9	5.6	14.2	39.1	0
Wheat germ	10.9	1.9	1.9	6.6	0
Bacon, raw	57.5	21.3	26.3	6.8	67
Roquefort cheese	33.1	21.1	9.0	.9	105
Sardines	9.4	2.1	3.7	3.9	85

g = gram
mg = milligram
Amount in 3 1/2 ounces unless otherwise noted

N/A = Not Available
TR = trace (less than 0.05 grams per 100 grams of food)

Cholesterol and Saturated Fat Content of Over 500 Foods

CHAPTER TEN

Holiday Meals and Eating Out

Holidays are, for most of us, a time of family, tradition, perhaps a renewal or deepening of religious connection and often increased tension. It may not be a time when you want to think of a diet. You may accept the loss of cheese, butter and whipped cream, and all the other foods you've had to give up the rest of the year but you'll be darned if you're going to deprive yourself on a holiday. The thinking is understandable. And it may be the choice you wish to make.

However, there isn't a holiday—from a Jewish orthodox observance of Passover or a Christian celebration of Lent, to a traditional Thanksgiving dinner—that can't be made healthier without disrupting either the religious observance or the feelings of great tradition. If you choose to lower the cholesterol and fats in your diet, you can do it easily without interfering with the tastes and feelings associated with the food and traditions that make holiday fare so deeply satisfying.

As soon as you are convinced lowering cholesterol and saturated fat in your diet is right for you and your family, anytime is the right time to start. You don't have to wait until "after the holidays." If it's the right choice for you to start now, this book will help you observe nearly every holiday without some foods and preparation methods that can be harmful, and you will continue these tips and practices gained here, hopefully, for the rest of your life.

Only a few holidays have either very religious directives or ingrained traditions we don't wish to change, and we don't have to. Most other holidays, such as Easter, with the usual but not obligatory ham, can be easily and gently shifted to foods healthier for the family. Ham, especially if it is low in fat (and many are) and if the portions are small, isn't the worst choice.

Most foods during Passover are not a problem. Apples and honey for a healthy and sweet new year are heart healthy. Only the egg yolk on the Seder plate shouldn't be consumed as it is a symbolic egg. Also, challah, a delicious egg bread prepared on Jewish holidays may be very successfully made with egg substitutes without losing flavor or texture but with a plus for your health.

A Low Cholesterol Thanksgiving

Thanksgiving is a holiday celebrated by nearly everyone. Thanksgiving for most Americans has very specific food requirements, and there is no reason to make major diet changes in this traditional celebration. Even drastic lowering can be achieved without giving up everything you love in food. Minor substitutions, cooking in a more enlightened way, and the lessening of certain ingredients can still give the same taste and texture.

Consider a "typical" Thanksgiving meal: dark meat and turkey skin, turkey giblets with liver, dressing made with butter and vegetables covered with butter, creamy crab soup, oily gravy, heart of palm salad, mince pie made with suet (a meat product), pumpkin pie with egg yolks and whipped cream. The cholesterol count in that single meal is probably over 2 grams or 2000 milligrams. Compare the cholesterol count when turkey, pie, vegetables and dressing are prepared with foods containing less cholesterol and fat and you can get 300 milligrams! With minor changes, Thanksgiving can be both traditional and healthy without feeling you're depriving yourself or your family.

Turkey: I prefer fresh over frozen turkey because if I'm going to have this sumptuous family meal once a year, I want the best flavor and texture I can get. The cost is usually higher for fresh birds, and often they have to be ordered a few weeks in advance. (Your grocery store meat cutter or your gourmet/specialty food store will know where to get fresh turkeys.) Remove the giblets and don't use livers or heart in the dressing or gravy; these are high in cholesterol. Serve more white meat than dark and don't eat the skin. If you like dark meat, eliminate whatever fat you can.

Stuffing: If you use a prepared bread stuffing, don't add the butter or margarine as indicated. Add the same amount of water or defatted, unsalted chicken stock to take the place of the omitted butter or margarine. Then add the extra stuffing ingredients you like. Excellent simple stuffing can be made with bread and a large amount of fresh chopped onions and celery, plus 1/4 to 1/2 teaspoon sage. If you like apples, prunes, or chestnuts, add these, too. You won't miss the butter or margarine at all. The bird drips enough fat and flavor into the dressing to make up for it. You can also stuff the bird rather tightly with the moist stuffing.

Gravy: It's better to not have gravy at all in a low cholesterol, low saturated-fat diet, but if you or your family insists, make gravy as usual, but thinner, adding slightly more liquid, either water or skim milk. Pour the broth into a stainless steel bowl and place in freezer for 5 to 10 minutes. When the fat rises, pick off, reheat the broth, thickening with flour or corn starch and serve. You can also use a defatting cup which has a low spout. The fat is left in the cup if you stop pouring at the right time; however it's difficult to remove all the fat this way.

Vegetables: Use margarine, instead of butter or cheese sauce and less of it. Use less sugar on sweet potatoes, add lemon to broccoli and asparagus or make a Hollandaise with imitation eggs.

Cranberry Sauce: Make as usual, reducing some sugar if you wish and using sugar substitutes.

Rolls: Serve rolls instead of biscuits and offer margarine for them. Most rolls are made without fat so you're fairly safe. Remember, the rolls and bread are fine; it's the added fats you put on that cause problems.

Green Salad: Use less salad oil to reduce calories or by substituting a diet dressing or plain vinegar or just salad dressing with less oil. Oils low in saturates are always recommended.

Desserts: Pumpkin Pie: Make with imitation eggs and evaporated skim milk. Use walnut, rapeseed, safflower, or sunflower oil in the crust. Ready-made crusts are usually made with meat fat so check the label. Or fill a custard dish with the pumpkin mixture and add a small round of crust on the top, baking as usual.

Mincemeat Pie: Make as usual but leave out the suet (meat fat). You will never miss the taste. Most prepared mincemeat no longer has suet in it. Use crust with no butter. Instead of ice cream serve Tofutti vanilla "ice cream."

Pumpkin Piettes: In a ramekin pour pumpkin pie filling. Place a round of pie crust on top and serve with a Tofutti ice cream dollop for a topping. There is no need to serve teeny tiny portions in such a diet.

Easter

Food at Easter is traditionally festive and colorful. Easter eggs are colored and eaten, candies are placed in the children's Easter baskets and are eaten heartily. Parents make bunny-shaped cakes with coconut shavings for fur and jelly beans for eyes. Ham is the usual traditional Easter fare. Believe it or not you can still make and eat many of these same things and keep them low in cholesterol and saturated fat.

For Easter, prepare a lean Canadian bacon roll instead of the somewhat more fatty and salty ham. Even ham though, if it isn't fatty, sometimes has less saturated fat than certain cuts of beef. Canadian bacon can be studded with cloves, pineapple, cherries, and brown sugar if you wish, just like a ham. Leg of lamb is also Easter fare but it is higher in cholesterol. Veal, especially if fatty, is slightly higher in cholesterol than beef and lamb. So make your choice whether Canadian bacon, ham, or leg of lamb. If lamb, an excellent butterflied, deboned, and defatted leg of lamb or mutton marinade can be made by combining 1/2 cup low salt soy sauce, 1/3 cup Worcestershire sauce, and 3 to 10 cloves minced garlic. Marinate the lamb for at least 2 hours, turning regularly. Grill the lamb on an indoor or outdoor barbecue until at least medium well, to cook out as much fat as possible. Then slice narrow, diagonal pieces. Keep meat servings small.

Other Easter foods include peas and potatoes. A dessert of fruit and angel food cake, page 248 (with no coconut) completes a healthy, traditional Easter meal with little cholesterol and which, although not low in saturated fats, isn't off the charts, either.

Passover (Seder) Supper

As we've already discussed, there are minor variations even in the classic Seder supper, depending upon the community and heritages of the celebrating Jews, but most often the charoseth for the Seder plate is a heart-healthy mixture of apples, raisins and minced nuts, sugar or honey, and wine. The hard boiled egg is symbolic and isn't eaten. Matzoh balls in the soup can be made with margarine instead of the cholesterol and saturated fat-laden chicken fat. (The fat should also be removed from the broth.) The roast chicken can be made fat-free too. (Recipe page 178) Meals for other Jewish holidays can be made by substituting honey for sugar (in some dishes) to celebrate a sweet year.

Lenten Menus

Many of the recipes in this book are ideal for Lenten meals because they contain no meat. A half-grapefruit, a potato dish, a vegetable soup, and sorbet make both an ideal Lenten meal and an ideal low cholesterol meal.

Christmas Dinners

Christmas or Christmas eve dinners are often turkey or goose or even duck, pheasant or, for some, roast suckling pig or stuffed boar's (pig's) head. I've seen no cholesterol figures on roast suckling pig and they may be acceptable if the piglet isn't fatty. A stuffed boar's head sounds astronomically high in cholesterol, but I've seen no figures. Pigs' brains and other animal brains, if included in the head, have the highest cholesterol of any other part of the animal. To keep Christmas festive and heart-healthy, substitute a guinea hen, pheasant, or lean Cornish hen.

Eating Out

Sometimes you may think, especially when you know a lot about food, saturated fat, and cholesterol, that some restaurants are out to poison you. Instead of having a pleasant lunchtime respite from a busy work day or a romantic candlelight interlude with someone very special to you, eating in restaurants when you're careful of the food you eat can be a frustrating, exasperating experience. You carefully select your choices with instructions of "no butter" or "sauce on the side, please." Waiters become grumpy, forget your special food requests, or are just plain indifferent and pay no attention. Busy or unenlightened chefs are sometimes less than enthusiastic, are uncreative, and your meal is often not only unimaginative but at the worst, downright awful.

But times are changing. Many more restaurants are becoming increasingly adaptive to special dietary needs. A few chefs are actually playful and very creative with the customer's requests for low cholesterol meals. Unusual food requests have to interrupt a chef's busy schedule and a kitchen that also might have obvious ingredient constraints. However, many restaurants now have low cholesterol meals starred or noted on their menu.

In California there are several places that specialize in low cholesterol, low fat meals. Many hotels and restaurants offer special low cholesterol, low fat menus approved by the American Heart Association. Just ask them. And most airlines will provide a low cholesterol meal if given 24-hours' advance notice. In fact, low cholesterol meals on airlines can be better because they're often prepared in a different kitchen than the usual fare. However, I recently saw a fatty steak on a supposedly low cholesterol airline meal.

How to Order in Restaurants

Many people are eating less meat and less animal protein (including fish and fowl), but most main dishes in restaurants are still meat, fish, or fowl, making it difficult in some establishments to eat heart-healthy food. Most of our finest French restaurants still specialize in rich, butter-based sauces; steak houses are still plentiful. It is difficult but not impossible to eat wonderful low cholesterol, low saturated fat meals in a restaurant. Actually it can be fun if you know how.

Main Dishes

One way to stick to a healthier diet is to select several appetizers or hors d'oeuvre instead of the traditional main dish. In fact, appetizer combinations and side dishes make excellent restaurant meals. Use these foods like the Spanish, eat tapas, which are several small servings of a variety of food.

You could order:

fat-free proscuitto (the chef or you can remove the fat) and melon

asparagus vinaigrette (dressing on the side)

roasted red peppers

Caesar salad (request it be made without the egg yolks and less oil)

various non-cream based soups

baked potato

wild or white rice

various interesting vegetables like the new baby or mini varieties

artichokes

green salads

aspics

bean salads

coleslaw (you may have to pour out some of the dressing)

pizza with onions, mushrooms, and green peppers but little or no meat (pepperoni is low in cholesterol and with light cheese

or imitation cheese which many pizza parlors use anyway, pizza can be very heart healthy)

smoked salmon

smoked trout

marinated herring without the sour cream or sour cream on the side

clams

couscous

most sushi and sashimi

cucumbers

mushrooms

some crepes

papaya

tofu

scallops

potato skins (baked instead of fried)

fruit cup

sliced tomatoes

Ordering this way can often be less expensive than going the usual appetizer, salad, main dish, vegetable, and dessert route. The amount of cholesterol ingested is usually far lower, too. But be aware that many of the above dishes such as green vegetables and mushrooms are often cooked or sauced with butter. Personally, I'd order it anyway and push most of the sauce aside. The selection of pasta with a tomato sauce for your main dish might be a good choice.

Salads

Salad, unless it is a Caesar salad, can be ordered with oil and vinegar dressing on the side. Omit the oil or use less of it. A Caesar salad is still excellent when requested without the egg. Salads may also be ordered with "house" dressing on the side so you can use just a dollop or blend it with some added lemon or vinegar. You can at least control the amount of salad dressing this way, and can be sure your salad isn't floating in high-fat creamy Italian.

Omit Thousand Island entirely as it contains heavy doses of fat. Some salad bars offer great varieties of vegetables you might not usually treat yourself to at home. Steer away from the cheeses and watch the hard boiled egg yolks and bacon bits. This is a great time to try new foods and new combinations. What we want to do is expand your food use, not limit the varieties.

Meat, Fish, or Fowl

If ordering meat, fish, or chicken be sure it isn't fried or sauteed but broiled or at least cooked without a breaded coating, which soaks up fat. Ask for any sauce's on the side so you can control the amount. If you really crave liver or sweetbreads, foods both very high in cholesterol, have them at your favorite restaurant at interludes of several weeks or months and enjoy them. The vitamins and nutrients will be good for you. But for your health's sake, just do it once in a great while. Otherwise stick to your better-health selections like vegetables or chicken breast, trout or halibut. If you really crave a good steak order a small portion and have it cooked medium-well or well done to burn off more of the fat and request that the chef cut off all visible fat. Remember cholesterol is in the muscle too.

Duckling, incidently, can be an excellent restaurant selection. The cholesterol in duck is fairly low, much like chicken. However, duck takes some skill and patience because you need to remove all fat. If you're lucky the chef will do it for you. Quail and dove have little fat, Cornish hens somewhere between chicken and quail. Guinea hens and pheasant are good choices. As for taste, guinea hens are less stringy than pheasant and are usually more moist (which is one reason why a pheasant was served under glass—to keep it more moist).

Soups

Many restaurants' soups, along with bread or rolls, a salad and fruit for dessert, make fine meals. Especially good are bean soups, vegetable soups, fish chowders, clam soups in a tomato base, and most noodle and rice soups. Both Chinese and Japanese restaurants have excellent soups although the salt content may be higher than you want. Incidently, many Oriental restaurants have lite soy—you just need to ask.

Desserts

Desserts are fun because good restaurants sometimes have wonderful fresh fruits that you can't get in the markets—raspberries, blackberries, boysenberries, fresh peaches, kiwi, tiny pineapples or lush orange slices—often beautifully cut and served. Just decline the creme fraiche and whipped cream. Other than that, select pies or fruit tarts (again without whipped cream) and just don't eat much of the crust; or order very small cakes, sorbets, sherbets or ices. Be aware some sherbets are cream based. Because of the egg yolk and cream content, omit custards, puddings, ice creams, mousses, souffles, cheesecakes, cream puffs, eclairs, chocolate, or cream cakes and obvious rich desserts containing lots of whipped cream, fat, or butter. If you are maintaining a low fat, low cholesterol diet at home for most of the time you can give yourself permission to eat that occasional hot fudge sundae or gooey dessert without fear of much impact.

Fast Foods

Fast foods can present special problems. An excellent book on the subject is *The Fast-Food Guide*, by Michael Jacobson and Sarah Fritschner published by The Center for Science and The Public Interest. The book says there are 15 teaspoons of fat in a Wendy's Triple cheeseburger, 25 teaspoons of sugar in a Dairy Queen chocolate malt, and many foods, including McDonalds' bread, fried potatoes, are cooked in meat fat, making them doubly dangerous in the heart disease department. Everyone interested in food, who has to occasionally eat at a fast food outlet should read this book. Companies do change their ingredients however. The addition of salad bars has been very helpful to those who want more variety and lower fat choices.

Animal and vegetable fats used in fast food restaurants often aren't changed for many days or even weeks. The fat is usually in a heated container that is on a thermostat causing the temperature to continually rise and lower for hours at a time, and if the restaurant is open all night, the same fat is used for days and weeks at a time. This continual high heat causes the chemical structure of the oil to change. This is especially true if the oil is at all burned or if the excess particles of food left in the oil (as batches of food are continually replaced) are burned. Although controversy surrounds the idea that the changes in the oil may be a causative factor in both cancer and heart problems, some studies show there is a connection in women who have breast or ovarian cancer and who continually eat foods high in fat (a recent study also refutes this). Although the continual ingestion of fried foods or food cooked in oils with food residual that change in chemical structure are considered dangerous only by some scientists, it is not controversial that consuming too much saturated fat, especially animal fat, is unhealthy for your heart and your arteries.

Here are some suggestions when going to a fast food restaurant:

• For breakfast, have a high carbohydrate pancake instead of sausages and eggs. Or fruit, cereal, and skim milk. Or get poached or hard-cooked eggs and just eat the whites.

• For your beverage, drink orange juice instead of malts, try diet sodas instead of sugar-based sodas or have decaffeinated coffee. If you want less caffeine in your iced tea or coffee, they'll thin the sometimes very dark, caffeine loaded brew with ice and water. (The chemicals in decaffeinated coffee varies but most are done with water now.)

• Stay away from croissants which are very high in butter and/or fat. The croissants with sausage and eggs are the worst as they are loaded with both cholesterol and fat. Egg McMuffins™ and ham or sausage are almost as bad. The muffin is probably the best part, high in carbohydrates. It may also be high in salt and vegetable fat, however.

• If you're going to eat pork, eat ham rather than patty sausage, and patty sausage rather than link sausage. Usually the link is highest in fat, especially if it isn't cooked thoroughly and for enough time for the excess fat to drain through the tough skin.

• Many fast-food items are actually pretty good as far as low cholesterol food is concerned. Coleslaws, potato salads (they both have some mayonnaise, however), baked beans, baked potatoes, corn on the cob (without butter), carrot raisin salads, and so on are good substitutes to the burger. Many are high in sugar as well as high in mayonnaise or salt, but ounce for ounce they are probably pretty healthy, at least more so than most of the straight hamburgers and fries.

• A single meat patty is better than a double patty (more bread per burger).

• Baked potatoes such as those at Wendy's are excellent choices especially if they will heavy-up on the vegetables and lighten-up on the cheese sauce. Just ask!

• Try to have a dry (any other than Wendy's as juicy usually means greasy), well-done hamburger instead of a hot dog which is usually higher in fat.

• Fried fish is usually higher in fat than hamburgers.

But, yes, you can get low cholesterol, high carbohydrate meals at fast food restaurants. Low salt? I'm not so sure!

CHAPTER ELEVEN

After Dinner Talk

*W*hen you read this, we hope that you have tried several recipes from this book and as a result have become even more convinced that reducing cholesterol and saturated fat in your diet isn't very difficult. Most of the foods you like are still acceptable on a low cholesterol, low saturated fat diet and may only require cutting the portion sizes, cooking it a bit differently or just not having it as often. Low saturated fat foods that can substitute for old favorites made from cream, cheese or eggs are now available at the market. The key issue is to develop the habits of planning, shopping, cooking and selecting smaller portion sizes which will sustain the change in eating patterns for a lifetime. It is several weeks before the full effect of a change in your diet can be measured as a change in your blood cholesterol level but when you do achieve this lower blood cholesterol, these new habits should provide increasing protection from vascular disease for the rest of your life.

Maintaining a good habit is often most difficult because those people with whom you work and live may not subscribe. We almost always eat with other people and their food choices directly impact ours. Did you ever try eating fruit, non-fat yogurt and cereal with skim milk when the cook has fixed buttered pancakes, lots of sausage and scrambled eggs with melted cheese? This type of problem is being solved as more and more people are becoming convinced that a low blood cholesterol is worth maintaining. Plus setting a good example for your children by beginning a tradition of healthy food habits instead of just relying on the old, high cholesterol, high saturated fat foods, gives them a head start in both their own health and their lifetime eating patterns.

Food manufacturers have certainly seen the growing market as reflected by the low or no cholesterol labels, or, "contains no palm oil" both on their products and in their television messages. Weis markets in the York, Harrisburg, and Lancaster, Pennsylvania, broadcast their television advertisements with a low cholesterol, low saturated fat philosophy and are certainly one of the more enlightened grocery chains in the country.

Many restaurants and hotel chain dining rooms are offering truly delicious entrees that meet the guidelines of the American Heart Association. On a recent visit to The Four Seasons Restaurant in New York, Chef Seppi, who graciously endorsed our book, told us of a banquet that he was preparing that evening for the executives of a large company who had requested that every course be consistent with a "Heart Healthy Diet." Chef Seppi who co-authored *Spa Cuisine* says his children are particularly interested in up to date health and diet information.

Is all of this just a "flash in the pan"? Is it all cooked up by folks who want to make money selling medications to lower cholesterol—or low cholesterol cook books? We believe that the excitement about being able to prevent heart attacks and the disability that comes from having vascular disease is well based in solid research studies. There is very strong scientific evidence that lowering blood cholesterol—even in mid-life and even in men and women with diagnosed coronary disease—can prevent heart disease from growing worse. The National Heart, Lung and Blood Institute, our major federal agency promoting research into the causes of heart disease, has come to the conclusion that the time has come to launch the National Cholesterol Education Program. This was done only after documenting that our leading scientists believe:

(1) that the majority of Americans are at risk from their high blood cholesterol and

(2) that lowering cholesterol will help prevent heart disease.

Actually doing this requires a consistent message to the American people. One of the major functions of the National Cholesterol Education Program is to develop sensible recommendations for identifying those who should lower their cholesterol and what they could do to bring about a more desirable level. The program is now run by a coordinating committee representing virtually every major medical society and voluntary health group concerned with heart disease in America. This is so important because for the first time, physicians and other health professionals have a link to the development of policy for identifying and treating high blood cholesterol through an organization that he or she knows is trustworthy. Armed and better laboratories, better dietary information, and better drugs, we expect your physician to be much more effective in handling your cholesterol problem in the future.

Our good friend and long time colleague, Dr. John LaRosa, chairman of the Nutrition Committee for the American Heart Association, who helped develop the recommendations to physicians, pointed out that the program must reach into the community as well. John has expressed the desire to open an Italian restaurant in his next life since he knows that so many healthy dishes can be prepared with the basics of that great cuisine.

The National Cholesterol Education Program has appointed a panel to develop specific guidelines relevant to public policy that should be of great help to restaurants and food producers as they try to provide information for meals and products that are lower in cholesterol, saturated fat and calories.

Another of the believers in this book's philosophy is Malcolm Forbes, who is surely the world's expert on how to celebrate life gloriously and enthusiastically. Malcolm serves lean meats and fish, the usual fresh fruits and vegetables—food that any of us can buy at our markets. He reflects his wish to live long and well by eating a beautifully prepared but prudent diet, low in cholesterol and saturated fat.

Larry King, our fourth endorser of our book, is about as serious a convert to healthy eating as you can get. Not only is his broadcast schedule backbreaking, often lasting from early afternoon to the early morning hours, but most important, Larry has had a recent heart attack and bypass operation. His book, *Tell It To The King*, is a best seller and he has another one due out soon about his heart attack and subsequent operation. Larry eats his own blend of favorites, matzos, chopped lettuce salad (often at the Palm or Duke Ziebert's Restaurant in Washington, D.C.), lean meat and a large plate of fresh vegetables.

Many people are becoming enlightened about diet. Learning what we should and shouldn't eat is an ongoing learning process, and we sincerely hope our book gives you more information to help you continue. We thank each of these four gentlemen for their generous support in their endorsements, Seppi in particular for his efforts and joint photograph.

In summary, there are a few reminders that we believe will always be useful to keep in mind.

- Know your cholesterol value.

- If it is above 200 mg/dl, it may be increasing your risk of heart disease. Ask your doctor for advice on how to proceed.

- If your cholesterol is over 240, or if you have two risk factors for heart disease or if you already have heart disease, you should know your LDL and HDL levels (see page 35).

- Dietary change is always the first and safest treatment for high blood cholesterol (or LDL-cholesterol). Examine your eating habits and do more to reduce the saturated fat, cholesterol and sodium content.

- Follow up with your physician to determine if the dietary change has achieved the desired degree of cholesterol lowering.

- Seek the advice of a registered dietitian if you do not reach your cholesterol goal.

- If after three to six months no further reduction can be achieved and your blood cholesterol is still too high, your doctor may consider medication as the appropriate treatment. With all medications, the cost and potential side effects must always be weighed against the estimated benefit.

- Always remember that high blood cholesterol is much more dangerous if other major risk factors are also present—so it is very important to:

a. control high blood pressure
b. stop cigarette smoking
c. lose excess fat tissue
d. control diabetes if present.

Heart disease can be prevented and with the correct approach, you can do it. We hope that this book will make your attempts to develop that approach a little easier and a lot more fun.

Glossary

Atherosclerosis—A type of "hardening of the arteries" in which cholesterol, fat, and other blood components build up in the walls of arteries. As atherosclerosis progresses, the arteries to the heart may narrow so that oxygen-rich blood and nutrients have difficulty reaching the heart.

Bile acid sequestrants—One type of cholesterol-lowering medication, including cholestyramine and colestipol. The sequestrants bind with cholesterol-containing bile acids in the intestine and remove them in bowel movements.

Carbohydrate—One of the three nutrients that supply calories (energy) to the body. Carbohydrate provides 4 calories per gram—the same number of calories as pure protein and less than half the calories of fat. Carbohydrate is essential for normal body function. There are two basic kinds of carbohydrate—simple carbohydrate (or sugars) and complex carbohydrate (starches and fiber). In nature, both the simple sugars and the complex starches come packaged in foods like oranges, apples, corn, wheat, and milk. Refined or processed carbohydrates are found in cookies, cakes, and pies.

- **Complex carbohydrate**—Starch and fiber. Complex carbohydrate comes from plants. When complex carbohydrate is substituted for saturated fat, the saturated fat reduction lowers blood cholesterol. Foods high in starch include breads, cereals, pasta, rice, dried beans and peas, corn, and lima beans.

- **Fiber**—A nondigestible type of complex carbohydrate. High-fiber foods are usually low in calories. Foods high in fiber include whole grain breads and cereals, whole fruits, and dried beans. The type of fiber found in foods such as oat and barley bran, some fruits like apples and oranges, and some dried beans may help reduce blood cholesterol.

Cholesterol—A soft, waxy substance. It is made in sufficient quality by the body for normal body function, including the manufacture of hormones, bile acid, and vitamin D. It is present in all parts of the body, including the nervous system, muscle, skin, liver, intestines, heart, etc.

- **Blood cholesterol**—Cholesterol that is manufactured in the liver and absorbed from the food you eat and is carried in the blood for use by all parts of the body. A high level of blood cholesterol leads to atherosclerosis and coronary heart disease.

- **Dietary cholesterol**—Cholesterol that is in the food you eat. It is present only in foods of animal origin, not in foods of plant origin. Dietary cholesterol, like dietary saturated fat, tends to raise blood cholesterol, which increases the risk for heart disease.

Coronary heart disease—Heart ailment caused by narrowing of the coronary arteries (arteries that supply oxygen and nutrients directly to the heart muscle). Coronary heart disease is caused by atherosclerosis, which decreases the blood supply to the heart muscle. The inadequate supply of oxygen-rich blood and nutrients damages the heart muscle and can lead to chest pain, heart attack, and death.

Fat—One of the three nutrients that supply calories to the body. Fat provides 9 calories per gram, more than twice the number provided by carbohydrate or protein. In addition to providing calories, fat helps in the absorption of certain vitamins. Small amounts of fat are necessary for normal body function.

- **Total fat**—The sum of the saturated, monounsaturated, and polyunsaturated fats present in food. A mixture of all three in varying amounts is found in most foods.

- **Saturated fat**—A type of fat found in greatest amounts in foods from animals such as meat, poultry, and whole-milk dairy products like cream, milk, ice cream, and cheese. Other examples of saturated fat include butter, the marbling and fat along the edges of meat, and lard and the saturated fat content is high in some vegetable oils—like coconut, palm kernel, and palm oils. Saturated fat raises blood cholesterol more than anything else in the diet.

- **Unsaturated fat**—A type of fat that is usually liquid at refrigerator temperature. Monounsaturated fat and polyunsaturated fat are two kinds of unsaturated fat.

  Monounsaturated fat—A slightly unsaturated fat that is found in greatest amounts in foods from plants, including olive and canola (rapeseed) oil. When substituted for saturated fat, monounsaturated fat helps reduce blood cholesterol.

  Polyunsaturated fat—An highly unsaturated fat that is found in greatest amounts in foods from plants, including safflower, sunflower, corn, and soybean oils. When substituted for saturated fat, polyunsaturated fat helps reduce blood cholesterol.

Gram (g)—A unit of weight. There are about 28 grams in 1 ounce. Dietary fat, protein, and carbohydrate are measured in grams.

Hydrogenation—A chemical process that changes liquid vegetable oils (unsaturated fat) into a more solid saturated fat. This process improves the shelf life of the produce—but also increases the saturated fat content. Many commercial food products contain hydrogenated vegetable oil. Selection should be made based on information found on the label.

Lipids—Fatty substances, including cholesterol and triglycerides, that are present in blood and body tissues.

Lipoproteins—Protein-coated packages that carry fat and cholesterol through the blood. Lipoproteins are classified according to their density.

- **High density lipoproteins (HDL)**—Lipoproteins that contain a small amount of cholesterol and carry cholesterol away from body cells and tissues to the liver for excretion from the body. Low levels of HDL are associated with an increased risk of coronary heart disease. Therefore the higher the HDL level, the better.

- **Low density lipoproteins (LDL)**—Lipoproteins that contain the largest amount of cholesterol in the blood. LDL is responsible for depositing cholesterol in the artery walls. High levels of LDL are associated with an increased risk of coronary heart disease and are therefore referred to as "bad cholesterol."

Milligram (mg)—A unit of weight equal to one thousandth of a gram. There are about 28,350 milligrams in 1 ounce. Dietary cholesterol is measured in milligrams.

Milligrams/deciliter—A way of expressing concentration: in blood cholesterol measurements, the weight of cholesterol (in milligrams) in a deciliter of blood. A deciliter is about one-tenth of a quart.

Niacin—A B vitamin essential for energy production in cells. The recommended daily allowance is about 14 mg for adult females and about 18 mg for adult males. When used in massive quantities under a physician's guidance, niacin is considered a cholesterol-lowering medication.

Protein—One of the three nutrients that supply calories to the body. Protein provides 4 calories per gram, which is less than half the calories of fat. Protein is an essential nutrient that becomes a component of many parts of the body, including muscle, bone, skin, and blood.

Risk factor—A habit, trait, or condition in a person that is associated with an increased chance (or risk) of developing a disease.

Triglycerides—Lipids (fat-like substances) carried through the bloodstream to the tissues. The bulk of the body's fat tissue is in the form of triglycerides, stored for later use as energy. We get triglycerides primarily from the fat in our diet.

Vascular disease—An ailment of the blood vessels often caused by atherosclerosis. Vascular disease may occur in the arteries to the brain and the major leg arteries.

INDEX OF RECIPES

INDEX OF MEDICAL TERMS